Third Time
LUCKY

Third Time
LUCKY

HOW BEN SHOWS US THE WAY

M<small>ICHAEL</small> G<small>EORGE</small>

iUniverse, Inc.
Bloomington

Third Time Lucky
How Ben shows us the way

iUniverse books may be ordered through booksellers or by contacting:

iUniverse
1663 Liberty Drive
Bloomington, IN 47403
www.iuniverse.com
1-800-Authors (1-800-288-4677)

ISBN: 978-1-4620-3918-0 (sc)
ISBN: 978-1-4620-3917-3 (hc)
ISBN: 978-1-4620-3916-6 (ebk)

Library of Congress Control Number: 2012918906

Printed in the United States of America

iUniverse rev. date: 11/01/2012

LOG

Week of: _Jan 3/93_

Weight, Height, Head Circum. (include date)	Jan 6 – 18 lbs – 65th percentile 27 1/4 in – 65th percentile	Head Circm: 40cm – same as last time but I'm sure Dr. Paras mistook it last time.
Milestones: e.g. sitting up, crawling, walking teething,...	First day weening off phenobarb (Jan 3)	
Doctors' appointments: -- who, why, outcome	Jan 6 – 6th month checkup c Dr. Paras. Had 2 needles : – DPT (without P), – Polio	
Sickness: e.g. colds, flu, ear infections, seizures,...	Just getting over flu, I guess. Slight diarrhea, some vomiting. But has kept all food down for past 2 days (Jan 2 & 3). Appetite returning to normal. Has had pablum in evenings. Still seems to have some sort of bug (Jan 6). Just takes a long time for Ben to get over illness.	
Special events: e.g. trips taken, parties, Christmas,...	Conor had his 4th yr. birthday party (Jan 3). Ben slept through whole thing – 3 1/2 hr nap.	
Our feelings: e.g. nervous, helpless, scared, happy, content,....	Minor setback c "flu" has caused us to get a little discouraged. With Ben he seems to take 2 steps forward & 1 step back. We both were quite nervous (even scared) at Dr. Paras checkup. Ben started clutching in usual fashion at beginning of examination but went into a frenzy when Paras cleaned out his ears – crying, sobbing, twitching uncontrollably. In some ways, though, that was good – did not progress into a seizure – has never been so "violently" clutching & crying. Was consoled within 10 mins. That evening (Jan 6), started crying uncontrollably & clutching after Jan tried to get him in his PJs – very frightening.	
General Assessment:	Seizures (even the thought of them) seem to be the worst to deal with. We seem to think that each time he clutches, he may go into a seizure simply because that's how his other seizures began. Dr. Paras, however, says this overactive moro reflex is not a precursor to a seizure, and Dr. Meek said he cannot have a seizure if he's crying. So, why does that not alleviate our fears? We have to stop (knowingly or subconsciously) comparing what Ben does with what a "normal" 6 month old does. Ben can never be measured with the standard yard stick – he will set his own standards and the sooner we accept this and accept that this is not something bad or something to be ashamed of, the sooner our fears will be lessened and dealing c setbacks will be easier. Do we forget the fears and the nervousness we felt when Conor was a baby? Perhaps. Conor said, "Ben just cries because he is a baby. He doesn't understand." He's right – crying is the only way Ben (and all babies, for that matter) can express that he is unhappy, he wants something or he is in pain. On the positive side, Ben seems to be holding his head up for longer periods of time – 15-20 sec on belly, beyond 1 minute when in your arms.	

Jan 9 (Sat). Yesterday thought he was getting a cold – first pneumonia, then flu, now a cold ! This morning, he got up early, no cold today – great. Got his appetite back. Wolfed down 6 1/2 oz. Maybe our imagination but seems to be more alert – yes like before – hold his head up for a long time whenever we hold him in our arms. Is the phenobarb reduction having an effect already ?

PREFACE

The story you are about to read describes my experiences with my son Ben, a perfect soul who was born with multiple disabilities, and is a personal account of how I saw things at different times, in different frames of mind, from his birth to age five. It is a story that goes beyond the medical and clinical aspects—a story that arose from a collection of weekly logs that I began keeping (and continue to keep) when Ben was six months old.

Each log contains a detailed account of his milestones and sickness episodes, the outcomes of his numerous appointments as well as any special events. Each also includes a description of how I was feeling that particular week. I did this so that I could remember what had happened in the previous week or previous month or previous year. However, I eventually realized that I could probably turn these logs into something useful for parents and care-givers in similar situations. I know that having a book written by a parent who had experienced the ups and downs of raising a child with even a single disability would have been invaluable to us, especially in the first few months.

Although this book talks about the effects of a particular virus, I believe (and hope) that it can be relevant for care-givers of any child with a disability, to help them understand and deal with the fears and hardships they may have to face. I hope it will also have a broader appeal so that readers may relate my experience to some aspect of their own lives, to reinforce an awareness of the fragility and miracle of human life.

Most individuals mentioned in this text have fictitious names although they do represent actual people. It is important to understand that my comments about them are purely my opinion and that nothing should be inferred about their effectiveness or ineffectiveness to care for others. My attitudes and assessments are a direct result of how I reacted and coped under the circumstances, for better or for worse. (That's my disclaimer!)

Early in the story, you will discover that I had some intense interactions with my parents, especially when they were disrespectful of Ben and our plight. I have chosen to share these to illustrate that those you expect to be closest to you in difficult times are often unable to provide much support at all, trapped by their own fears and prejudices. As time passed, my parents did have moments of compassion and, despite numerous disagreements, we are still family.

If you are a parent of a child with "special needs" (though I hate that term), it is also important to understand that your child will progress at his or her own rate, possibly faster than Ben did, or not. Draw encouragement from your faster developer but do not get discouraged if your child is slower. Share the pain and the joy of each day. Draw strength from my experience if you can. Keep as positive an attitude as possible. Get educated. Persevere. But most of all, remember that you are not alone; there will always be people to help you along the way.

I hope that I am one of them.

ACKNOWLEDGEMENTS

I must begin by thanking the trio of physicians who were such a big part of Ben's life and ours in the first few years, not that any of us really had a choice about that.

Dr. Emile Paras is Ben's paediatrician. Tireless, dedicated, compassionate, and funny. He was and is there for us day and night, without fail. There is no one quite like him nor do I think there ever will be. If he ever retires, the medical community will have lost a giant.

Dr. Cecil Ojah, one of the first specialists we saw, told us to take Ben home and just love him like we would any child. His kindness, sincerity, and willingness to help us at any time are characteristics we will always cherish and something that is lost on many in the medical profession—a true gentleman.

Dr. David Meek we nicknamed "Dr. Bleak" because his prognoses were never uplifting. His steady hand and uncanny ability to listen were strangely comforting at the worst of times. A genuine desire to help was evident in all that he did.

There are several other people I must thank, as well.

Long Huynh is my good friend and mentor. This book would not have been possible without his unwavering support. Our days as master/apprentice that spanned two successful IT companies helped to mold my critical thinking and soften my edges. Long's commitment to proof-read (and tear apart) my early writings is something I can never repay. What I thought would take six months lasted two-and-a-half years but Long never strayed from the goal and repeatedly thanked *me* for the opportunity to help. That says it all.

Conor and Tori are the rocks that we leaned on far too often. Their common-sense ideas and innocent loving nature are what parents dream about. Ben knew this every day, especially during those times when Jan and I were completely lost.

Jan is the love of my life who never stops bringing sensibility to my life. She picked me up every time I was down, no matter how wild things got. Our bond is truly unbreakable, truly unique, and no one else really knows what that means. Jan, you know I love you too much, and that's not good!

And, not least, Ben! You have unleashed a passion in me that makes me whole. I hope I am equal to the task.

1

"MRS. GEORGE, WE HAVE A PROBLEM!"

Confident. Complacent. Perhaps a little of both. I'd even go so far as to so say "experienced" as THE day finally arrives. That's what's in the air today. I had witnessed two previous births up close, though I like to call them two previous miracles. Each came with no surprises and the imminent arrival of baby number three has become very predictable. It is a scheduled birth, for 10 a.m. on Wednesday, June 29, a caesarean-section like the others. It is almost too easy, ". . . you will have a baby today." Yes, today is going to be a good day.

It wasn't always this way. We weren't really excited about having another child. The sleepless nights, the diapers, the middle-of-the-night feedings: we thought all of that was behind us. We needed some sleep, having been deprived of it for two years. Not only that, but how could we afford to raise three children under four years of age?

Our life was so perfect with just Conor and Tori. Two young children, one son and one daughter, 15 months apart, and two young professionals, Jan and I. A millionaire's family, people remarked. Jan blamed herself, she blamed me, we blamed others around us for not doing something to prevent any more pregnancies, and I battled with my religious faith. It was such a contradiction. In the end, we did nothing but argue about it. We did nothing because we had little confidence that the confidentiality of any preventive measure would be guaranteed. It's a small town. People talk. Each time we argued, it proved self-defeating. And, of course, it was pointless. We were having another child.

It was very different when Jan was first pregnant with Conor. I was very much on edge with both anxiety and anticipation, barely 25 years old, just a kid, and just finishing graduate school in the far-off Canadian prairie lands. I remember my fears being washed away following that first ultrasound. Those images were so life-like: I could see Conor moving very slowly, lifting his hand and putting his finger to his cheek, as if he had an itch that had to be scratched. For several months after, a mark remained on his cheek and I'm sure he did it that day. During that eye-opening experience, I realized that I was watching a living being, growing, moving, developing. It made it all seem so real, and I counted all of his fingers and toes. Kind of silly when you think about it, and really, quite shallow of me.

The clock inches ever so close to the top of the hour and I am feeling very prepared. The pregnancy had been uneventful (easy for me to say, of course). All tests over the past nine months have revealed a so-called "healthy, normal fetus." The other two deliveries had been fine. Jan takes care of herself as she always does. It is all so familiar to us. Was that experience? . . . complacency? . . . confidence?

*   *   *

The birth

I am in my greens by 9:45 a.m. and wait, impatiently, for them to call me. At least 20 minutes pass and I start pacing. In an agitated tone, I ask a nurse how much longer. It is close to 10:20 a.m. before they allow me into the O/R.

Dr. Losier, a tall, gentle man, is well underway with his team of nurses when I sit down on a cold, metal stool next to Jan. I ask her why the delay and she nervously tells me that she had passed out and they had to bring her around. She had had that fainting feeling just before Tori's birth, too.

We wait what seems like an hour until, at 10:29 a.m., Dr. Losier calls out that it is a boy. Jan is able to hold him almost immediately and the anaesthesiologist asks us his name.

"Benjamin," we say in unison.

Ben's newborn skin is quite slimy and bloody—a normal sight.

I watch while they clean and weigh him (6lbs 6oz—a little more than Tori but a lot smaller than Conor), and score him Apgars of 8 and 9. While they are weighing him, one of the nurses points to a little rash on his tummy. Another nurse shrugs it off as nothing important.

A short time later, the three of us are in the recovery room. We start making the necessary phone calls to Ben's grandparents to announce his arrival. My parents, as expected, are not impressed by the name we have chosen, believing that all male grandchildren should include their grandfather's name. Why can't they just be happy for us?

It is close to noon when a nurse comes to get Ben and mentions that she is going to stop into the Unit to get his tummy rash checked. I tell Jan that I will meet her back in her room and leave for the cafeteria to get some lunch.

Proud and self-assured, and with sandwich and cola in hand, I stop at the nursery to peek in at Ben. Oddly, he isn't there. Something doesn't feel right. About 10 minutes later, while I am sitting in Jan's hospital room waiting for her, a nurse pops her head in and says, "They want to see you in the Unit."

Who are "they" and why do they want to see me? Where is the Unit?

The "something-is-not-right" feeling is starting to grow and the closer I get to the Unit the faster my heart beats. My face is flushed and my head is beginning to pound, thinking that there's something wrong with Jan. As I arrive at the doors to the Unit, Jan is wheeled out of the adjacent recovery room with a troubled and puzzled look on her face. I ask her what is happening and she says that they won't tell her anything.

*   *   *

Haunting words

We wait at the back of the Unit as one of the neonatologists approaches us. Dr. Dunphy is a compact woman with tight, curly hair and very round glasses. I fixate on her glasses that sit so perfectly on her short nose. Her face is expressionless so I know it is serious, whatever it is. Ignoring me, Dr. Dunphy turns to Jan and calmly says, "*Mrs. George. We have a problem.*" Her calmness seems ice cold and is making it hard for me to breathe.

And then what seems like a run-on of words . . .

"You have a very sick baby. He has an enlarged liver, an enlarged spleen, his head is too small, and his platelets are dangerously low. He may not live the day!"

Then a barrage of questions.

"Did you ever have rubella?"

"Were you sick during the pregnancy?"

"Did you have any high fevers?" . . .

No. No. No. What kind of monster is she? How can we remember anything after being told that our son may not live the day? There must be some mistake. We had just held him less than an hour before and everything was fine. We thought, "You must have the wrong baby!"

With my heart coming through my chest, I find myself speechless, motionless, and scared, all at the same time. What is happening to us? Someone must have screwed up. Why weren't these problems discovered before now? The stress is building, the questions are mounting, my worst nightmare is a reality.

After that first tortuous conversation, we are permitted to see Ben. That's exactly what it feels like, that somehow we have been granted some special dispensation to see our own child. He is lying in an incubator, appearing almost lifeless, with wires and monitors surrounding him. The little rash that was discovered on his tummy, the very reason why he was brought to the Unit, has consumed his whole body. A purple-like skin covers him from head to toe (petichiae, it is called), an indication of his low platelets. As we stare at his transformed body, Dr. Dunphy informs us that Ben's platelet count is in the low 30s compared to a normal value of at least 300. She also points out that his tummy is, indeed, a little large, an indication of the enlarged liver and spleen. I just want to hold him. I feel so helpless.

I am not grasping much of what she is saying. I still can't believe that Ben could be so sick so quickly. It has been only a few hours. Her diagnosis must be wrong. Maybe we'll have a few rough days but that's all. I can't imagine anything else.

After we provide Dr. Dunphy with little in the way of answers, she instructs Jan (I appear to be a non-entity) rather matter-of-factly,

"You may go back to your room," and calmly walks away.

*   *   *

Devastated

Sitting in the starkness of Jan's hospital room, I am in disbelief. It is as if someone has decided that my life as I knew it is over and that I will have this incredible burden to carry for the rest of my life. The scars of this day will never heal. The more I think about it the more I ask why we are so deserving of this. I am starting to feel deep anger and resentment towards everyone. Babies are born every day with no complications. What did we do wrong?

My mind is consumed, focused on our venture to this year's Christmas party, and getting away for the weekend, how this is now in danger. But that is six months away. I am troubled about why this seems so important to me now. I'm trying to block it out, to toss it aside, but it won't go away. I'm beginning to feel that our freedom has been taken away—taken away without our permission. Either Ben will be under our care for the rest of our lives, and I mean round-the-clock-care, or he will die and we will be grieving forever.

No matter what happens, I have just experienced what seems like a permanent loss of happiness from my life. Like some massive, impenetrable door has just slammed shut in front of me, the kind you'd find in a medieval castle.

It's all over.

The fun we had with each other, with Conor and Tori, will never return.

I am completely useless in helping Jan deal with anything that has just happened. I have no idea what to say, what to do. After so pleasantly announcing (to some) Ben's arrival such a short time ago, I have to call everyone and explain the turn of events. I don't know what to say, what to do. Things are becoming blurry. Things don't seem real.

*   *   *

So many questions

By chance, I spot the stocky frame of our paediatrician, Dr. Campbell, walking down the hall. Despite the summer heat, he is wearing a wool sweater; he always wears sweaters but his choice today seems out of place. My whole life is out of place today.

I dash towards him realizing that he is completely unaware of the situation. He is someone I trust unconditionally, someone who can cut through the clutter and solve problems. Someone who is undeniably reliable. And maybe even today, a shoulder to cry on. I relay to him the facts as I know them and ask him about CMV, one of the potential causes, we were told, of Ben's problems. Cytomegalovirus derives its name from its appearance under a microscope, where the cells (*cyto*) are significantly large (*megalo*). It's a common virus that often goes undetected and to most people is harmless. "So, if it's so common and so harmless, how is it that Ben is so affected?", I ask Dr. Campbell. His fifty-year-old rugged face curls up with worry. I know he knows something and is not giving me any answers right now. His unwavering dedication to both his profession and the well-being of his patients is instantly brought to the surface, and he assures me that he will find out what it all means.

My ambush is rather unfair but I need to talk to someone. I need answers. I need someone to tell me everything will work out. A small dose of panic is creeping in. I am beginning to realize that uncertainty is really tough to deal with.

A short time later, my father, a physician for 40 years, arrives on the floor. I can't remember whether or not I asked him to come. My head is such a scrambled mess right now. I begin asking him about CMV since Dr. Campbell was short on answers. In his serious, teacher-like tone which comes out when he really wants to make a point, he says that he knows little about the effects it can have on newborns but understands it is often a complication with transplant patients who are taking immuno-suppressants, as well as with AIDS patients. I pause, not knowing what that sentence has to do with Ben.

No one has any answers for us. The fear of him dying is growing larger by the minute.

*   *   *

Sadness

Before June 29, I really didn't know sadness. I thought I did. I thought I had done all the right things and didn't expect anything less than a perfect baby. But today, I'm being told that it doesn't matter what I had done, thought I'd done, expected would happen. Today, my world has been destroyed.

Never in my life have I experienced feelings of such intensity. They are overwhelming me, consuming me. I want to run but there's nowhere to run to. There is no one to turn to for comfort, for answers, for anything.

We are quickly seeing that everyone we talk to knows very little about anything to do with Ben. As the hours pass, we begin feeling more and more isolated, more and more alone, more and more like outcasts. No one knows quite what to say to us.

In six years of marriage and the six years I knew Jan before that, I have never seen her this way. I have never felt this way. Sitting at her bedside while she dozes, I am swept away to the summer of our high school graduation. The memory is so vivid right now, I can taste it. That humid summer evening. A perfect setting. No one else around. Just the two of us. Swaying on the park swings. Talking. Planning our future. Where we would live. Picturing our lives together forever. Always in love. Always happy, though not sure how we would do it since Jan would be going to Sackville to college and I to Halifax. A two-hour train ride apart. Short but still apart. That night, it didn't matter. Nothing could dampen the moment.

Something special was being born then. A deep sense of peace and happiness, unlike any other time. Something we both knew no one could take away. A connection, a bond that would keep us together forever, that we would thirst for every day, that would never allow us to be apart for very long, that would intertwine our thoughts and emotions so completely that we always would know what the other was thinking. A oneness that few people ever come to know.

Watching the rising and falling of her chest, I feel that that once-indestructible bond is now crumbling around me. I didn't think that was possible. There was nothing stronger, I thought. For this first time I begin to believe that something could actually tear us apart. It is making every cell in my body ache, like an itch that can never be scratched. The more I dwell on this the more it drives me crazy, making me jumpy, spinning me out of control.

What is happening to us?

*   *   *

2

THE FIRST (WORST) WEEK

They have no beginning or ending, these first few days; they just happen, all pretty much a blur, a constant run-on of events. We are told that there would be no confirmed diagnosis for several days but it is one of three culprits: cytomegalovirus, which was already suggested, rubella, or toxoplasmosis. Talking in this language makes me ill. The birth of your child is supposed to be a joyous event, a time for celebration, unlike any other. The hours and days that follow are a time when you begin to form and nurture that important bond with your child, one that will last a lifetime. Instead, the only thing that will last a lifetime are those haunting words of Dr. Dunphy. They keep playing over and over in my head.

". . . You have a very sick baby! He may not live the day! . . ."

". . . You have a very sick baby! He may not live the day! . . ."

By Day 3, I give in to Conor's relentless requests to see his brother. My attempts to shelter his 3-year-old mind from this awful place are no match for his burning desire to welcome Ben to our family. We cautiously enter the rear of the neonatal unit, through the same doors that Jan and I had entered for the first time a few days ago. Conor searches the aisles with his energetic eyes looking for Ben until we lead him to the incubator where his brother is lying, peacefully. His eyes widen as he examines the complex of wires and monitors that surround Ben, perking his ears at their unfriendly tones, their beeps and warbles. We aren't able to hold Ben but that doesn't stop Conor from letting him know that his big brother has been to see him.

He reaches into a side pocket of his shorts that he has willingly donned to combat the summer heat and pulls out a yellow miniature toy truck. He's certain that Ben will love these toys as much as he does, as much as I did at his age. We talk to the nurse about leaving it with Ben; no problem, we're told. And without hesitation, Conor places his little hand inside Ben's incubator and gently parks the truck next to his sleeping head. The haze that has enveloped my head for the past three days is suddenly lifted.

A new bond is forming, a new friendship has begun.

Some early tests

I just want someone to tell me that Ben will be all right, that maybe he'll have some difficulties in the first few months but "... *if you do these things, follow this list, it will all work out fine* ..." I can't seem to find this person.

Learning the results of each test brings a new set of information to digest but it's difficult to put it all together. Ben has long-bone scans, CAT scans, liver-enzyme tests, and on and on. We have nothing to compare with other than "normal" values, so the information isn't really informative at all.

One afternoon, the door to Jan's hospital room is opened by a stocky woman dressed in a yellow hospital gown. Like Dr. Dunphy a few days earlier, her face is expressionless. Without even a simple, "Hi," she walks over to Jan, introduces herself as Jennifer, one of the audiologists with the hospital. Again, in Dr. Dunphy-like style, she proceeds to tell Jan that Ben has failed all of the screening tests that she has performed. As far as she can determine, he has a very severe hearing loss and she is not really sure how much he will ever be able to hear. She does, however, recommend having the tests repeated in a month since, under "better circumstances", the results may be better.

Jan just nods and replies, "Okay".

What are we supposed to do with this conversation other than add ". . . *failed all screening tests* . . ." and ". . . *never be able to hear* . . ." to our vernacular. Did we really need to know this now? Does it really matter whether or not Ben is deaf given all of the other issues he's been handed?

What am I saying? If we had been told that about Conor or Tori, we would have been devastated. But somehow, learning that Ben could likely be deaf almost seems insignificant. Who cares about his hearing ability when he may not "live the day"?

It kills me that I can't be with Ben every second of the day, especially during his tests and throughout the night. How do I know if all these experts really know what they're talking about? Do they even know how to conduct these tests on a person so small, so fragile? One of the neonatal nurses told us he was having seizure episodes earlier in the day. I mean, how can you tell? He always sleeps whenever we are with him. Does he even know we're there? Does he know who his parents are?

A short time after Jennifer imparts her words of discouragement, my mother arrives. We have had many visitors over the past few days but most are unable to provide any comfort. Most don't know what to say to us or what questions are appropriate to ask. It doesn't matter since we have no answers. Some avoid discussing Ben altogether. My mother is one of them.

Our relationship has always been one of Dr. Jekyll and Mr. Hyde, like a heavy pendulum that swings unimpeded. Both of us are "the babies" of our respective families and some days I think she longs for the days when I was a 13-year old living at home. Young enough to be admonished and controlled. Perhaps me being the last to leave the nest, despite that being more than a decade ago, makes it all the more difficult for her to develop any sort of adult relationship. And me calling Jan "my wife," she has never really accepted. I was too young to get married and Jan certainly wasn't good enough for me, in her mind. The grief she put us through only weeks before our wedding still lingers with me.

This afternoon, she knows enough not to chastise me for my usual faults but chooses to carry on a very one-sided conversation with us. I am mystified why she makes no attempt to see Ben, to talk about him, or to ask us what she can do to help. It seems more important for her to talk about the chaos she is dealing with having the carpet replaced on the outside steps of her house. At the best of times, that topic would have only mildly interested me. Today, I'm angry. I don't even want to talk to her. I want her to leave if that's the best she can do. Bring back Dr. Dunphy! At least she cares about helping Ben.

*   *   *

The baptism

By the weekend, the migraine-inducing buzz of the hospital dims to a barely audible hum. All of the clinics are closed and the routine 7 a.m. to 3 p.m. staffers are nowhere to be found. I won't say it's refreshing but it gives us a breather, though the quietness is a little eerie. With no tests scheduled or doctors poking at Ben, we spend some time comforting him. Jan cradles him in her arms despite the countless wires attached to his little body, tenderly rocking in a soothing rhythm. He just sleeps and sleeps. I want him to open his eyes so I can tell him how much I love him.

The soft footsteps of a visitor interrupts the rhythmic ticking of the rocking chair. It is our parish priest, Fr. O'Reilley. Word of Ben has obviously spread throughout our circle of friends. Sitting beside Jan, I immediately jump to my feet to greet him. My reaction is a conditioned response, ingrained from years of Emily-Post-training by my mother. I am glad to see him though, and his presence begins to bring a momentary calm to me, a welcomed relief to the bombardment of negativity that has been heaped upon us.

We describe to him the sequence of events of the past few days, a jumbled synopsis told in a nervous manner. He can feel our suffering. Most of all, he can feel our desire to know why we have to deal with this. We tell him our faith has been greatly tested and we're very unsure of ourselves. He can't answer our questions or lessen our anxiety but his gentleness and compassion is a perfect mix for us today.

Uncovering a small bottle of holy water and a leather bound book, he asks us if he can baptize Ben. I have never truly considered the importance of this first sacrament until right now. It would not have been something I would have thought could be done in the hospital but I'm glad he's here. The ceremony takes less than 10 minutes.

Ben is really not aware of what has just been accomplished but we are. In an instant, our pain is suspended, like we have just entered the calmness and serenity of the eye of a hurricane. There are no projectiles swirling overhead anymore, waiting to inflict more injury and suffering. For a few moments, I don't feel alone or abandoned, but start to think that maybe things will get better very soon. I really don't know what to think but I like what I'm feeling.

*   *   *

"He may never . . ."

The next day many of the results of the early tests are available and Dr. Dunphy's colleague has requested to speak with us about them. His name is Dr. Smythe and he leads us to a somewhat private corner at the opposite end of the Unit so we can talk without interruption.

His body language exudes a thoughtful and caring person, a welcome atmosphere, and his long, well-manicured beard tells us he is very approachable.

Dr. Smythe begins by confirming that CMV is the cause of all of Ben's troubles. For most people, this virus is quite innocuous and adults are often unaware that they have contracted it. But to a developing fetus it can be very destructive, especially if it is contracted during the first trimester. All indications are that's what had happened in Jan's case. He goes on to describe some of the results and the impacts they may have down the road, focusing especially on a list of cognitive and motor delays. We aren't surprised to hear a lot of this since we have had access to some medical texts that described about a dozen cases related to CMV. It was not easy reading but we are now somewhat prepared for the list of the problems Ben may face.

After 15 minutes of quiet discussion with Dr. Smythe, a tall man with a gangly frame approaches us, almost tentatively. His name is Dr. Norris, a paediatric neurologist. Probably of similar age to Dr. Smythe, in his late forties, he introduces himself in a relatively soft voice, appearing unusually shy for a physician, perhaps even a little awkward.

The tone of his conversation is altogether different—very monotone and serious—as he bemoans Ben's lack of normal brain development as a major concern. Of course, most of his patients have serious conditions, since neurological issues can be quite disturbing and very depressing. He speaks of all of the neurological tests that Ben has received but focuses on Ben's microcephaly (i.e. his head being smaller than normal) as a key indicator that his brain has been significantly impacted by the virus. The results of the CAT scans clearly highlight extensive calcifications in the brain which indicate that many areas are not functioning normally and likely will not ever do so. There is also a noted extra concern regarding the enlarged ventricles in Ben's brain, an indication of an overabundance of fluid. He mentions the possibility that shunts would need to be inserted if this condition persists to help drain the fluid and prevent any pressure from occurring.

I sit motionless, in disbelief. It is all too much to rationalize. Essentially, Ben's brain is a mess, or at least that's the message I'm hearing. How can someone so little have so many major things go wrong? My God, we are only into Day 4 of Ben's fragile life. The peace of the baptism the day before has been rudely and completely swept away.

Dr. Norris tries to relate what it all might mean down the road by summarizing it into one disturbing sentence:

"Ben may never be able to walk, or talk, or go to school."

Wow. I'm trying really hard to grasp what all this means. While he continues to speak, I try imagining what life would be like for any parents whose child could not walk, or talk, or go to school. Not all three, just one of those conditions. But then add to it a profound hearing loss, an enlarged liver and spleen, seizures . . . What is happening to us?

We don't want to hear any more. We have been presented with this laundry list of problems but shown no path to resolving any of them. This bleak diagnosis makes us feel even more helpless and more isolated. The eye-wall of the hurricane has quickly descended upon us. The sunshine has vanished and the swirling projectiles are back, this time even stronger. Oh, how I want to rewind my life to a week ago when I didn't know about any of this, to a year ago before Ben was conceived, to see what I missed, what I did wrong or didn't do to be put in this desperate situation.

We slowly make our way to the far corner where Ben is sleeping, leaving Dr. Smythe and Dr. Norris behind. Looking at Ben's tiny body, the rising and falling of his chest, I hold Jan tightly and begin to slip into a downward death-spiral, believing that our dreams are forever dashed, our lives forever burdened. We are left without direction or purpose, and keep asking ourselves, why?

* * *

Day 7—going home

Tuesday, July 5 dawns another sunny day. The weather has been perfect since the day Ben was born, which hardly seems fair. It almost feels like the world is bragging how wonderful life is. After seven days of immersion in the artificial life-support world of the Unit, almost to the point of drowning, we want out.

Quietly, throughout the week, Ben has shown steady improvement. His platelet count has crossed the 130 level, having more than quadrupled from Day 1 and his condition is now noted as "stable." We are seeing that he is showing signs that he is a fighter, making Dr. Dunphy eat her words.

Both she and Dr. Smythe are present today. We grab Dr. Smythe's attention and eagerly express our desire to leave this wretched place. Quite willingly, he agrees and believes that we will all do better in the familiar surroundings of our own home. But our eagerness is tainted with much anxiety and uncertainty. What will we do if he starts having seizures at home? Would we even recognize a seizure? What if he doesn't eat for us? That "experience" of being parents twice before is worth nothing right now. In his calm and reassuring manner, Dr. Smythe simply tells us to forget everything, to just take Ben home and love him. That's all we should focus on.

His words are a cure for our nervousness. But to keep things in check, we will be kept on a short leash, needing to return every two weeks for the foreseeable future to have Ben's bloods done, at least until his liver functions are closer to normal and his platelet count is out of the worry zone.

Wrapped in a blanket and donning a brand new blue outfit, Ben seems ready to go. I haven't really noticed his eyes until now. They're big, they're beautiful, they're normal. These guys have to be wrong.

Ben doesn't really know what home is, of course, but he seems very content to come along with us. His mood and expressions are not unlike those of Conor and Tori at that age. Our lives are so very confusing and unsettling right now. Maybe the horrific predictions will not come true and the worst week of our lives will finally be over.

We walk out of the main doors of the hospital as new parents again having no idea what tomorrow will bring. The warmth of the July sun is soothing and relaxing. The buzz of the traffic and the bustle of the crowd continues without the slightest clue of what we have just been through. No one knows and no one cares. Life does go on and so must we.

* * *

3

THE FIRST SIX MONTHS

Stumbling into the boys' room as the clock nudges past 7 a.m., having been awakened by the murmur of little voices, I am met with the smiles of two brothers enjoying each other's company, their faces aglow in the morning brightness. Ben rolls effortlessly from his back to his tummy with the experience of a toddler and pushes his face against the crib's rails, peeking above the side cushions to get a good look at me and his brother. It is a wonderful scene, in complete contrast to the past two weeks. It's as if those painful, empty days had never happened.

For a moment, I am awash in a river of tremendous peace.

I approach Ben's side to pick him up and give him a big hug. Somehow, my legs don't want to move—there's something blocking them. I look down and see there's nothing there. I don't seem to be standing on anything. Very quickly, my head feels disconnected from my body and I find myself drifting up and away from the bedroom. I am transplanted outside and Conor and Ben are running around the front lawn. When did Ben get big? How did he learn to walk? Something isn't right.

I'm feeling agitated and restless. I can see them but I can't touch them. Everything around me is moving very fast.

Suddenly, I am back in bed, feeling myself tossing and turning. I open my eyes and feel Jan's body beside me. Confused, I sit up and look at the clock. It reads 7:02 a.m. I tiptoe into the boys' room which is still in darkness.

Both are sleeping and Ben is just as he was yesterday. Dejected, I fall back into bed as tears slowly trickle down my cheeks. The emptiness returns stronger than ever.

2:30 a.m. feedings

Middle-of-the-night feedings are a killer but they're unavoidable. And they are my small contribution to giving Jan the rest she so truly needs and deserves. Despite all of his problems, Ben very much enjoys eating, liquid-form of course, and he behaves like clockwork in this regard. Predictable and punctual.

After a few days of initiation, my body becomes adjusted to the 2:30 a.m. wakeup call, responding to the 45-minute feeding routine in a very mechanical if not zombie-like manner.

It begins with an occasional cry or rustling from Ben in his antique cradle. This is my signal that I must haul my tired body out of bed with eyes half shut and find my way to his side. To avoid waking up Jan, I gently but quickly scoop up Ben's little body and quietly take us both to the family room downstairs.

A couch substitutes as a change table for this punishing time of day though it doesn't take long to freshen him up. Ben's reaction to a clean diaper is no different than that of any child—relief and comfort.

Before settling in to a tasty 4 oz meal, Ben waits while I start up the next episode of *Star Trek* on our well-used VCR. I have viewed these adventures dozens of times, knowing much of the dialogue by heart, but watching them helps fill the void in this early hour.

Ben loves his *Isomil* and drinks it effortlessly, even through those moments where I really am a zombie. After several productive burps, he falls back to sleep . . . and sometimes I join him. My body doesn't completely relax since it somehow remembers that Ben is still within my grasp but my mind flies off to a world of fast-changing events that are completely unrelated to each another. Often, I am transported to the hospital where I can't seem to find Ben. The sounds and the smells are familiar but nauseating. The images are recognizable and novel at the same time, a reality that leaves me restless and confused.

The whirring of a kitchen appliance or the ticking of a clock often extracts me abruptly from my dream world. My eye lids quickly unfurl like two roller shades that have been snapped open and I slowly gather my bearings. I'm not sure which world I prefer.

This morning, I am awakened by the TV. The final scene of the episode, "Space Seed," is just beginning, in which the villain, Khanoonian Singh, played by Ricardo Montalban, is about to be transported to a barren, uninhabited planet after his attempt to commandeer the *Enterprise* has been foiled.

Before departing, he remarks to Captain Kirk,

"Have you ever read Milton, Captain?" His reference is to the epic poem *Paradise Lost*, in which Lucifer states that "it is better to reign in Hell than to serve in Heaven." But this reference to Milton, the classic poet whom my father tried desperately to get me to read as a young adolescent, is really resonating with me this time, evoking a passage from the one and only sonnet of his that I did read:

> "... *God does not need either man's work or his own gifts; who best bear his mild yoke, they serve him best . . .*"

As I recite these words in my mind, I feel the hair on the back of my neck stand up and a tingly chill race down my body. I'm a little frightened by it all.

With the closing credits rolling up the screen, I come back to life just in time to carry Ben to his waiting cradle at the foot of our bed. Somehow he has magically snuggled into my neck. You'd never know there was anything wrong.

*   *   *

My parents' 40th wedding anniversary

From early July to early August, five wedding anniversaries are celebrated in our families, with mine and Jan's rounding out the list. This year my parents are celebrating their 40th wedding anniversary and for my mother, it is a big deal. Bigger than Ben's birth, it seems, for despite all we have gone through since June 29, it is full steam ahead for this celebration.

The guest list had been prepared in the weeks prior to Ben's birth with my mother handling all the invitations herself. Rather than allowing her offspring to manage this affair, she has organized everything—and, though this is one of her strengths, things just have to be done her way.

The only item she hasn't managed is booking the photographer. Eleven years ago, my sister had a bad experience with a local professional (though he is probably one of the top photographers in the country) but once you fail with my mother, it is rarely forgotten. It would have been suicidal for any of us to select this same individual, so we opt to choose another bidder.

The number of guests streaming through the front door is a lot fewer than I was expecting so it's not a crowded, congested atmosphere. I get the sense that my mother has had a number of declines and that she is somewhat disappointed. Perhaps she took on too much of the planning herself and didn't give people enough lead time. A handful of those who do show up make an effort to greet the newest addition to the George family but it's clear they're only being polite.

When it comes time for the family portrait, the second-rater we have hired is just that and we realize at that moment that you get what you pay for. The resulting print holds the memory quite well but the quality is just . . . well . . . average. In it, my mother is cradling Ben's tiny, 12-day-old body in her arms but her smile and the awkward manner in which she holds him very much shows her discomfort, and even, perhaps, embarrassment since he isn't "normal." Deep inside, I want to believe that she wants to love him but doesn't really know how. I hope this is the case.

Try as I might, I just can't feel good about this milestone that so few ever reach. Ben is where the focus should be, something my family should realize. I really don't want to be here.

*   *   *

Pain, and more pain

An hour after his supper bottle, Ben turns very irritable. It's Day 21 of Ben's already burdened life and he is not happy. Nothing is able to console him as his lungs blast out his pain in a continuous shrill. For six solid hours, his crying is incessant, though it ebbs and flows between whimpers and piercing screams. As the clock slowly ticks past midnight, he falls asleep on Jan's shoulder—sheer exhaustion has finally taken over. Jan and I are frazzled, not quite understanding what has just happened or how Ben could have the energy to cry for that long.

He awakes the next morning the same way he has the other mornings—content, smiling, generally happy. No signs of any discomfort or anything that would have provoked last evening's wailing. His day carries on in a rather normal fashion. As evening approaches, his irritability resurfaces for no obvious reasons. I check every inch of his body looking for signs of redness, soreness, or pinched skin. After listening to an hour of crying, Jan and I strap Ben into his stroller and go for a walk through the neighbourhood. The summer evening air is somewhat consoling to Ben but he still isn't very happy. His wailing isn't as painful to hear outside the confines of our home but there is clearly something bothering him. Like the previous day, he somehow musters the energy to cry and sob for another six-hour period. Again, falling asleep from sheer exhaustion.

After two nights in a row of this uncontrollable sobbing, we are very confused and concerned. We come up with a dozen reasons why he is inconsolable—he has a bowel obstruction; he has a hernia; he has some sort of virus that is causing him pain; and on and on.

Night after night, his little body writhes in pain and he screams it out to the world. No position makes any noticeable difference, no talking or singing or reading stories changes his mood or the volume of sobbing. Three weeks into this inhumane cycle, we are becoming numb. Jan and I take turns walking the basement floor with him, taking 90-minute shifts. When one is trying to comfort Ben, the other just has to get out of the house. Each night, we feel ourselves nearing the breaking point.

One evening, we think we can get ahead of Ben's pain by changing his surroundings. We choose to take an early evening stroll near the city's boardwalk. Ben's eyes are wide with excitement at the bustle of pedestrians and corner musicians. So far, so good.

Without warning, Jan's knees buckle and she doubles over in pain, as if she were shot. She can't move nor can she talk. The methodical flow of people continues past us though a few passers-by pause and stare. I am taken completely off guard and have no idea what to do. Rather than attempt to console her, I stand beside her, motionless. My world doesn't seem real right now. After 10 minutes of agony, Jan straightens up and continues walking, but it ends any hope of a relaxing evening. Neither of us are sure what has just happened but her pain is gone. On the ride home, Ben picks up where he left off last night. Our excursion has only slightly delayed the inevitable. No matter what time he crashes after his wailing, he somehow finds the energy to awaken for his 2:30 a.m. feeding. I'm not sure I can continue at this pace.

Jan's pain episodes return within a few weeks and become more frequent, with each one just as excruciating and immobilizing. A routine appointment with Dr. Losier finds the source of her debilitating pain, a pain second only to childbirth I'm told. It is her gall bladder and she is booked for a laparoscopic procedure to remove it. Dr. Losier tells her that the stress of the physical and hormonal changes of a pregnancy can sometimes affect the body's equilibrium or expedite some conditions to their logical conclusion. Apparently, her gall bladder was destined to be removed sooner or later. Whatever the reason, it doesn't seem fair.

The day of Jan's procedure, I cut short my work day to coincide with her departure from the recovery room. I arrive a little early (which is unusual for me) and wait about 30 minutes before she is shuffled up to her room. We're both surprised to discover that she is still in moderate discomfort. We expected total relief. I find a nurse to tell her how Jan is feeling, indicating that her abdomen is still throbbing. She's a bit stand-offish, not really thinking too much of it, and tells Jan to get some rest, that she should feel better soon. Something is not right here but no one is paying attention. I don't have the energy to demand answers.

A week out of hospital, Jan's pain is back, though not as severe. Two days later, she is re-admitted to remove two gall stones that are making their way through her body. Why they weren't noticed and removed the first time around is unclear. Finding gall stones isn't a medical rarity. No one wants to be responsible. No one really cares. Our lives are turning more and more complicated and our care-free approach to life is just about gone.

On a cool evening several weeks later, our house is still and quiet. My watch innocently displays the time of day as 7:20 p.m. Conor and Tori are playing outside with a neighbour's dog and Ben is nicely propped in his chair. The wailing, the sobbing, is no more. Our evenings usurped by Ben's relentless crying have come to an end. It is over. This is unfamiliar territory for us and I expect Ben is as glad as we are.

However, I can't remember any of the activities I did with Conor and Tori during that time. Whatever I participated in was done without feeling, without enjoyment, without wonderment, without noticing. I have lost 65 days of my life.

* * *

Awful thoughts

I am nearly to the 75th floor on the *StairClimber*'s display when a female voice interrupts the music playing over the fitness club's PA system.

"Michael George, please come to the front desk. Michael George, please come to the front desk. Thank you."

I am perplexed that I am being summoned. Dripping, panting, and red faced, I disembark from the exercise machine and make a path to the front desk. After introducing myself, the staff member hands me the phone and says Charmin wants to speak with me. My brow wrinkles. Charmin? The *receptionist-at-my-office-Charmin*? What could she want?

"Hi Charmin," I answer, trying to slow my breathing.

"Mike, your wife just called. Ben had to be rushed by ambulance to the hospital. I think she said that he had a seizure!"

"Oh, okay. Thanks." And I hand the phone back. No one is aware of what I had just been told nor does anyone really care. They all continue to answer phones, greet members, and work out. The music has returned, blaring some ridiculous song to the whole club.

I rush back into the men's locker room and change. No time for a shower. My head is very fuzzy but I know I must get to the hospital as quickly as possible. Fumbling through the locker, I stuff as many of my belongings as I can into my duffle bag and head for the exit.

I hail a cab, jump in and blast out a command to get me to the hospital. My mind is racing a thousand miles an hour and my body is still sweating. Suddenly, I realize that I don't have any money on me to pay for the ride.

Once at the ER entrance, I burst inside, still panting, and ask the first person I see where I can find Ben. After a few minutes of moving in slow motion, trying as hard as she can NOT to find out for me, this person, who now realizes that she shouldn't have come to work today, responds,

"Ah, he's in bed #10. Just go through the doors down the hall. Down there."

When I get to Ben's side, I discover him lying on the gurney, nearly stripped bare of clothing and hooked up to a monitor. I am a bit surprised to see that he doesn't look in any discomfort. Jan is standing there, telling the nurse something. As I focus on Ben, Jan quickly directs her voice in my direction to explain how Conor had run over to a neighbour to get them to help . . . and how Ben had reacted . . . and how frightening it was . . . and how she rode in the ambulance with Ben while Conor and Tori stayed with the neighbours. It is just a hodge-podge of statements that make no sense. I just want to take Ben home. I hate this place.

A few days later, it really hits me. The stress of the last four months, of the endless doctor appointments and now the ER visit. I can't even exercise for a half hour without something going wrong. I am starting to realize that maybe the horror stories are coming true. Ben is not getting any better.

What kind of life is he going to have? What if he can't walk, play games, or talk to his friends? What friends would he have anyway if he can't talk? How will he get to school? If he can't to sit up by himself, how can he ever do something as simple as hold a crayon?

Standing over his cradle, I feel my mind slipping into a dark place. He is so peaceful, sleeping with his head resting on a little Jan-crafted pillow. I begin to wonder if everyone would be better off if he suddenly just stopped breathing. The stress would be gone. We could return to a normal life again and finally be free.

As I say my nightly prayers, I ask God why was he even allowed to be born? We can't possibly build a happy life with this massive load placed upon us. This is his "mild yoke"? It's not fair to Conor and Tori. They are so young and have their whole lives ahead of them. There is so much potential there. They shouldn't be burdened with this. I begin to ask God to take him. There's no way I can handle this.

I feel that I have nothing to be thankful for. The future is so dark, so uncertain. I can't understand what I did so terribly wrong to be given this enormous cross to carry. No parents' magazine tells you about what to expect in this situation, where to turn, or what guidelines to follow. I am feeling so lost.

And now I have to deal with seizures? Rushing to the hospital every time? There's no way I can do this. I want to run away from it all. I want to give him up to someone else. How can I get through this? And, really, why should I have to? Who's going to help me? My family is nowhere to be found. What will I do if he's a teenager, drooling in a wheelchair, staring at the ceiling? Who will look after him? We can't afford 24-hour care!

All these swirling thoughts somehow transport me to my childhood neighbourhood as a 12-year-old, playing street hockey with some friends, one of whom had a "retarded" brother (the generally accepted label of the 1970s), who could only sit in his wheelchair on the sidewalk, wearing a football helmet, watching us. I could never understand a word he said. He just moaned and mumbled.

Is that Ben's life 15 years from now? I'll never make it.

*   *   *

1992—A bad year

Three months before Ben was born, my father's only sister asked to be released from hospital so she could spend her final days at home. Stricken with cancer, having smoked very heavily for many years, she had spent the past year in and out of hospital battling a host of issues.

She meant the world to me, so much so that Tori (Victoria) is named after her. She spoiled me as a kid, herself unmarried with only nieces and nephews on whom to shower her love. She would faithfully take me and my friends places on Friday evenings, as long as we could walk there—she didn't have a driver's license. And in later years, she would counsel me on the struggles I had with my parents, both as a teenager and in the months leading up to my wedding.

Today, she is lying in her bed, barely awake, struggling to take every breath. I just have to be there with her. My parents are in San Diego attending a medical convention and no other members of my family are close by—they live in different cities across the country. Ummi (that's "uncle" in Arabic), Vicki's other brother, is with me but he is very distraught, telling me how she's not going to make it, hugging me, kissing me, like he has never done before. He is also somewhat angry that my father isn't here. Midway through the afternoon, one of our parish priests visits, someone who has known Vicki for most of her life.

By this time, she is not conscious. I try to speak to her, to tell her who's with her, but there is no response. As the minutes pass, her breathing becomes more laboured and the colour is slowly disappearing from her finger nails. The years of smoking have finally caught up with her and there's nothing anyone can do. My uncle paces the floor, getting more and more agitated. The priest anoints her, praying for her soul, and bestows upon her the last rites. After we all bless ourselves, it is over. Her chest stops rising and there isn't a sound, except the weeping of those present.

It is an awful day and I am angry, too, that I am the only one of my family here to be with her. A big part of me has died. And I feel some regret that I probably didn't tell her often enough how much she meant to me.

I have never watched someone die until right now.

Several months later, sometime after the nine weeks of Ben's colic hell, I receive a call from my father telling me that Ummi had been admitted to the hospital. Also a heavy smoker, he has fallen victim to the same cancer that took Vicki from us. It's all too much for me. There's nothing left in the tank. Vicki's passing was hard enough but dealing with Ben in these early days has put me over the top.

A week or so later, I meet Ummi sitting on a bench on King Street in the downtown core. Every day for the last 40-plus years, he has taken long walks throughout the city, even into the seedy sections of town, which is rather risky for a provincial court judge. Over the years, I have witnessed his well-crafted skill of understanding people and their behaviours. He has a reputation for being very fair, astute and compassionate—not lenient necessarily, but he commands much respect.

My encounter with him today is just as he is beginning one of those walks. I sit down beside him and begin to chat. He is happy to see me and I him. He had been released from the hospital the day before and wanted to enjoy the early September air, since he realized that he didn't have many days left. That's one of the remarkable things about him—always very matter-of-fact, even in the face of death. His mind was still sharp that day and he wanted to talk about Ben. He doesn't know the full story nor does he have any idea what we've been through the past few months but he tells me to never give up, and kisses me in true Middle Eastern fashion.

It is the last conversation we have. I must heed his advice.

* * *

Searching for answers

Jan and I need to find people who have gone through the same hell we've been through in the past few months. We need to find out more about CMV, talk to people who actually know about CMV, talk to other families, tap into their experience, their learnings, their wisdom.

Our *ad hoc* search leads us to a CMV support network headquartered in Minneapolis. Speaking to one of the coordinators, we are given the names of a few families in Ontario who are part of a parent network. We are eager to share our story and learn from them.

Within a few weeks, the responses to our letter arrive in our mailbox. One family tells of their two sons, the youngest, now three years of age, born with CMV just like Ben. The mother talks of many of the same things we have experienced and describes her son, Jake. Included is a photo of Jake and his brother, both standing beside a tall wooden stool, with Jake holding onto the seat. Seeing that wonderful picture, I am filled with hope and encouragement, foreign to say the least. This image is making me believe that Ben could learn to stand. In the last paragraph is an open invitation to visit them if we ever find ourselves in Toronto. Susan Ward is her name. I write it down.

Another letter describes a family with two girls. Jamie, the youngest, is Ben's CMV-mate. They tell of a different set of experiences but mention how they have visited Jake and his family from time to time. Obviously, this parent network is useful. At the end of the letter, the mother writes,

> "When Jamie was little, I always wanted to see another CMV child, just to see what they looked like, so I am enclosing a picture of Jamie for you to see."

Wow. Her thoughts are our thoughts.

A third letter arrives about a month later and it is very different from the others. In it, the mother writes (I am curious why it's never the father),

> "We don't want to discourage you but our daughter's birth has put a very big burden on our life. Don't get me wrong. We love her more than anything in the world and she has brought us a lot of happiness but the battles, the letters, the phone calls, the trips, and sacrifices that we had to go through have been enormous. She is only 6 ½ years old and we have had to fight for everything she has now. This was not easy because people do not come knocking at your door to offer all these services—you find out by hard work. Through the years we have shed many tears and the anger that we felt towards agencies and government was very exhausting for everyone."

A little voice in the back of my head is whispering that this is somehow a more realistic outlook for Ben. I try to shut it down but I can't.

She goes on to say that she has recently been treated for depression which was a shock to her family since she was always described as a very strong and capable person. She encloses a school picture of her daughter who is very thin.

This one is tough to take. We went looking for answers and we got them, right between the eyes. It doesn't quench our thirst for knowledge, however. We need to sit down with specialists who have treated CMV children, who can give us proper guidance, set us in the right direction, get access to the best services, the best therapy, and the best people. We need to visit a larger centre where there are more kids like Ben, Jake and Jamie.

Following some referrals from Drs. Campbell and Norris, we are booked for a few consultations at Toronto's Hospital for Sick Children (known as Sick Kids). On a chilly, late November day, we make the trip to the big city. Ben's first plane ride and the commute from the airport are both uneventful. Upon arrival, we check ourselves into a low-cost hotel in the downtown core, just steps away from Maple Leaf Gardens.

As we ride the elevator up to our room, Ben is babbling away, repeatedly saying, "Ah, goo. Ah, goo . . ." Standing next to us, smiling, is an older man. He looks down at Ben and asks with a thick accent,

"Why do babies always say 'uncle, uncle'? They say 'uncle'?"

We simply return a smile to him, not really understanding what he's trying to say.

A short time later, the phone rings in our room. It's Susan Ward, one of the CMV moms. She is just leaving work and offers to take us to her home for supper so that we can meet her family, and Jake, of course. We're delighted.

Waiting in the lobby, we see a professionally dressed woman enter, sporting a long overcoat and winter gloves to combat the lingering snow flurries. Her flaxen hair is a bit tousled from the wind and she looks to be our age, late twenties/early thirties. She smiles as she approaches us; Ben is a giveaway. We all climb into her car and head for Oakville, about a 30-minute ride at this time of day. Ben seems intrigued by the car ride—the speed, the darkness of early evening, the passing lights.

Susan's husband greets us as we pull in front of the small, two-storey, well appointed home. This is true suburbia—the kind you read about—with houses and courts and playgrounds as far as the eye can see. Entering their foyer, we can feel the warmth of their family. We go in a little further and meet her two sons. They are both good-looking kids and we can instantly sense their closeness. Jake doesn't speak but seems eager to greet us. Ben is just satisfied to take in his new surroundings.

We spend a very relaxing few hours in their home, sharing stories, but most of all listening to their advice. They instruct us that while it is certainly important to include Ben as much as possible, not to do so at the expense of his siblings, nor focus so much on Ben that their needs are ignored. It's so easy to do, to get caught up in all of Ben's needs.

Before dropping us back at the hotel, Susan insists that we keep in touch, and says she would like to meet Ben's brother and sister some time. We thank her again, and promise her that we will certainly do that. Getting the opportunity to meet her and her family is something very special. Perhaps I do have something to be thankful for.

The next morning, we hail a cab to Sick Kids hospital. It is a huge complex nestled among several office towers, close to the main campus of the University of Toronto—a little intimidating and overwhelming, needless to say.

Our first appointment is with Dr. Crowley, an ear, nose and throat specialist. After being escorted to an examination room, we are greeted by a young man who fails to introduce himself. We assume he is a resident since he looks to be about our age. Sitting abruptly onto a metal stool, he flips through some paperwork, occasionally catching a glimpse of Ben.

"So . . . ," he pauses. "You're here for a consult on a cochlear implant for your son?", he impatiently asks.

Jan and I look at each other, a bit confused. This isn't the first impression we were expecting. We thought they would know why we are here. We thought Sick Kids was supposed to be the Mecca of children's hospitals in the country. Doesn't he understand that Ben is only five months old and wouldn't be a candidate for this type of procedure? We have just spent a tonne of money that we didn't have so that we could talk to some real experts . . . and he thinks we want Ben to have a cochlear implant?

We politely respond that we've traveled a long way to see Dr. Crowley not to discuss a cochlear implant. He slams the file folder shut and tells us that Dr. Crowley will be along shortly but he needs to get a history from us first. The questions he asks seem redundant, since we expect the answers would have already been provided in the referral from Dr. Campbell but we cooperate. We wait an additional half hour to see Dr. Crowley and the outcome is benign, much to our disappointment.

Later in the morning, we meet Dr. Forester, an infectious-disease specialist who, we are told, knows everything there is to know about CMV. She tells us that she has been looking forward to meeting us. Through an insightful 20-minute interaction, she gives us a broad perspective about the disease and how it is managed. In particular, she informs us that it is unlikely that it will cause any further damage, which means that Ben's condition and challenges should stabilize over time. Basically, all of the damage has been done. What remains to be determined is the long-term impact of that damage, and that is anyone's guess. I suppose that's a positive message but I'm not sure. Although her message is somewhat ambiguous, she is a wonderful person to talk to.

Her office is in a brightly lit corner of the first floor of the hospital and is very close to that of Dr. McDonald, a paediatric neurologist who has seen many kids like Ben. She knows Dr. Norris quite well as she tells us that the contingent of such specialists is a small group across the country and everyone knows each other. In contrast, she is much more expressive than Dr. Norris could ever think of being and sets aside an extended amount of time examining Ben and addressing most of our questions. Our discussion is actually positive, as neurology discussions go.

The long and tiring day comes to an end, eight hours after it began. It hasn't been the epiphany we had hoped to have. We didn't discover any magical treatments or new insight into what the future holds for Ben. Perhaps my expectations were too high. As time passes, it is becoming painfully obvious that we're going to need the support of as many people as possible. This trip, at least, has begun some new and important relationships.

Hailing another cab, we head for nearby Union Station with little time to spare. We scurry to catch the 6 p.m. train to London so that we can visit my sister and her husband for a few days. We need a break.

*   *   *

4

THE FIRST WINTER

People seem to disappear in the winter, locking themselves away during frigid, snowy evenings when the punishing wind is relentless. Other than darting from their front steps to their vehicles, our neighbours are rarely seen. Winter's fury chases each of us to the warmth of our homes, eliminating any possibility of relishing enchanted evenings under breathtaking, starlit skies, suspending any nurturing of neighbourly relationships.

Lonely, that's the word. Winters are lonely. Escaping the darkness of winter for soothing, tropical destinations is a common occurrence only for those who are fortunate enough to be able to afford such a rest. This isn't us. Even in its most optimistic form, winters are still readily associated with flu season, SAD (seasonal affective disorder), hibernations, shorter days, longer nights, and a suspension of all growing seasons.

I can find no complimentary words for this unavoidable period other than, perhaps, it helps me to appreciate the other seasons more fully. Under normal circumstances, it's definitely a taxing time of year so I'm not sure what to expect in the coming months. We were told that the first year with Ben would be the hardest to endure but mixing in the starkness, desolation, and gloominess of a winter season could very easily send us over the edge.

These past six months have kept us in a constant daze, not knowing what the next day, or even the next hour, will bring. We are trying to grasp what Ben is all about with nothing to guide us.

Nothing to look forward to.

Locked inside and away from normalcy.

Trapped in a frozen wilderness.

Organizing the chaos

I'm not sure where I stand on any given day. There have been so many
heart-stopping events, so many panic incidents, so many interruptions,
so many hospital visits, so many specialist appointments. It hasn't been
anywhere close to being a normal family life and my fear is that it is
only going to get uglier.

To reach for some control over all of this, I began to write down
everything into a crude list of notes. It is the only way I can remember
what happened that day, what happened the day before, and what is
scheduled tomorrow. A few days after Christmas, I actually find an
hour to myself and start thinking about these notes. Doodling on
some wrapping paper, I get an idea to take it one step further. And
during that creative hour, I sketch out a weekly chart of key topics that
I commit to writing about every day, much like a diary:

THE LOG

Week of: _____
Weight, Height, Head Circum. (include date)
Milestones: (e.g., sitting up, crawling, walking, teething . . .)
Doctors' appointments (who, why, outcome)
Sickness: (e.g., colds, flu, ear infections, seizures . . .)
Special Events: (e.g., trips taken, parties, Christmas . . .)
Our feelings: (e.g., nervous, helpless, scared, happy, content . . .)

General Assessment:

It is my analytical side pushing through. It's what I know best and
where my comfort zone lies. I haven't felt comfortable about anything

for quite a while. I need to know everything there is to know about Ben and everything that has occurred.

The new year of 1993 doesn't start off very well. Ben has no sooner recovered from a bout of pneumonia early in December when, by month-end, he contracts the flu. In the first official Log entry for the first week of January, I write these notes in the "Sickness" section:

> *"Just getting over the flu, I guess. Slight diarrhea, some vomiting. But has kept all food down for past two days (Jan. 2 and 3). Appetite returning to normal. Has had* Pablum *in evenings. Still seems to have some sort of bug (Jan. 6). Just takes a long time for Ben to get over an illness."*

It's so hard to tell—one symptom seems to blend into the next—but it appears that his flu symptoms are now turning into cold symptoms. Is this two steps forward and one step back, or one step forward and two steps back?

Jan and I are feeling down and overwhelmed. Before going to bed a few nights later, I write down in the Log:

> *"Seizures (even the thought of them) seem to be the worst to deal with. We seem to think that each time he throws out his arms (we call them "the clutches"), he may go into a seizure simply because that was how his other seizures began. Dr. Campbell, however, says that this overactive Moro reflex (his clutching) is not a precursor to a seizure and not only that but Dr. Norris said he cannot have a seizure if he is crying. So why does that not alleviate our fears?*
>
> *We have to stop (knowingly or subconsciously) comparing what Ben does with what a "normal" six-month old does. Ben can never be measured with the standard yardstick—he will set his own standards—and the sooner we accept this and accept that this is not something bad or something about which to be ashamed, I believe, the sooner our fears will be lessened and dealing with setbacks will be easier.*

Do we forget the fears and the nervousness we felt when Conor was a baby? Perhaps. Tonight when Ben was crying uncontrollably and we were having trouble coping, Conor came to us and said, 'Ben just cries because he is a baby. He doesn't understand.' He's right—crying is the only way that Ben (and all babies, for that matter) can express that he is unhappy, he wants something, or he is in pain."

As I write these words, it hits me that this is my four-year-old talking! How does he know this, telling me something I should already know? Have we muddied the waters so much with all of Ben's problems? If Ben had not had any problems and was crying uncontrollably, we would probably have reached the same conclusion as Conor.

It's like being new parents again, only this time, there doesn't seem to be anyone close by with whom we can share our fears, our anxiety, our stress. It's as if no one has done this before.

* * *

Diagnosis reflux?

Winter is revving up. The days are short and the air is biting, keeping us all locked inside—I'm sure it's a big reason why Ben is stuck in a chronic state of sickness. Though his alertness seems to be increasing, his clutchiness is nearly off the scale, throwing out his arms stiffly no matter if he is sitting or lying on his back. He has been on an antibiotic (*Amoxil*) for the past few days to help him shake this latest cold/infection (or whatever it is) and I am beginning to think that it is bothering his tummy.

Dr. Campbell gets to see Ben having the clutches repeatedly as he examines him. He goes back to the theory of gastroaesophageal reflux, to what we hypothesized in the early days, to when Dr. Smythe surmised that Ben's seizures could really be a bad reaction to severe reflux since his nervous system is so immature.

Dr. Campbell wants to try Ben on *Prepulsid* for a couple of weeks to see if there is any noticeable difference. He tells us that it is a motility drug that will help his stomach to empty more easily so that the food has less chance of coming back up. And it may just help to quiet his tummy overall. To that end, he suggests we stop the *Amoxil* even though there are still 4 days of doses remaining.

A few days later, winter takes a break as a welcoming January thaw arrives. With the afternoon temperature hovering at a balmy 7°C, we decide to get some much-needed fresh air and take a half-hour stroll around the neighbourhood. Ben enjoys the wide-openness of his surroundings and is very alert.

In the "Feelings" section of this week's Log, I write,

> *"Clutchiness is almost gone and he is showing more response to us and surroundings. Always looks at you (Jan 25*th*); starting to feel he enjoys us more. And I think we are definitely enjoying him more. He is certainly no real extra care like we thought he'd be. His 'off day' (Jan 27*th*) made us feel a little nervous, although the thought of seizures seems to be far away. Our worry about Ben, however, translates into a short temper when dealing with Conor and Tori—seem to yell at them more—and tires us out."*

*   *   *

Jan's notes

Jan will readily admit that she is not a detail person and so capturing daily notes about Ben is not helpful to her. Some things are too difficult and painful to write about: she simply wants to forget about them. But as we hit the end of the first full month of winter, life with Ben isn't all that bad. He is now completely off of his night-time *Phenobarbital* dose (for epilepsy), ingesting only half the daily amount of a few months ago, and there isn't even a hint of seizures. One evening, she finds the weekly Log and wants to enter her perspective:

"Jan can write this week because it was not scary. Although the Prepulsid seems to make him less choky, it's hard to say if he would have been that way anyway. He laughs when we 'raspberry' his face, and when we do patty cake."

As the week ends, Ben is showing signs of developing another cold. What's this, number five? six? Despite his frequent sneezing and coughing, he performs well for Lisa, a physiotherapist we have been seeing for a few months, and for her partner, Marsha, who is an occupational therapist. Both are part of the early intervention team coordinated by Dr. Norris. They are very pleased with Ben's progress to date, especially now that he is starting to roll over on his own. Ben is able to lift his trunk, supported by his forearms, and move his head from side to side, which requires him to shift his weight—a good sign. Marsha comments that she can usually predict which children will never sit on their own and that she is sure that Ben is not one of them. It is both heart-warming and encouraging.

Following the appointment, it's clear that Ben's energy level is down. Dr. Campbell suggests holding off prescribing another antibiotic so soon and wants to see how well Ben can fight this one on his own. We tend to agree but, like every other decision, we're really not sure.

* * *

"I'm not convinced there's much vision . . ."

Several days pass and Ben's cold is hanging on, taking a lot out of him. He is both irritable and jumpy—no clutches but he has the "heebie jeebies"—and can't get a restful sleep. I am wiped from waking up with him for the past four nights. His worsening cold is making us all miserable.

Ben cries whenever he coughs or burps and is very slow swallowing. It's obvious his throat is raw. We have tried to let him overcome this latest infection on his own but after five days, it's time to call Dr. Campbell.

He prescribes *Ceclor* this time which should be a little easier on his tummy, he believes.

Within two days, Ben is back to his normal self; the coughing, sneezing and irritability have just about disappeared and we are all starting to regain some lost sleep. We are also pining for the end of winter and the end of this relentless cold season.

One of the troublesome effects of CMV is scarring of the retina which can lead to vision problems. We have been referred to a local ophthalmologist, Dr. Goderich, to start investigating whether Ben has been affected. There isn't a lot of choice of eye specialists in this town but Dr. Campbell believes Dr. Goderich to be helpful, and my parents also know him.

His office is in the downtown core, in a small office building with a very small elevator. When we arrive for the early afternoon appointment, the waiting room is overflowing with patients, mostly seniors. It seems Ben isn't the only one with a 1:30 p.m. appointment. Running several minutes late, as most physicians do, Dr. Goderich escorts us into his examination room. He is soft spoken and not really adept at carrying on any sort of conversation. He is not quite sure why we are here today. Not another cochlear implant scenario! We tell him that we are somewhat concerned about one of Ben's eyes that sometimes turns inward and are wondering if it would help if Ben wore glasses.

Without explaining anything, he dims the lights and begins looking in Ben's eyes, while I support Ben on my knee in the exam chair. He takes out a small pen light and waves it in front of Ben's face. Ben is interested in looking at everything but Dr. Goderich's light, especially since the room is so dimly lit. After 30 seconds of trying to get Ben to follow the light, he drops it back into his lab coat and turns on the overhead lights.

We ask what he thinks about his turning eye. He sighs, and says, "I'm not convinced there's much vision!"

I stop breathing for a few moments. I want to think he hasn't really understood our question, that he was telling us of some other patient he just examined.

Timidly, we ask what would lead him to that conclusion. He admits that he doesn't see too many kids like Ben but he doesn't have a good feeling. Now, that's really scientific. In an effort to wash his hands of Ben, he refers us to a physician at the IWK children's hospital in Halifax to "brain test" Ben's eyes. The test is called a VEP (visual evoked potential) which can determine if Ben's brain responds involuntarily to any light stimulus.

Jan and I can't believe how callous this guy is. What an idiot! Furious, we pack up our things and leave in a hurry. Our minds are muddled as we drive home. We begin to question ourselves about Ben's vision. How can Dr. Goderich make a snap diagnosis after such a quick 15 minute examination, and a "not good" feeling? Are there not some rules to follow when dealing with such fragile parents? Can he just say anything he likes? C'mon, he didn't even have a clue *why* we were seeing him. He has no idea what Ben is like. After all of the problems we have encountered so far, Ben can't be blind, too . . . can he?

Later in the evening, I have a lot to write in the Log:

> "... There is such an overwhelming number of examples of when Ben must be seeing that we are just trying to chalk this experience up to one of those times when the doctor has no idea. Wow, there are a lot of them. Doctors, that is, who have no idea. We are the only ones who can pull all of the "expert opinions" together and make some sense of it. No one else can. No one else wants to.
>
> Goderich has seen him three times in the last eight months and has no idea how Ben acts during the day, night, the alert times, the stressful times . . . His question of why Ben's head was the shape that it was (asymmetrical, like a letter D) and his response that we were sleeping him on one side too much shows just how little knows of, cares about, or has seen babies with CMV.

> *How can one 20-minute visit shake our confidence so much? I*
> *have to believe that it will only serve to strengthen our resolve*
> *and our bond with Ben. It may take a few more days . . ."*

We are both anxious and eager to have this VEP test. It can't be all that bad. And even if it is bad, all it means is that he failed the test on a particular day. We know that when he is alert, there is no question that he can see—just ask Lisa or Marsha or . . .

We learn that this test can't be scheduled until May. That gives us several months of fretting and questioning. Great.

*   *   *

A roller coaster

One of Jan's sisters has recently lent us Erma Bombeck's *Motherhood—The Second Oldest Profession.* As I read each sentence of the chapter, "The Special Mother," tears begin to well up in my eyes and I become very emotional. My usual stoic and "I never cry" demeanour has been broken. It's a little scary that the written word can so easily conjure up such intense feelings. I had often joked with my father that "his bladder must be near his eyes," myself proud that I was so much stronger. But Bombeck's words are such an apt description of our lives (in which being overwhelmed is now a permanent part of our existence) that they bring instant comfort and reassurance, dispelling all feelings of isolation and loneliness. My tears weren't from sadness but from something spiritually deeper.

Bombeck pictures ". . . God hovering over Earth selecting His instruments for propagation with great care and deliberation." At one point, he instructs an angel to give a mother "a handicapped child."

Then Bombeck "transcribes" a fascinating conversation between God and the angel.

"Why this one, God? She's so happy."

"Exactly," smiles God. "Could I give a handicapped child a mother who does not know laughter? That would be cruel."

"But does she have patience?" asks the angel.

"I don't want her to have too much patience, or she will drown in a sea of self-pity and despair. Once the shock and resentment wear off, she'll handle it.

"I watched her today. She has that sense of self and independence that are so rare and so necessary in a mother. You see, the child I'm going to give her has his own world. She has to make it live in her world and that's not going to be easy.

". . . Yes, here is a woman whom I will bless with a child less than perfect. She doesn't realize it yet, but she is to be envied.

"She will never take for granted a spoken word. She will never consider a step ordinary. When her child says 'Momma' for the first time, she will be witness to a miracle and know it . . . .

"I will permit her to see clearly the things I see—ignorance, cruelty, prejudice—and allow her to rise above them. She will never be alone. I will be at her side every minute of every day of her life because she is doing my work as surely as she is here by my side."

"And what about her patron saint?" asks the angel

God smiles. "A mirror will suffice."

* * *

Pneumonia, seizures, ear infections . . .

Ben is making a few new sounds and generally verbalizing more. Several times throughout the day, he shows just how much he likes to be around Conor, who can make him laugh. Clearly, Ben recognizes him. Sitting on the couch without his hearing aids, Ben follows Conor's movements back and forth in front of him. I'm convinced there's all kinds of vision!

After a seven-day run, Ben's *Ceclor* regimen is coming to an end. This is good timing since his tummy is showing signs that it isn't really tolerating the chemical concoction any longer. No clutchiness from this round of drugs but he is in noticeable discomfort.

Less than 24 hours later, Ben turns lethargic and his breathing is a bit laboured. It makes no sense.

Before the weekend, we manage to see Dr. Campbell, yet again. I'm sure he's getting tired of us. Listening to Ben's chest, Dr. Campbell doesn't like what he hears and orders a chest X-ray. It's hard to believe but Ben has developed pneumonia in his left lung, and it's quite serious. Dr. Campbell decides to put him on *Ceclor* for another run even though he has no idea why Ben isn't getting better.

A few days into his second run of the antibiotic, Ben has a "blippy" day, a term we created to describe a time where it appears the neurons in his brain aren't firing quite right. He is somewhat jumpy and has jerky eye movements. Not sooner do I place him on the couch when he outstretches both arms as far as they can go. Thinking he is in pain, I pick him back up. He begins choking and gagging, turning quite red, and not breathing very well. I pat his back a few times and he vomits. Where did that come from? He becomes very sleepy but his breathing has improved. Without warning, he stiffens again, turns his head as far to the left as physically possible and locks his eyes even farther to the left. Once again, his breathing is shallow and he doesn't look right. Pats on the back this time have no effect. A minute later, he relaxes, looks at me and smiles.

I'm not smiling, though. There's something wrong. I call my neighbour, a nurse, to come over to take a look at him. She isn't home. I carry Ben to our upstairs bathroom as he locks his head to the left. This time his eyes are bouncing in rhythmic fashion, trying to turn completely inside his skull. It lasts less than a minute. This has to be a seizure. I call Dr. Norris, who happens to be on call tonight, to tell him. He wants us to come to the hospital.

On the drive, Ben cries non-stop. Dr. Norris decides to keep him in the Paediatric Intensive Care Unit (PICU) overnight for observation. By 9:30 p.m., we are escorted to a corner bed. It's not busy tonight and, for the first time, it doesn't bother me to be here. Ben awakes a few hours later and looks confused. It doesn't look like a seizure but how would I know. He quickly falls back to sleep and stays that way all night.

Morning arrives and Ben awakes in a normal fashion. Dr. Norris asks about his night and concludes that Ben is likely having some seizure activity. He decides to return his *Phenobarbital* dose to 30 mg a day—the level he was on in January—and will likely keep him at that level for the next 9 to 12 months. He tells us that as Ben grows and gains weight, his increase in size will act like a natural weaning process.

As the next few days slowly pass, my anxiety level diminishes. Perhaps I'm becoming hardened to the fact that seizures are part of Ben's life though they are very disturbing to watch. A "blippy" day seems to be a precursor to seizure activity. It's a strange example of predictability. But removing any degree of uncertainty is really a good thing I keep telling myself.

The month of March, the last month of winter, starts off well with Ben having two really good days, back-to-back. On one of those days, we take a cross-border day trip to Calais, Maine, his first true outing of the winter. It is as if there is so much for him to take in, that he has been starved of fun for far too long. Good days like these give us the strength and hope that we can take anywhere.

A few days later, our world does an about-face with all three kids getting sick: Conor has an aggravating cough, Tori has a throat infection, and

Ben has developed another ear infection. This is really unbelievable—a cold, the flu, pneumonia, seizures, and an ear infection, all in the last three months. And when he's miserable, no one sleeps. Chronic fatigue makes our life even more difficult to tolerate. Going back on *Ceclor* is a nightmare this time, causing Ben a lot of belly pain and even some slight diarrhea.

Jan is getting ready to spend a much-deserved four days with her Aunt Rita in Rhode Island. She wants to get away but is quite nervous. We both are. Two days before she is supposed to leave, Ben is acting "blippy" again, similar to his behaviour that stressful night when he had multiple seizure episodes.

Nothing happens this time. No seizures is good but my predictor was wrong.

On her departure day, Ben is irritable and out-of-sorts. It's hard to know whether this is the lingering effects of his ear infection, the antibiotic or some new problem. Jan is reluctant to leave. I get in touch with Dr. Campbell and make an appointment to see him in the afternoon. This relieves a tiny amount of her anxiety and she follows through on her travel plans.

Our 3 p.m. appointment with Dr. Campbell is delayed an hour. He is always late arriving at his office. I describe the events of the last week while he examines Ben. He is a little surprised that the multiple runs of *Ceclor* have really not been very effective but admits that it doesn't work with all kids. He recommends trying *Sulfa*, a different antibiotic, one that should be much easier on his tummy, but may not be as strong.

As we leave the office, Ben is quiet. After traversing the awkward set of stairs leading to the street, I notice that Ben seems a little "far away" in his eyes. Even the cold March air doesn't seem to make a difference. When we arrive home, his face is a somewhat flushed as I slowly remove his winter gear. For what seems like forever, he gets that terrified look on his face, like he is going to have a seizure. His breathing is very shallow and his complexion isn't right. I am instantly hyper and nervous, realizing that I'm all alone, with Jan somewhere near Massachusetts. A few minutes pass. Nothing comes of his reaction and he falls asleep in my arms.

That evening, he swallows two doses of *Sulfa* with little trouble. Our first night without Jan is a peaceful one. Ben decides to sleep in until 9 a.m., and awakens goo-ing and lively. I am relieved. His energy level is noticeably up today and there is no sign of any tummy discomfort. *Sulfa* is a miracle. I am so fickle.

*   *   *

Anniversary Mass

Winter is wrapping up but we are feeling overwhelmed. Ben is not doing as much as he did last month, not holding his head up for very long, especially in the morning and at meal time. We have a sense that the increased dose of *Phenobarbital* is dragging him down. It's such a delicate balance. We want his abnormal brain activity calmed but not so much that his energy level is noticeably reduced. Dr. Norris suggests that we take away Ben's morning dose for a few weeks to see if it makes a difference. It's a double-edged sword, of course. After a few days of this trial, Ben seems a little more active. It could be that that's what we want to see.

We are quickly approaching the one-year anniversary of the passing of my Aunt Vicki as we remember her at an evening mass. Not much is said by the priest other than telling the congregation that the mass is ". . . being offered for Vicki George . . . ." Ben is having a good day and attends with us, the first time he has been able to go to church in quite a few months.

As the homily begins, I feel a certain emptiness. Not only have I lumbered through the last year without her love and kindness, so have Jan, Conor and Tori. I am troubled by the fact that Vicki didn't get to see Ben. What a loss for Ben. He will never have the opportunity to be spoiled by her, as were his siblings, as I was as a child and even as a teenager. Things don't seem very fair. I can't imagine what purpose has been served depriving Ben of her caring and love.

With the homily nearly complete, most of which I have completely tuned out, I begin to ponder the effect of both my parents having no living siblings. And how I have no family close by. There is such a large age difference between me and my mother's nieces that we have little in common. All of my father's nieces and single nephew live in other cities. Vicki never married so no cousins there. And my siblings are all living in other parts of the country, too.

Rising to recite the Creed, I start to wonder what is keeping us here in Saint John.

*   *   *

Planning the move

As Ben has battled infection after infection over the past few months, Jan and I have wondered if moving to a larger city would provide us with more of the things we need—answers, insight, hope, support. To be around parents like Susan and Don Ward and specialists who have dealt with kids like Ben has to be a good thing. Conor and Tori aren't in school yet so picking up and starting a new life shouldn't be that difficult, we ponder.

Here in our hometown, every time we encounter an issue with Ben, it's like starting over. No one is really sure what the outcome will be, what the cause of the issue is, or what action should be taken. Is it a seizure? Is it a severe reflux attack? Is it some sort of spastic torticollis? The last one is a new possibility that has been suggested; it involves involuntary contractions of the neck muscles.

It would be comforting to hear something like "... *oh that's this and typically it occurs when . . . and here's what can be done to help . . .*" instead of "... *well it could be this or it could be that and, well, you could try this for a few days and see what happens or you could try that . . .*"

It's hard to believe that no one in the Saint John region has ever given birth to a child like Ben. We seem to be the first, or at least the only ones seeking treatment for such a wide range of problems. You'd think someone would mention something or someone would come forward and tell us that we should talk to ". . . this person . . ." about what they've experienced and what to expect.

My employer has offices across the country, including Toronto, and I begin to inquire about taking a short-term transfer, something less than a year. Even though our fall trip to Sick Kids hospital didn't produce the miracle we were looking for, perhaps living in the community for an extended period would produce the fruit we're starving for. I am put in touch with the HR manager in the Toronto office to start the process. Because it's a short-term move, we decide to keep our home in Saint John and seek out a semi-furnished dwelling that's located in a family-friendly neighbourhood not too far from Sick Kids. My colleague in Toronto is very eager to help in any way she can and informs me she will also begin to look for a consulting assignment. She says she will even video tape the interiors of some possible locations to help us decide. Fabulous.

We give ourselves six weeks to get ready and circle May 1 on the calendar as the target to be settled into our new "home."

* * *

5

NO EASY ROAD

I view life as a virtual journey through a complex, interconnected series of roads. The imagery in my mind is similar to what is portrayed in Robert Frost's poem, "The Road Not Taken." These roads are always changing. Most don't exist until you approach them though the entrances always lie in wait for you. Each decision you make or don't make at any given moment can change the make-up and direction of the road you're travelling. Even your mere presence can affect its nature, and consequently, the experiences in your life.

Take, for example, driving your car along a busy thoroughfare and some distracted driver slams his vehicle into yours. Such an event, happening in a few brief seconds, can change your life forever. How you respond will determine the next series of roads that are placed before you, assuming you survived the crash. If you had chosen to take an alternate route, you may have avoided that head-on collision and have a different series of roads in front of you.

On my life's journey, I know that I can often choose which road to take but I'm never really sure to where I will be carried. Even if I could somehow fly overhead, to get a glimpse of where these roads lead, to see what is just over that hill or around the bend, it wouldn't matter because each road and its surroundings are never constant. Our choices are all that controls them.

The road that has taken us out of the winter wilderness is very confusing and unsettling. We remain without any map to guide us, often afraid to see what's just around the corner, not knowing how much further, unable to recognize anyone or anything.

We strive to build a safety net to catch us when we fall or come dangerously close to falling off the edge. And we look to our compass that we hope is pointing us in the right direction, helping us make the right choices, the right decisions.

But it is never easy. It is a constant battle.

In the blink of an eye

Approaching one year of age, Ben is starting to behave in a so-called normal fashion. His alertness and energy level seem to be in lock-step with the advance of spring. The hours of daylight have become noticeably longer and his afternoon naps correspondingly shorter. His recent checkup with Dr. Campbell—a calm, methodical meeting—shows he is progressing at the same rate as "normal" kids though still way off the scale.

Everyone is buoyed by these results. Even Ben senses our upbeat mood. With growing confidence, Jan decides to try Ben with a little bit of milk, an attempt to move away from baby formula. Most of the liquid dribbles out of his mouth, covering his chin and soaking his bib. The cup is likely not the most efficient utensil to use but he does manage to get the taste.

As Jan wipes up the mess he has made, she notices that his chin has broken out into an angry, bright red rash that is hot to the touch. His neck is even worse, with welts and bumps forming in rapid succession. A wave of fear drowns her as she wonders how long it will be before his windpipe begins to close over from this allergic reaction.

She calls me at work in a panic and then hustles Ben to the hospital. I scramble to find my coat and rush to the uptown bus depot to find one that will take me to them. I have no money for a cab today. At this non-peak time, the buses run only every half hour. Through nothing but luck, I don't have to wait long to get the next one but it meanders through a long, circuitous route that lasts a torturous 40 minutes.

Running through the hallways of the hospital, I find Jan and Ben in the paediatric clinic waiting room. Everyone seems to be quite calm. Panting and sweating, I ask how things are, a little mystified, expecting to see something terrible. Obviously, he didn't suffocate the way I feared and his rash is quite mild looking. Dr. Norris is holding his regular clinic today and, though we don't have a scheduled appointment, he examines Ben anyway. That's just the way he is and we are grateful. Despite his haunting words of "he may never . . ." during those early days that have permanently damaged my psyche, his presence is strangely comforting today.

His examination of Ben turns up nothing—breathing is fine, temperature is fine, and reflexes are normal. Dr. Norris's conclusion is that it was simply a skin reaction and nothing more. What occurs externally does not necessarily indicate what would take place internally. He suggests that we stay away from milk for a while and at some point have Ben tested for allergies to get a complete picture.

Our confidence is shot. Nothing is simple with Ben. We try something new and it's a disaster. Our world can be turned upside-down in the blink of an eye. Ben is unfazed by the afternoon whirlwind so we have to find a way to calm ourselves. On the drive home, we talk each other through the events and realize that this incident is likely completely unrelated to any of Ben's other problems. But it is another problem we must deal with. What other dreadful things are lurking, waiting to be randomly discovered? Nervousness and paranoia are things we have never experienced until Ben came into our lives.

* * *

Very tense

To make Ben's first morning appointment at the IWK hospital for Children in Halifax, we have to extend the trip over two days and stay with Jan's grandmother overnight. She has become known by her grandchildren as Nana Brook, since her sprawling homestead is situated adjacent to a fast-moving brook that streams out of the large hillside at the rear of her property. The picturesque setting that she has called home for decades cannot be enjoyed by any of us this time. Our heads are filled with clouded thoughts, unable to share the churning anxiety of whether or not Ben "has much vision."

The next day, we arrive at the IWK with 10 minutes to spare and find our way to the sixth-floor eye clinic to see Dr. Tripper, a Ph.D in neuropsychology, who will conduct the VEP test. Down a long hallway lined with office doors, this institutional setting is devoid of people. As we approach a fork in the corridor, a tall man rounds the corner and introduces himself as Dr. Tripper. He leads us to a large room where the test will be conducted.

Soft spoken and articulate, he describes how the test will be conducted while gently attaching three electrodes to Ben—one on his ear and two on his head. These are connected to a monitor that will read Ben's brain waves.

After dimming the lights slightly, Dr. Tripper flashes a strobe light in front of Ben. He waits several seconds and flashes it again. Ben is quite fixated on the source of this light. Next, he shows Ben a small, red and black display of a checkerboard and observes Ben's reaction as the red and black squares move, exchanging their positions. For the last part of the test, he moves Ben in front of a large television screen where small black and white squares dance around on it.

Dr. Tripper is pleased that Ben is so cooperative during the 15-minute exercise and disappears into another room to read the results. From what we observed, it seemed quite obvious that Ben saw everything.

The minutes pass like hours.

Finally, he emerges holding a printout, confirming quite emphatically that Ben's optic nerve is working normally and that his brain is receiving the signal.

"In essence, all of the parts are working," he tells us but he qualifies that statement by saying he is unsure what Ben's brain does with that optical information.

Who cares? Ben can see!

The suffocating blanket of uncertainty that we've had to carry for the past few months has been lifted and tossed away. Like shackles removed from our limbs, we are free to move. It wouldn't have been this way but for a doctor's cavalier and incompetent remarks. But that's the system we're living with, little to no accountability, so Dr. Goderich will not be reprimanded. What a waste of our energy.

Our next appointment is with Dr. Lavoie, a paediatric ophthalmologist. In contrast to Dr. Tripper, he is small in stature. His tone and manners, though, exude a great deal of confidence.

The first test he conducts is a visual acuity test using Teller Acuity Cards. Each rectangular card is actually a large board, measuring about 1 by 2 feet. On one side, half of the board has alternating black and white stripes of a certain thickness (these contrasting images seem to be a trend), the other half is blank, and in the middle of the board is a pinhole. Dr. Lavoie holds the first card in front of Ben and peers at him through the pinhole. The contrasting lines stimulate vision and draws a person's eyes towards it, including mine. Almost instantly, Ben finds the patch of stripes with both eyes. Dr. Lavoie then flips the board around so that stripes are now on the left side. Ben follows the pattern.

Dr. Lavoie continues this six more times, each time the lines becoming a little thinner, and more difficult to see. After about five minutes, Ben stops playing the game; perhaps he's bored. His response is in the normal range, although at the low end.

After putting the cards away, Dr. Lavoie wheels his stool to the other side of the examination room and picks up a small bottle. He tells us that he needs to dilate Ben's pupils to find out why his eye is turning. Ben jumps and jerks his head as each drop lands in his eyes. With roughly an hour to kill while the drops slowly take effect, we wander the hospital, stopping in the gift shop to pick up some small sunglasses for Ben.

Returning to the eye clinic, we find it empty of patients, perhaps because it's nearly 4 p.m. Dr. Lavoie comes to get us and we follow him to the same examination room. He dims the lights, catching Ben's attention, and places a headset on himself with a large light in the centre. He holds a small lens in front of Ben's eyes and shines the light through, striking the back of the retina. By doing this, he is able to examine the inside of Ben's eye including the start of the optic nerve, which he describes as "perfect." No one has ever used that word before in describing Ben. He notes a small scar on the back of his left eye but it is not concerning and should not affect his vision. By interchanging these lenses, he is able to tell that Ben is far-sighted, and observes Ben left eye turning.

Dr. Lavoie says that Ben needs glasses and we will need to patch his right eye once a day for up to an hour to help him strengthen the muscles in his weak eye.

"Come back in three months," he tells us.

Feeling comforted and assured, we ask him if he has had kids like Ben as patients. He tells us that he has seen close to 10 other kids born with CMV, some with quite extensive calcifications, where the CT scan looks terrible. Most are able to see quite well despite all of their other problems.

Wow.

We pause at the doorway.

Imagine, actually talking to a physician who has experience with kids like Ben. The trepidation and isolation of believing we're some sort of freakish outlier has been lessened a few degrees.

But the best, of course, is discovering that his vision is "perfect."

* * *

Always there to help

With just a little more than a week before our move to Toronto, Ben develops a cold. Of course he does. Life just hasn't been complicated enough lately. His energy level is noticeably suppressed and his sleep is very restless. Perhaps he senses our anxiety. Last night, he tossed and turned, and we tossed and turned with him for a steady five hours.

Dr. Campbell's office accommodates our ridiculously hectic schedule by squeezing us into a late afternoon appointment to make sure Ben is OK.

". . . Chest and ears are clear so it's just a cold . . . ."

Dr. Campbell is sentimental today and extends his hand to wish us well, knowing that we'll be gone for close to a year. It is a comforting moment, taking us a little off guard. He has been so helpful to us over the past several months. We know that finding as dedicated and caring a physician will be a nearly impossible task.

Exiting the examination room, we discover his office is empty—even Julie, his secretary/receptionist/organizer has gone for the day. It is an odd sight. He expresses his surprise on how far he has seen Ben come and gives him a gentle pat on the head. This is really the first time he has shared his thoughts that Ben is actually progressing, a welcomed boost to our spirits.

A few days pass but Ben isn't getting any better, and his nose is now running green. Jan and I are in the throes of packing, our stress level on a steady climb. We can't really wait out this infection and pressure Dr. Campbell to prescribe something.

Ben's sleep improves but his appetite grows weaker. By the end of the week, just one day before we are to start driving to Ontario, Ben is acting a little "blippy." He has developed a rash on his face and is experiencing abdominal cramps. We stop the antibiotic.

On travel day, Jan awakes to intense nausea and a high fever, vomiting several times. Tori has wet her bed—something she's never done—and feels sick to her stomach. Conor is like Jan—a high fever and vomiting. Ben's rash has spread and is redder. And for the first time in months, he clutches wildly the moment he is placed on his back, his face enveloped in terror as he screams in pain.

What is happening? My whole being starts hurting as it fills with panic and anxiety. There's no way we can hop in a car today. Jan is the sickest I have ever seen her. She can't even lift her head.

I frantically attempt to reach Dr. Campbell, again! He's not on call today—it's some doctor I've never heard of. There's no way I'm going through the whole "Ben Story" with a complete stranger—not today. I call my father to see if there's some way he can get in touch with Dr. Campbell for us. An hour passes and he calls me back with Dr. Campbell's home phone number. An unlisted number, of course, but told me Dr. Campbell wouldn't mind.

The number just rings and rings until finally an answering machine kicks in. I leave a frenetic, detailed message, telling him we're supposed to leave today but everyone is sick, including Ben. By mid-afternoon, he calls me back. I apologize for calling him at home. It doesn't matter to him but he wonders how I got the number.

After I describe things more calmly for him, he guesses that Ben must have the same bug that everyone else has. He also tells me that he has recently seen a lot of sick mothers but not a lot of sick fathers. Whatever bug is going around, it seems to affect mostly females—which explains why Jan and Tori are so sick. The only treatment is to wait it out and ensure that neither Ben nor Conor nor Tori get dehydrated.

Emotionally exhausted, I thank him once again for his incredible dedication and support for us. I am completely lost today. To have everyone sick at the same time is more than enough but pile on the stress of the past week, that most of our everyday items have all been packed, and our routine is turned upside down . . . It's an anxiety level I haven't felt since Ben was born.

It will be at least a few days before anyone can travel which means we'll have to get on a plane if we want get to Toronto before the end of the week. And that means I'll have to figure out how we can get our car there, too.

I'm not sure if someone is trying to tell us not to go but this isn't how it's supposed to happen. Nothing is simple anymore.

After three days of hell, Jan is finally able to get herself out of bed. She is very weak and looks terrible but the nausea has thankfully ended.

I don't even want to go anymore. Every ounce of excitement and enthusiasm has been drained from me. For God's sake, I'm only 29 years old. How can I be so spent?

* * *

"I'm not going to be sick or anything . . ."

The bright morning sun awakens my gritty and tired eyes earlier than expected. Everyone is still not truly travel-ready but it's now Thursday, and we need a few days to get settled before I report to work. Ben seems back to normal but Jan is still dragging.

I load the car with our suitcases while Jan gets Ben ready. We arrive at the airport well before our flight time and Tori isn't feeling well. She has a worried look on her face when she tells Jan that she has messed her pants. I feel a little helpless and wonder if I should be asking her to travel today.

The two-hour plane ride is smooth except for the final 30 minutes—Tori needs to go to the bathroom again, and quickly. Jan carries her to the back of the cabin and they both squeeze into the micro-lavatory. Landing is no problem and the drop in altitude does not bother any of us, including Ben.

As we make our way to the luggage carousels, Conor tells me that he needs to go to the bathroom. It is really to clean himself up since he, too, still has the diarrhea. He removes his soiled underwear and I discreetly dump them in the garbage can; there's no place to clean them and we have no place to store them. We gather our belongings and find the rental car desk.

I attempt to pay the deposit with cash since my Visa does not have enough available credit. The service rep refuses to take the money, saying she has no place to take cash. She only will accept a credit card. As I'm telling her how she is not making sense (I really want to tell her how small her brain is), Jan says that Conor needs to go to the bathroom again. I don't believe this. We're going to be trapped in the Toronto airport.

In the meantime, Jan gets in touch with the Visa contact centre, telling our story, and they allow the pre-authorization to go through. The rental car rep, in her disgust, accepts my signature, putting as little effort as possible to describe where to find the car and how to exit the parking lot.

"You have a nice day, too," I snap back at her.

The maroon coloured Dodge Spirit we've rented is just large enough for our bags. This was one detail I hadn't considered. I guess everything can't go wrong all at the same time.

Tori buckles up in the front seat while Jan rides in the back with Conor and Ben. Speeding along highway 401 at 100 km/h, I check my mirrors before making a lane change. Ben and Conor are content in the back and Tori is just staring out her window.

Breaking the constant whooshing sound of the car zipping along, Tori exclaims, "I'm not going to be sick or anything," even though no one had asked her the question. I whirl my head to see her eyes wide and her face devoid of any colour.

"What do you mean?" I foolishly ask, in a bit of a panic. "Jan, she's going to be sick!"

Jan reaches down into her bag and whips out a small, plastic container she had brought ". . . just in case . . ." Still traveling the inside lane at a rapid pace, I reach for it and hand it Tori. She delicately places it under her chin and lets go, quite coordinated, too, for a 3-year-old. Instantly, an awful stench fills the car but Tori feels better.

Fifteen minutes later, I loop off the expressway and head north. The exit to Sheppard Avenue comes up more quickly than I expect and I make a bit of a panic manoeuver not to miss it. The long exit ramp takes us to the heart of Willowdale, just a few blocks from our new home. I try to turn into the roadway to the condo complex but it is blocked off with yellow tape. Nice. I guess almost everything *is* going wrong.

I walk into the row of condos and find a few people standing outside what I think is our condo. One of them, a tall man, very slick in his dress, approaches me as I introduce myself.

"Oh, hi, Michael. I'm Andy Battison." He is the real estate agent we have spoken with who helped to arrange our accommodations. He apologizes for the chaos but the court was just newly paved today and we can't drive on it until tomorrow. He also informs me that the moving company had called him to say that they would be delayed delivering our belongings. He gives me a contact number to reach them.

I know that none of this disastrous day is his fault but I'm ready to smash him. He is much too cheerful for me right now and has no idea the stress level twisting inside my head, having two kids with diarrhea, one who had just thrown up in the car, having to park a block away with all of our stuff, and now telling me that our belongings have not even arrived! Once Jan catches up with me with the kids and Andy shows us into our new place, I whisper to her that the mover got lost.

We softly cross the postage-stamp lawn in front of the three storey structure. Opening the front door next to the single car garage, we are greeted with a long staircase. We had seen a video of the inside but didn't quite realize how many stairs there were, and the kind that have open risers—a great way for toddlers to kill themselves. From the front door, we climb the 16 stairs to the living room. It's large, very bright and clean smelling, and the furniture looks like it was just unwrapped. My mood is slowly changing. Perhaps this place might just work.

A few steps more leads to the dining room, with a wide open railing overlooking the living room. Adjacent to that is a large kitchen that overlooks the court. Conor and Tori follow us but don't say very much—they're exhausted—and Ben, well, he's just indifferent. Another 14 stairs take us to the bedrooms. At one end of the hall is the master which is quite roomy with a small *en suite*. Opposite to that are the other two bedrooms—the small one court-side barely fits a bed and a dresser. It will be Tori's room. The third bedroom is big enough for our crib, fortunately, and the bed that is already there.

Andy hands us the keys and leaves us to get settled. Conor and Tori head for the TV and we prop Ben in his car seat beside them. The floor-to-ceiling living room windows run the entire length of one of the walls. I stand quietly in front of them, first looking at the calm street below and then gazing to the horizon, eastward to Saint John. I remember standing in one of the science buildings at Dalhousie University in my first year of undergrad, almost a dozen years ago, on melancholic Sunday evenings, looking then to the northwestern sky in the direction of Saint John, where Jan was, wishing she was with me in Halifax. There was an emptiness and a feeling of being stuck in a place you just can't like. We're all together today but that same lonely feeling is creeping back.

I hope that this is a good move for Ben.

*   *   *

Getting settled

The alarm buzzes at 6:15 a.m. Everyone is still asleep, including Jan, as I haul my exhausted body out of bed and into the shower. A short time later, after kissing everyone, I exit the front door of our condo and am ambushed by a wall of humid, southern Ontario air. It's my first official work day in Toronto. The walk down our street is very different today than it was when we first arrived. There is a noticeable buzz coming from the main drag, Sheppard Avenue, even though it is a few hundred feet away.

As I get closer, I see bus after bus rocket by the corner. Last night, I looked at the public transit schedules, trying to find the most efficient route to get me downtown by 8:15 a.m. Efficiency is a relative term, of course, since I expect to need at least 1 hour to reach my new place of work: two buses, a half-hour subway ride, and a 15-minute walk east of Yonge St. near Front St.

As I disembark the transit system, I spot a Treats coffee shop. I need to get some sustenance to keep me going. I also order a chocolate mint-flavoured coffee, hoping that will give me a boost. I don't really like coffee but this morning I feel I need it.

My work day unfolds as I expect—meeting lots of people, finding a workspace to call my own, and getting oriented on a new project. Ben has a great day but Jan and I are both somewhat nervous about him. We're realizing that there's no quick way for me to get home if needed and Jan doesn't know a soul to call on. But a bigger concern is finding a babysitter. Jan starts work next week, another evening position, so we'll need someone to cover the late afternoon/supper hours.

By the end of the week, we're feeling slightly more settled but Ben has developed a cold. We can't imagine putting him on another antibiotic. My sister Cathy and her husband arrive on Saturday, spending the long holiday weekend to help us get settled. They're a welcome sight, a familiar sight, and the kids enjoy their company. A family doc, Cathy determines that Ben's ears are fine but his throat is a little red. She suggests letting him fight this infection on his own for a few days.

Our second full week runs a little more smoothly but we still can't relax. Ben seems to have fought off his latest infection without any drugs but he has developed a new movement where he sticks out his tongue while hyperextending his head. I guess that's okay but it does look strange. He is not very energetic though he does enjoy the hour-long outing on Friday afternoon to the neighbourhood park, which is only a ten-minute jaunt. Conor and Tori love it, happy to be able to run free. The condo complex really has no back yard to speak of, the price paid for living in a megalopolis.

That evening, Ben cries out shortly after going to bed. Perhaps the day was too tiring for him. Jan is worried he is going to have a seizure. We panic a little, worrying what to do if we had to take him to a hospital. No one knows a thing about him and we don't know any of the physicians, at least not yet. His crying lasts for almost an hour. Still reeling from the stress of the move, I am very unsure of myself. Somehow we have to learn to not expect the worst each time, but it's tough. It's tough when you're emotionally and physically tired. It's tough when everything is new and you have no confidence of whether or not you're following the right path.

A month of routine days pass by quickly until our first set of appointments at Sick Kids is upon us. This is what we came for and our expectations are high. Approaching the hospital's downtown location is a bit confusing and finding a parking spot nearby is a challenge. The front atrium of the hospital is stacked with lines of parents, grandparents, children, and patients. We stumble to the Audiology department after following a round-about set of directions and are introduced to a young, energetic audiologist named Stephanie. She is conducting a hearing test today to get a baseline of Ben's hearing ability. Before she shows us to the booth, she checks Ben's ears and notes that he has some fluid in both canals. God, I hope she's wrong. We tell her that we're seeing his pediatrician tomorrow and will ask about it.

Once Ben and I get seated inside the booth, another audiologist joins us to help monitor Ben's reactions very closely. This is a different approach than what we're used to and one that I think would be more precise. After 10 minutes of "Ba ba ba . . ." and high-pitched squeals, Stephanie reports quite excitedly that Ben responded to speech at about 70 dB. This is one of the best results he has ever received. Feeling surprised and just a little upbeat, we head for the Neurology Clinic.

Our 11 a.m. appointment with Dr. MacDonald is delayed for nearly three hours since she is tied up with two emergencies. Filling in the void is not easy. I just want to sleep. When Dr. MacDonald finally makes her way to the clinic, she apologizes for keeping us so late. She remembers Ben from last fall and says he looks quite healthy. Gee, two positive comments in one day.

Choosing not to examine him this time, she simply listens intently to our description of his seizures over the last year. Hearing of his regimen of antibiotics, she notes that the *Ceclor* he had taken in February could have interacted with his system and led to the seizure episodes. We pause. No one had ever suggested that an antibiotic could do this. I am both relieved by this comment and perplexed as to why Dr. Campbell, or a pharmacist, or anyone, wouldn't know this.

Dr. MacDonald assures us that we shouldn't be concerned about Ben's apparent laughing "at nothing." nor about him stretching his neck and thrusting his tongue. She believes that it's simply him stretching his head and neck muscles since he doesn't move much on his own. It may look odd but is it not seizure-related. Before heading to her next patient, she books a follow-up appointment for us and hopes to have more time when we see her in a month or so.

It is now 3 p.m., a full six hours since we arrived, and I feel very drained, like I hadn't slept all night. Everyone's a little cranky on the drive home, which takes nearly an hour at this time of day. It's a bit ridiculous having to take six hours out of your day to see two specialists.

The day has been a bit too much for Ben. Shortly after supper, he gets into a coughing fit and throws up. For the next two hours, he is very irritable, crying intermittently. His evening nap is not restful nor can he fall asleep later in the evening. I decide to lay my head next to him in his crib to try to calm him.

"You had a big day," I tell him. "It was tiring but you did great. Just try to calm down."

His eyes fixate on me as I talk to him. His breathing slows and his body stops fidgeting. Coincidental? Maybe. But there must be some level of understanding. Can you reason with a one-year old? Not likely but something worked.

The next day we get the opportunity to meet our new pediatrician, Dr. Toms. His office is located in North York General Hospital, less than a 10-minute drive from our condo. The adjacent parking lot is huge and we have no trouble finding a suitable parking spot. Entering the main doors of the hospital, we find a completely different atmosphere. There is no chaos, no wall-to-wall people—quite welcoming, in fact. The antithesis of Sick Kids.

Dr. Toms' office is on the main floor and is easy to find. It's yet another hospital for Conor and Tori but they are so adaptable and readily tag along. They want to participate in Ben's care. It's all they know when it comes to Ben.

Our morning appointment takes place within minutes of its scheduled start time. I like this doctor already. Dr. Toms is a fit, tall man who appears to be only a few years older than Jan and me. He actually introduces himself—a great start—and welcomes us into one of the treatment rooms. It is bright and spacious, with lots of natural light and pastel-washed walls. His tone and demeanour is very calming and he gives us all the time in the world, intently listening to every detail of Ben's history. Part way through, he begins to examine Ben . . . thoroughly. Looking in his ears, Dr. Toms confirms that there is fluid but no sign of infection. And that it would clear itself in time, so not to worry.

He offers to look after Conor and Tori, too, and says that we can call him anytime, especially if we have questions about Ben.

Wow, this guy must be heaven sent. Someone who has never met us until now, who is willing to take a complicated person like Ben, who is so self-assured, who respects our time by being on time, who genuinely listens to our rambling stories, challenges, worries, concerns.

We have found another safety net and real relief to our increasingly complex and stressful lives.

I know that this move to Toronto is a good one for Ben . . . and us.

*   *   *

6

HIS FIRST REAL SUMMER

The mid-afternoon summer sun radiates through our large living room windows, drenching me in its warmth. There's too much of it right now, to the point of being uncomfortable. I press my forehead against the heated glass to watch Conor and Tori playing in our tiny backyard, two-and-a-half stories below. Their large, green plastic sandbox, in the shape of a good-natured turtle, is filled with white dusty sand, some strands of grass and small rocks, and a collection of shovels and pails. The two of them are sitting on the sandbox's edge, shirtless, their feet buried underneath a thin layer of soft granules. Their smiles and giggles show the world how much fun they're having. I can easily see their every move but they are far out of reach. If I move my eyes only slightly upward, I can focus on the sidewalk and the roadway on the other side of the wooden fence that separates them from the secure surroundings of our condo. The fence isn't much of a barrier against the madness of the outside world. Despite seeing their carefree and excited demeanour, I feel I can't leave them alone, worried that they could be snatched in a heartbeat. In a moment of paranoia, I dash to the family room below to watch them from only a few strides away.

A few hours later, I am sitting restfully in that same living room, a short while after Ben has fallen asleep. A small crescent moon is barely noticeable through the upper corner of our wall-to-wall windows, even with the living room in darkness. Conor and Tori are getting ready for bed while Jan, her Mom, her Aunt Rita and a visiting cousin are gathered around the dining room table engaged in a very competitive game of 45s.

The teardrop bulbs of the overhead chandelier are almost too bright, glaring down on me while I quietly follow a Blue Jays ball game on the near-new television, the sound turned way down. It's somewhat reminiscent of a summer evening at Jan's Camp—so comfortable, so homey, so familiar. A thousand miles from home but yet it somehow feels like home.

For a few moments, I am actually enjoying my life.

How can the same room give me such contrasting feelings? It's a kind of metaphor for our lives.

Still getting settled

The rustling of blankets and the creaking of Ben's vinyl crib mattress crackles through the monitor at the painful hour of 3 a.m. I am stirred awake by these intermittent sounds, hopeful that they will go away. A few more minutes pass and Ben's breathing gets a little more forceful, almost panting. I enter his darkened bedroom and discover his eyes wide open, a big smile across his face, and his legs kicking back and forth. He is lying on his back, ready to play. I place him on his side, snuggle him into his pillow, and go back to bed.

He isn't interested in going to sleep. Within minutes, he rolls onto his back and starts to verbalize. I return to his crib and flip him onto his other side. We play this game for two hours until he decides that he's had enough and closes his eyes.

As the Sunday morning sun brightens our bedroom a short time later, I pull my fatigued body out of bed to prepare for a much anticipated visit to Ontario Place. It is a kid's wonderland of entertainment and activities, stretched across three man-made islands along the city's waterfront. The highlight today is a Fred Penner concert.

Despite the early wakeup call, the five-hour outing is exciting and refreshing for all of us, including Ben. He is more than willing to participate. I marvel at the intensity of his gaze at the over-stimulating attractions as he tries to drink everything in. By the time the concert begins, he has had enough, and falls asleep in Jan's arms. We sit near the perimeter of the round, outdoor stage which gives Conor and Tori some extra room to stretch their legs. Our seats are perfectly chosen to shelter our heads from the hot June sun.

Returning home late in the afternoon, I am swept with a feeling that the day was a bit too much for Ben. Part way through eating, he appears to drift into a state where his eyes are empty looking. I pick him out of his high chair and start to give him his bottle. He isn't interested. His eyes are still far away and I notice that his breathing is not right, very irregular. I sit him up and he chokes, as if he is going to vomit. His breathing gets more shallow and his colour is very mottled. A worrisome three or four minutes feels likes an hour until his colour returns to normal. This altered state takes its toll on him as his body goes very limp, and he falls asleep. A half hour later he awakens with a start and begins to cry forcefully, off and on, for about 45 minutes. This must have been some sort of seizure.

It is awful, that terrible sick feeling that rushes through me, that takes control of my mind. During these moments, I experience the worst feelings I have ever felt, like those of the day he was born. These feelings don't build like a crescendo, they envelop me instantly, like some electric shock, and I want to panic. Within a couple of minutes, I can usually calm myself once I realize that he'll get over it, that it's not life threatening, that I've been through it before. But through it all I feel completely out of control.

Later in the evening, Jan has a brief conversation with a neurologist at Sick Kids about this seizure-like episode. She suggests to us that Ben's *Phenobarbital* dose may need to be increased and she would speak to Dr. MacDonald tomorrow morning. Another helpful and understanding person. We must write down this person's name.

A few days later, Dr. MacDonald calls us to discuss Ben's episode. Not surprisingly, she tells us it certainly sounds like a seizure and that it will be probably be a good idea to increase his meds. The levels in his blood are well below the therapeutic range so really it is not much help. She wants to try the increased dose for a month and then have his blood checked again.

This is a tough decision for me. A part of me concludes that Ben has been able to reasonably control his seizures much on his own, since the *Phenobarbital* has been too low a dose to have much impact. But another part of me says that he certainly needs extra help to stabilize his nervous system, especially those times when he is over-tired. It's clear that he is not ready to come off the medication, if ever.

* * *

A Good Experience

Ben is active and feeling wonderful today, his eyes bright and his appetite hearty. Even an hour-long drive to downtown doesn't bother him. We have our first appointment with a private audiologist, Pierre Keleher, who is going to make new ear molds for Ben. His office is a short walk from Sick Kids.

As we turn the corner, a parking spot opens up directly in front of the non-descript, 18-storey structure that houses Mr. Keleher's office. Piling out the car, we feel our hair tousled mercilessly by a continuous funnel of wind that is artificially manufactured by the imposing pale, concrete monsters erected on each side of the street. As I load Ben into his stroller, a large Greyhound bus roars past us filling the air with a choking smell of diesel, its brisk speed an indication that it is devoid of any passengers. I am startled by the noise and look up to discover that a large bus terminal is located in the next block, and the street is lined with more than a dozen blue buses.

Jan and I gather everyone close and scurry into the lobby of the office building. Off to the right is a very bright and welcoming deli restaurant. It looks like a chain. We promise the kids that we'll get a treat once the appointment is over. They nod in agreement.

A short elevator ride climbs a dozen floors and opens into a long, narrow hallway. We hesitate for a moment before turning ourselves to the left. Mr. Keleher's office is set up at the end of the hallway. It sports a clean, glass entrance way. Inside is a spacious waiting room with several doors leading from it.

Within a few minutes of our arrival, a tall, hulking man enters wearing a wrinkled white dress shirt and royal blue tie. His face is round and his mannerisms remind me of my grandfather. In a booming voice, he introduces himself as Mr. Keleher and leans over to greet Ben. He takes us into a side office, its windows looking directly down over our car. With a quick tug, he hauls Ben's hearing aids from both ears. Holding them in both hands and turning them over repeatedly, he snorts and clicks his false teeth.

"I don't like this material," he states in a somewhat gruff tone, referring to the earmolds of Ben's hearing aids. "This is something I might use on an adult but never with a child. It's too stiff and brittle."

I think I'm going to like this man. He exudes confidence but not arrogance, though his tone could be less biting. With the skill of someone who has done this for a long, long time, he takes impressions for new molds—new silicone molds. Since the manufacturer is in Toronto, we should have them in only a few days.

Mr. Keleher does a quick check of Ben's hearing aids, giving them a thumbs up. He makes another appointment for a week out and politely says goodbye to everyone, again clicking his teeth as he speaks.

The journey back to our condo is uneventful and the hour trek seems to fly by. I dare say that we are getting accustomed to these long commutes that should take only 15 minutes. As we pull in our driveway, a neighbour is standing in his, washing his car. We exchange hellos and introduce ourselves. His name is Sam.

"Hi, I'm Mike. This is my wife, Jan. And this is Conor . . . Tori . . . and Ben."

Jan takes Ben inside to get changed and Conor and Tori have no interest in making small talk. At that same moment, a boy and girl run into Sam's driveway to greet him and hug him. These are his two kids who look to be about 10 and 12 years of age. Sam's ebony complexion brightens as they embrace.

He welcomes me to the neighbourhood which he describes as very quiet and very safe. There are a few other families with small children, he tells me, in this 36-unit condo complex. I mention that we're from the Maritimes and have moved here temporarily to get some specialized care for Ben. I give Sam a very compressed version of Ben's first year and tell him how I hope he continues to progress.

"Oh, he will. By the power of God," Sam exclaims.

His words catch me by surprise but I have to agree with him. I've only known him for five minutes but it's as if we're kindred spirits. Walking up our stairways, I am left with a sense of security that we are not alone, that there are always people who will help and support us, if only by the words they say.

* * *

Great conversations

One lesson Ben has taught us is to continuously look for answers. At times, my driver personality takes this learning to another level, to the point of obsession. I recognize this weakness in myself occasionally but am unapologetic when it comes to helping Ben. Through some diligent fact finding and research, we land a phone conversation with Dr. Richard Gehrz, Director of the Children's Biomedical Research Institute in St. Paul, Minnesota, which has become a centre for CMV research. Having the opportunity to connect with him is huge since he is someone who knows everything there is to know about CMV, who can give us a glimpse into the future, and maybe, provide us just a glimmer of encouragement and hope.

He tells us many things, giving us a much more mature perspective about the disease. His most interesting comment describes that although CMV causes all sorts of problems, from epilepsy to cerebral palsy and so on, the outcome of these conditions is very different than if they were caused in other ways, such as a head injury or a genetic defect. Why has no one ever told us this?

But his most energized comments reveal that Ben's first year is really a write-off. We should not worry about what has already happened. Kids with CMV have their most difficult time in those initial twelve months. Since Ben has almost reached his first birthday, his learning is just beginning.

Wow. If this is true, then we have just been given the opportunity to start again. This is unbelievably rejuvenating to Jan and me. Looking back to last June, I feel both amazed and overcome with emotion, wondering how we got through those ungodly months. There are days when I feel a little too self-assured, perhaps, but with that comes a warm sense of accomplishment, that we have the "experience" now, a medal of honour in a sense, that we did, indeed, survive the intense and prolonged pain of initiation. Now we're onto stage 2. Nothing could be as bad as that first year. Could it?

Following close on the heels of this mind-blowing conversation, we get to meet Genevieve. Referred to us by Dr. MacDonald, she is an OT associated with a non-profit community-based rehabilitation health service provide called COTA (Community Occupational Therapy Associates). She is eager to meet Ben. Her warm smile tells us she isn't afraid of him and wants to help. She tells us she deals exclusively with children and has worked with kids born with CMV. She is also cross-trained in physiotherapy and can work on gross motor skills, as well, during her weekly visits.

"Ah, c'mon. A real expert? Who will come to us? Once a week? Don't play with my head," I think to myself. "Really? You've worked with 'CMV kids' before?"

In describing Ben, we refer to his clutchiness and she immediately says that many CMV kids are affected in this way, that his infant reflexes are not suppressed despite his age, and may never be completely. My eyes widen as she tells us this. No way! She knows exactly what we're talking about and even uses the same words that Dr. Gehrz used to describe this.

Seeing him in his high chair, she comments that he appears to sit up quite well—she has seen kids who are better than Ben but also many who are not. She looks over the insert that was made for Ben and tells us that she believes it is serving him well.

Today, I'm glad we made the move to Toronto.

A subsequent visit by Genevieve is another eye-opening experience, with her focus on stretching exercises, ones that should be done every day. She admits that although stretching alone cannot change the neurological impacts to the tension and contractions of the muscles, she has seen evidence that it does help to keep them healthy, since they may not otherwise be used. At the very least, stretching just feels good.

She sits on the floor with Ben lying in front of her, his legs resting close to her, and shows us how to stretch his legs slowly. We had been doing it too fast. The routine begins with bending his foot gently to stretch the calf, moving his hips each time we change his diaper, slowly extending his arms and massaging his biceps to help them open more easily, rubbing his back to encourage it to stretch so he can more easily straighten it, and when sitting with him, twisting his trunk from side to side. There is so much for us to learn but we're ready.

Not long after Genevieve's training session we receive a call from Dr. MacDonald. Ben's blood results from a few weeks ago indicate that his *Phenobarbital* level is at the low end of the therapeutic range, with a value of 65. She wants to increase his morning dose to 15 mg.

We tell her that he seems to be more wakeful late at night, not falling asleep until at least 11 p.m. We wonder if giving his evening dose at supper time versus just before bed would make him less wakeful. She is excited to hear this, saying that it is encouraging that he is becoming more wakeful and active. When kids get their seizures under control, they can concentrate on more activities and not worry about the seizures.

Are we at that stage? Crossing the one-year mark, is it really a whole new beginning?

* * *

Confidence

We are starting to get good at this, everyone piling into the car for a daily excursion. Jan's shift begins at 4 p.m. and Ben has an appointment with Mr. Keleher today at 6 p.m. With only one vehicle, our options are few. But the kids don't mind shuffling Mom to work and then heading downtown.

Once Ben's belly is full, we head downtown to see Mr. Keleher to pick up his new ear molds. Ben is content to look out the car windows in between pulling off his glasses. He has found a way to hook his index finger around the arm of the frame and drag them part way across his face so that one nose-pad is lodged just inside a nostril. Conor helps to reposition the glasses and scolds Ben like any big brother would.

We pull up in front of Mr. Keleher's building with a few minutes to spare. The side streets are remarkably quiet. A little eerie. The working population has vacated most of this section of town and there is little trouble finding a parking spot. A continuous warm breeze swirls about as I gather everyone to the front door. I can't believe I'm here alone, with my three kids, all of whom are under five years of age. And Ben, well, he could have a seizure and I'm not sure what I'd do. But the feeling is different today. Dare I say, a small ray of confidence has crept into my demeanour. Jan is 50 km away and it doesn't matter.

Conor and Tori know the way and dart down the 12th floor hall, bursting through the office door. Mr. Keleher is pleased to see us and doesn't mind the evening appointments. He finds this hour of day a time to catch up and prepare for the next day's madness.

On the drive home, Ben falls into a deep sleep. Carrying him onto our living room couch does not wake him and his eyes remain closed nearly 45 minutes. When he does wake, he is a little confused, perhaps forgetting that he is no longer at Mr. Keleher's. Waking up can sometimes be difficult for him, though his reactions are certainly more normal than those of even a few months ago. This late evening nap has messed up his bedtime and he lies awake until nearly midnight.

Most times, this would frustrate me since it would leave no time for myself to unwind, to do something mindless. But this night, I gladly exchange my "me" time for Ben having a "great" day.

* * *

Visits I couldn't enjoy

The weather at the beginning of August is hot and humid in fine, southern Ontario style, perfect for many outings. Conor and Tori have a great time even if it's just a quick trip to the park behind our condo. Ben doesn't participate much—it's too hot for him to enjoy. Ben's only outing is to see a new ophthalmologist, Dr. Buckley, who is the chief of the department at Sick Kids. Given the choice, Ben's siblings remain at home today with their Nana (Marg) who is visiting us for a week together with Jan's Auntie Rita.

Typical of most of our appointments, we are forced to interact with a bumbling resident first—one of the drawbacks of a teaching hospital. The whole conversation focuses on Jan's pregnancy. I'm not sure if he is just very nervous or very clumsy but it's a complete waste of time. What does the pregnancy have to do with Ben's turning eye? He fumbles around for so long that Ben falls asleep and the eye drops really don't get a chance to work.

An hour and a half past our appointment time, Dr. Buckley finally gets to examine Ben. He suggests that his glasses are a little strong and, most importantly, that his turning eye problem isn't very significant. He confirms the slight scarring on Ben's left eye but says that it should have no effect on his vision. He recommends that we continue patching and return in October. It's not the educating experience we were hoping for.

In the evening, a cousin of Jan's, now a resident of Toronto, comes over for a visit. None of us have seen him in a long, long time and, of course, Marg and Auntie are delighted. They spend most of the evening playing match after match of 45s. I've never really learned to play cards with any decent level of skill and have little desire to participate. I'm content to watch the Blue Jays game. Tonight, it feels like home to me.

The week is over much too quickly and we are sad to see Marg and Auntie leave. Conor and Tori are quite melancholy and Ben seems a little off. My parents are arriving tomorrow for a week's stay too, and I'm hopeful it will be a good visit. They will be in unfamiliar territory which should help them focus on enjoying their grandchildren instead of nitpicking at me and Jan.

At midnight, Ben awakes crying and is burning up with a fever. As I stand over his crib, he starts choking a little. I hold him upright and he starts clutching. Yelling for Jan, I scurry him into the bathroom believing he is going to throw up. Ben continues to hold his arms outstretched and cries, getting that terrified look in his eyes, and turns grey. My heart is racing and my head is pounding. Just like that—boom—into a seizure. Sound asleep one minute and in distress the next. No warning. Oh, how I thought that these episodes were behind us.

After a few minutes, he comes around. We stick the thermometer under his arm and it beeps once, reaching 39°C. Jan doesn't want to fool around and insists we go to Sick Kids right away. I resist, suggesting it will make matters worse going there so late at night and having to bring Conor and Tori with us. With the dining room lights glaring in our eyes while the rest of the condo in darkness, we pause, not really sure what to do. As a compromise, we contact the neurologist on call at Sick Kids to get some advice. From our description, and, of course, she knows nothing about Ben, she believes that his actions were a seizure and most likely a febrile one. She gives us some tips on keeping him cool and says to call back as often as we want . . . for anything. By 4 a.m., Ben's little body finally settles. He is much cooler and stays asleep for several hours.

By late morning, he is quite listless. His limbs exhibit very little tone, his eyes look drawn, and he is not the least bit interested in eating. My parents arrive on schedule and are greeted with Ben's shrill cries. He is miserable and can't get comfortable, his cries becoming more and more painful. His night's sleep is even more restless.

The next day—our 7th wedding anniversary—he is showing signs of dehydration. I come home from work early, unable to concentrate. Ben really looks sick. He has no life in him, and I can see that my father is concerned. We shuffle Ben to see Dr. Toms at North York General Hospital on short notice. Even his usual calm demeanour seems a bit rattled at Ben's condition and this noticeable unease heightens my anxiety. He tells us that Ben should be admitted right away to determine what is going on. If we go home, he thinks Ben would only get worse. I am both relieved and anxious. I hate the thought of spending more overnights in a hospital. It's so discouraging.

We are quickly shown to what will be Ben's hospital room. It's huge—a ward, actually—spacious enough for four patients but Ben is the only occupant today. Consistent with our first impression of this place, the atmosphere is almost welcoming, as much as a hospital can be. The dusty rose colour of the walls is clean and soothing, and the lighting contributes to a sense of calmness.

Ben is placed in a crib identical to the ones at the hospital in Saint John. He can only lie there while they poke and prod him to get some blood. They can't find a vein. What a disaster. My calmness fades and I want to say something caustic. The specialists at Sick Kids were much more skilled when it came to this. Ben is too wiped to complain and so I don't say a word.

A few more punctures of his tiny hands finally lead to a successful connection of the IV. It is like magic juice to him. In only a few minutes of the fluid running through him, he starts lifting up on his arms and gooing, even attempting a faint smile. It's not supposed to work that quickly. Almost instantly, I feel the same small burst of energy rising inside of me, draining the crippling tension from my body, the kind of tension that hardens your arteries and shortens your lifespan. It's as if I just finished a marathon. I'm relieved but too tired to stand.

A few hours pass and Jan returns with everyone. Conor and Tori are excited to see their brother and I think my parents are a bit reassured, as well. I am starving, not having left Ben's side all afternoon, and decide to take my father and Ben's siblings to McDonald's to grab a bite. It's the only place that's close and quick.

After this condensed reprieve from the confines of the hospital, I feel strong enough to spend the night with Ben: someone has to. A loud audio broadcast reminds us that visiting hours are over, and Jan gathers the crew to head home.

The hissing of the room's white noise is all that can be heard as Ben lies still and quiet. The darkened summer sky helps to wind things down and Ben comfortably closes his eyes by 9:30 p.m. Gently, I drag a fold-out chair from the corner of the room and place it next to his crib. Attempting to stretch out across the vinyl-covered cushions is nearly impossible since the gaps between the cushions are so ergonomically incorrect. I can't stay in one position for very long but the arrival of a duo of nurses every two hours to check Ben's vitals ensures that I'm not cramped in the same awkward position for very long.

By 6 a.m., Ben is awake and seems rested. Not me. My eyes are crusty, my back is a little tender, and I feel like I have a hangover. I get him out of his crib, avoiding his IV line, and feed him his morning bottle. He sucks slowly at first but then gets into a rhythm. Dr. Toms pays us a visit several hours later to say that all tests were negative. He surmises that once Ben got into a cycle of not eating well because he wasn't feeling well, it became a downward spiral, and with his small size, it didn't take much for him to become dehydrated. By late afternoon, Dr. Toms lets us go home.

As the week passes, Ben becomes stronger and more like himself. We try to make my parents' visit enjoyable but I can't let go. I'm still worried about seizures, their unpredictability, their suddenness. Spending our wedding anniversary in the paediatric ward is demoralizing. So much has changed in seven short years.

*   *   *

Steady improvement

With that exhausting week behind us, Jan and I look to regroup. Conor and Tori enjoyed having a visit from my parents but it was all a blur to me. Ben has such control over me and my emotions that some days I don't remember anything I did or needed to do.

A week later, both Genevieve and Sandra, his new physiotherapist, visit to try a new insert she has made for his high chair. It fits like a glove. We're amazed at how well he holds himself upright. Genevieve instructs us that the way to improve head control is to improve trunk control. The new insert holds his hips more securely than the old one, allowing him to forget about supporting his trunk and focus on keeping his head up. This should help with eating, too. She's amazing.

Both Genevieve and Sandra are encouraged with his progress and remark how Ben always seems to be happy. He has a spark in his eye, they tell us. This is really important since they see many children who don't seem to have any life at all.

"The small steps should be celebrated," Genevieve tells us. "Because Ben's progress will be measured in grains of sand!"

Genevieve returns a day later to construct an *Ethafoam* insert for Ben's stroller so that he will be able to sit more supported on long walks and outings. Since her time with Ben has been filled with seating needs, she tells us that Sandra will become more involved and help us with Ben's exercises. This is personalized service.

Feeling a rise in our confidence following Genevieve's visit, we decide to go window shopping for a new car—a minivan, actually. We find a Mazda dealer on the western side of the city who is very keen to sell a new 8-passenger MPV. Ben isn't at all interested in what the salesman has to say and falls asleep in the showroom. I'm dreaming, of course, if I believe for a second that we can afford a car payment.

We let the salesperson chat much too long about a deal that's just not going to happen. As we get ready to leave, it hits me that we won't be able to make it home in time to feed Ben his lunch. We didn't bring anything with us, either, and I get a little panicky. Jan tries to assure me that we will be able to find someplace close that sells baby food. I hope she's right. This part of the city is completely foreign to us. Ben is getting a little antsy before we spot signs for Woodbine Mall. We pull into a nearby parking spot and hustle inside.

Once inside, we locate a Shoppers Drug Mart to purchase some baby food for Ben as Conor and Tori discover a McDonald's a short distance away. It is unbelievably noisy inside the restaurant but Ben doesn't care. Between spoonfuls of sweet potatoes, he looks at the yelling toddlers running crazily throughout. He is eager to join the mayhem.

On our stroll back to our car, we discover that the mall is equipped with a large indoor amusement park. Needless to say, Conor and Tori want to stay. We acquiesce, feeling their desire to enjoy life. Getting ambitious, we take Ben on his first merry-go-round ride. Jan sits on one of the stationary benches with Ben while I stand beside Conor and Tori as they bob up and down on the backs of the wooden ponies. The jack-in-the-box type music blares from the large speaker in the centre of the ride as we revolve in a clockwise fashion. Bright, clear light bulbs flash all around us. It is a little mundane for Conor but Ben is very stimulated, his eyes wide for the full three-minute ride. Jan was right. Our unplanned afternoon turned out fine. Another example of how well we complement each other.

On my drive to work the next day, I mull over Ben's streak of good days and the "blippy" ones that can arise at any time. I stick to the collector lanes for most of my westbound journey down Highway 401. You're really not supposed to do that but the flow of vehicles is much more uniform and predictable in these outside lanes. And, moving west, I'm traveling opposite to most who are heading to downtown. Every morning at 7:45 a.m., CHUM-FM plays the "morning mystery hit" and this morning I have no idea what it is. The caller into the show, though, is familiar to me.

"Hi. Who's this?", the DJ asks.

"It's Genevieve," the caller responds.

"Well, Genevieve, we're going to the play it one more time for you . . ."

I can't believe it. I actually know the person on the radio—it's *our* Genevieve. A familiar voice in a town of 3 million strangers. Another moment when this place feels like home.

* * *

7

THE FIRE

On a Saturday morning, the journey to downtown can be accomplished in less than 15 minutes but during the week, it's anyone's guess. Ben needs new ear molds (again), and since Mr. Keleher doesn't work weekends, we have no choice but to eat up an hour or more of our lives.

Jan is preparing for her usual evening shift and so I am on my own (almost) to handle this appointment (again). Tara arrives early today to help me, her soft smile always welcomed by the kids.

Tara Ramos is all of 16 years old but a remarkably mature teenager who enjoys kids and is unafraid of Ben. Over the summer, we had begun to ask our small network of co-workers and neighbours about finding a teenager who could look after Conor, Tori and Ben for a few hours after school, at least until I got home. This was an incredibly huge step for us. With only two months on the ground, we needed to find a person who was responsible, fun to be with, and capable of managing an emergency situation with Ben.

When Tara showed up at our doorstep, our prayer had been answered. She was so pleasant, had a well-balanced manner, and was someone who immediately connected with each of us. In our opening conversation, we talked about how Jan would leave for work at 3:30 p.m. each day so it was important for her to be on time. And how I might not get home until 6 p.m. or later.

During the "interview," we gave her a rundown of the late-afternoon routine, when to feed Ben, what medications to give him, how to lay him down for a nap, and on and on. She took it all in without a hint of hesitation. When Jan asked if she thought she could handle it, even if Ben got into trouble, she responded that it would be no problem. She wants to be a pediatrician and helping a child like Ben would give her great experience. She also said that she could always call her parents to come over if something happened and we couldn't get home quickly—they lived only a few minutes away.

With little effort, we buckle up for the downtown ride to see Mr. Keleher—Ben is locked into the middle of the back seat, Conor sits behind me and Tori is propped on her booster seat behind Tara.

"Always great"

For the first day of September, the sun is particularly strong and we feel it as we creep along the Don Valley Parkway; in these situations, it is easy to see why it is sometimes labeled the "Don Valley Parking Lot." Ben doesn't mind the stop-and-go motion . . . nor sitting for nearly 45 minutes . . . nor hustling out of the car in front of the now-familiar, windswept concrete tower where his audiologist is located.

Today, Mr. Keleher is ever the eccentric individual we've come to know. He is only months away from retirement, he tells us, and every story that he conveys, in between the clicking of his false teeth, is always entertaining and informative. He has no trouble sharing his views about the health-care system but his 35 years of working with it and against it demonstrate his wisdom and care.

Instead of taking the ear-mold impressions separately, where the pink goo would be placed in one ear, carefully removed, examined and set aside, and then the other, Mr. Keleher chooses to take impressions in both ears at the same time. Ben sits contented, both ears plugged, as the compound hardens amid the cool air flow of the office. Tara watches over Conor and Tori as they very quietly entertain themselves in the play corner. Attending appointments with Ben rarely tests their patience—they're quite remarkable.

After only 15 minutes, Conor is rushing into the narrow hallway outside of the office to press the "down" button. I can remember when Jennifer, Ben's first audiologist in Saint John, took ear-mold impressions, how insecure she seemed, never quite knowing whether or not she had taken a good one, sometimes re-doing them, sometimes more than once. An hour of our lives would have been eaten up, at a minimum.

No matter how you look at it, though, we need to set aside a good two hours of our day to get new ear-molds made: whether it's 30 minutes of driving and a 90-minute appointment (as it used to be) or 90 minutes of driving and a 15-minute appointment, it's never quick.

Despite the long day, Ben remains in a great mood. His evening bath is enjoyable for me and for him as he repeatedly kicks and splashes anything he can. The worry of him having the "clutches" while in the tub is beginning to wane.

Jan and I talk about how Ben is "always great" whenever she calls from work. The adverb "great" has a special meaning for us—it means that there are no major concerns or issues and we can rest easy for the time being. It's our way of putting life in perspective, of being thankful for not having to rush to a hospital's ER. A day without seizures is a "great" day. A day without a hospital visit is a "great" day.

We remind ourselves of some of the fears we originally had, like his enlarged ventricles or losing the ability to swallow. Perhaps they're no longer a problem. Certainly, as time passes, they become less and less important.

A whole day ends without incident, with Ben being great. You can't ask for much more.

* * *

A Falls weekend

For a moment, life seems quite normal as we pose for the camera. With the deafening roar of Niagara Falls whipping along fifty or so feet below us, Conor and Tori stand fearlessly on the thick stone wall, gently holding onto the black tubular railing that separates them from nature's fury. In between them, Jan cradles Ben in the afternoon sunlight while I extend my arm to provide a little extra support. It has been an enjoyable but tiring day and Tori's expression can't hide her displeasure of having her picture taken.

We arrived in the border town yesterday and connected with Care and Charlie, Jan's cousin and her husband, who ventured from Rhode Island. Quite often, when we need Ben to rise early, he doesn't cooperate, or when we can laze in bed for an extra hour, he chooses to wake up the household. But he awakened shortly after 7 a.m., which was early for him, perhaps in anticipation of spending Labour Day weekend away.

He was in good spirits when we pulled up in front of our motel. Following a lunch break, we made our way for an afternoon at Marineland, driving past a large group of demonstrators who were protesting the captivity of the sea creatures. We spent a full five hours in the park and Ben enjoyed every minute. He watched curiously while Charlie and I took a roller coaster ride. He even slept, reclined in his stroller, as Shamu and Baby Shamu jumped, dove, and splashed in the outdoor aquarium.

In the evening, Ben accompanied us to La Parmigiana, a local Italian eatery. Despite rising at that early hour, he was "great" in the restaurant, quite content to kick, punch, laugh, and goo, while exploring his environs with his dancing eyes. Usually such a long day without a decent sleep is enough to send him into wacky-land but not this time.

This morning, Ben decided to rest a little longer. And he had earned it, given Saturday's lengthy itinerary. Charlie and I, along with Conor and Tori, spent the morning in the room while Jan and Care went to Mass.

The photo shoot was great, the afternoon was great, and the evening is winding down very nicely. Care and Charlie stop in and offer to stay with the kids so that we can get an hour to ourselves. After Ben drifts off to sleep, we find the courage to take a walk in the crisp evening air that is starting to smell like fall.

About 10 minutes away is Niagara's most famous landmark—the Skylon Tower—and we decide to ascend to its revolving restaurant. From nearly 800 feet skyward, it provides a spectacular view of the whole Niagara region, and the evening lights of the city bordering the rushing Falls help us unwind.

For a moment, life seems quite normal.

* * *

"Everyone, get out!"

Entering our 2nd floor motel room presents us with shades of darkness plus three sleeping, little people. Whether it is luck or providence, we are allowed to enjoy an hour alone and have the task of getting three toddlers to sleep already done for us. Jan and I take advantage of this rare opportunity and decide to get an early start to our own sleep.

Our restful evening is rudely interrupted by the rhythmic ding of a fire alarm. Glancing at the clock, it displays 12:40 a.m. I briefly freeze while I attempt to make sense of it all. Jan awakes to me calling her name and we debate about what to do. The dissonance of the same alarm pierced the evening stillness at about the same time last night, and it had turned out to be a false alarm. I convince myself it is a recurring problem with this budget motel and want to simply ring the front desk to confirm my suspicion. Jan overrules and wants me to physically transport my weary frame downstairs and speak face-to-face with the front desk staff.

After another 10-second pause, I find my way to the stairwell. At this late hour, descending the set of unfinished, metal stairs reminds me of my dorm room after a Saturday night of over-eating and over-drinking. I can even remember the distinct odours of the men's residence, as my feet reluctantly make their way to the bottom floor. When I open the door to the hallway that spills out into the motel lobby, I am almost knocked down by two policeman frantically running through hall yelling for everyone to get out.

IT IS FOR REAL!

I sprint back up the stairs, my heart coming through my chest. Suddenly, I'm not so tired. Charlie is outside in the hall rubbing his eyes as I blurt out that the alarm is real. We look down the hall and can see smoke on the other side of the hall door. I rush into the room and tell Jan. Conor and Tori wake up, a little confused but not crying. I tell them that this is a fire alarm and to go with Mom. I am able to find shoes for Tori but don't have time to get Conor's on him. The room is in total darkness so I really can't see.

Conor and Tori walk out into the hall to find Jan. When I realize that Jan is actually in the bathroom, instant panic grips me, having just sent Conor and Tori into the hall with no one! Jan dashes to the stairwell and discovers that they are both going down the stairs with Care.

In military fashion, Charlie grabs the stroller and proceeds to head outside. I snatch Ben's heavier blanket from the side of the playpen where he is sleeping, wrap it around him and scoop him up. I also manage to get the room key, car keys, some loose money, my wallet, and oh yes, Conor's sneakers. You're not supposed to waste time doing this, of course. You're supposed to just leave.

In the mêlée, I yell at Jan to get Ben's hearing aids and glasses. She can't find them! We can't afford to leave them, we can't afford new ones, and it will take forever to make an insurance claim to get replacements. Our life is so complicated. As we are searching for these few things, a policemen reaches our room, his flashlight panning the area looking for people, and tells everyone to get out.

Somehow, Ben stays asleep as I walk down the stairwell. Once we breach the night air, he opens his eyes. He does not appear confused, nor breathe rapidly, nor behave seizure-like. We all huddle in Care and Charlie's Ford Explorer to escape the coolness of the night and Ben just goos. I am relieved that a tiring weekend and an abrupt end to his night's sleep doesn't push him over the edge. I glance at Conor who has walked down the cold stairs and out into the parking lot in his bare feet. He doesn't seem to mind and is quite fascinated by the turn of events.

Realizing that we need to find a place to sleep, Charlie and I search out some neighbouring motels. All are fully booked—it's a holiday weekend, after all. Care thinks she saw a Red Roof Inn close by. It turns out to be the "Red Carpet Inn," kind of sleazy, kind of 1970s, kind of *Planes, Trains, and Automobiles*—like, you know, where John Candy tries to pay for his room by bartering his Casio watch. They have *one* room available. A very small room.

After getting the kids settled for what is left of the night, Charlie and I make our way back to our old motel to pick up our belongings. The clock in his Explorer rolls to 3 a.m. as we turn the corner.

Approaching the front steps of the hotel, we overhear some guests gossiping that it was an electrical fire while others were convinced it started in the laundry chute from oily cloths. It doesn't matter to us. We can't stay here.

The unmistakable stench of smoke hits us as we enter the lobby. Strangely, the upper floor has no smell of anything even though this is where the fire supposedly had started. No one seems to care that we leave the premises with our bags and armfuls of items. This place has some serious issues.

Ben takes quite a while to get back to sleep with Jan gently massaging his back. Since there are only two queen beds in the room, I sleep with Conor on the floor, on top of the dust-mite-infested, rust coloured shag fibres of the floor covering, and Care sleeps with Tori.

Did I say life seems normal?

* * *

Setting the bar too high

From the moment that Conor was born, my life changed. My role as a father had become real and, like most important things in my life, I committed to putting my heart and soul into doing the best job possible as his father. Now, with three children under five, my life *is* my children.

The test of just how wonderful they truly are comes not only from glowing compliments of others, commenting on how well behaved they are, but also from their responses in critical, important situations. It very much demonstrates that they have mastered the principles of what is the right thing to do, an undeniable sign of their maturity, even at such a young age.

This sudden evacuation of our hotel has reinforced their centrality in my life and reminds me not to sweat the small stuff. When Conor was replaying these events for his grandparents, of how he walked down the cold stairs in his bare feet in the middle of the night, without me or Jan going with him, and innocently interjected with,

"*Well, sometimes I don't listen . . .* ," my heart sank.

All of the times that I was angry with him, yelling at him for totally meaningless and irrelevant things, came flooding back to me. I was instantly crushed under a tremendous mountain of guilt, being nothing more than a twisted, pathetic mess on the floor.

The intensity and the desire to be the best father possible can prevent me from believing that I'm actually doing a good job and making progress. I tend to set the bar higher than it needs to be, especially when it comes to them. The result is that I wind being much too hard on them when I should just be thankful that they are such precious human beings.

My absence of patience is made evident mostly when I'm tired, when the stress of Ben's care is too much. And they feel the brunt of my exasperation.

I have to learn to overcome this all too frequent reaction. I need to find another outlet.

8

HAVING A ROUTINE IS POSSIBLE

My first day back to work after the Labour Day holiday is a busy one. The summer coasting has come to an end and everyone is getting antsy about all of the things that have to be completed by the end of the year. It is as if a big switch has been flipped—on Friday, things were laid back, no worries, but today, everything seems to be behind schedule. Our team leaders have called an end-of-day status meeting to bring the group onto the same page and share their sense of urgency. Finding this out at the last minute, I call home to ask Tara if she could stay an extra hour.

The chain of subway connections and bus rides deposits me home at 6:30 p.m. Tara is a little flustered, telling me that Ben was quite irritable and wasn't interested in eating. She tells me she had given him some Tempra, which calmed his crying but felt concerned about his lack of appetite. I tell her not to worry, that his teething of late has been difficult for him, and thanked her for managing through the extra hour on such short notice.

Before I snuggle Ben into bed, I give him another dose of Tempra and it further calms his crankiness. Through the night, he cries out a few times but does not wake up. A minor inconvenience.

The next few days are much the same for Tara. I get home late, Ben is irritable, not really hungry but eventually settles. By Thursday, Ben is realizing Tara is all he's got until I get home. I don't arrive home until 7:30 p.m. but all is well. She has him in his pyjamas and he is content.

On Friday, I get bold and ask Tara to watch over the supper hour again while I pick up Jan from a training session she is attending downtown. Ben finally eats for Tara and she is pleased with her success.

It has been a good test for everyone. For Tara and her coping abilities. For the kids and their ease of adapting to a new person and a new routine. And for Jan and me, that we can both be away from Ben at the same time and feel comfortable enough to do that. In light of this new reality, Jan increases her work week to nearly full-time, in part because we need the extra income, but also that life is slowly allowing us to develop a normal routine. There's that word again.

Marginalized, again!

No two aspects of our life ever fire in sync. If Ben is having a great day (which is truly all that matters), then something in our work life goes sideways, or Conor and Tori aren't feeling well, or we have to deal with a useless specialist appointment. Overall, though, things do feel as if they are starting to come together. Genevieve and Sandra have set up a coordinated therapist session with Ben, and both are scheduled to visit today.

Piercing the morning stillness, the phone rings. It's 7 a.m. It never rings this early. It's Sandra. Her voice has a nervous, almost sheepish, tone to it. She reveals to Jan that she won't be coming today since she has just learned that she is pregnant. In fact, she has decided to not see Ben anymore to eliminate any chance of catching CMV. Jan calmly explains that Ben has long stopped shedding the virus so there should be no concern, that the virus is so common, so widespread that she likely has already contracted it in her day-to-day interactions with so many children.

I try to control my anger. It's not good to be angry so early in the morning. So much for the mecca of the health-care world. So much for the centre of the universe. They're just as backward here as they are in Saint John.

If Sandra believes she's less at risk by not seeing Ben, she is oh so wrong. Why doesn't she know this? For every child like Ben—less than one in a thousand—there are 10 others who have had the virus and show *no* obvious symptoms. None. And you have no idea who they are. In fact, because it is so widespread, you cannot possibly control contracting it from other children, from your neighbours' children, or your neighbours themselves. Hell, you can pick it up at the grocery store.

We were just beginning to develop a physio routine and suddenly we're abandoned. No warning, no replacement, no support. Just gone.

Sandra shouldn't be allowed to get off that easy. She should have to personally explain to *Ben* that she's afraid of catching the same disease that caused all of his problems and that she's not going to see him any more. But deep down, she is really saying something like,

> "Good morning, Ben. I have some bad news for you. I'm not going be able to help you any more. You see, I can't run the risk of giving birth to a retarded kid like you. My pregnancy is way more important than helping you. I mean, really, you have so many problems, your physical rehab is not going to change anything. Let's be honest, do you really think you're ever going to be able to walk?"

Our doorbell rings. It's Genevieve, on time for her appointment with Ben. She apologizes for Sandra's decision, agreeing that it is misguided and understands how hurtful it is. She tells Jan that she will fulfill her OT duties and the physio ones that Sandra would have done. Someone with an unwavering commitment to her most vulnerable patients. We want to keep her forever.

* * *

Chronic fear

There is something to learn every day, whether we choose to do so or not. There are days when I am so eager to understand everything there is to know to help Ben. And then there are days when I don't want to hear another word.

Seizures continue to scare me. I want them to go away but, perhaps, if I learn more about them, they wouldn't bother me so much. The Bloorview Children's Hospital is holding an information session on childhood seizure disorders. Here's my chance.

The first speaker is from Epilepsy Canada who provides an excellent overview of seizures. She is joined by a physician from the hospital who remarks that if you have ever caught yourself staring off into space, what some people might refer to as "day dreaming," that can technically be classified as a form of epilepsy. That would mean 90% of the population, or at least 90% of people I know, have epilepsy. Intriguing but difficult to believe. During the Q&A portion of the presentation, Jan asks about Ben's laughing spells, in which he seems to laugh uncontrollably, wondering if they could be seizures. We are told that it's very unlikely. Interesting. Another piece of the puzzle unveiled for us. I'm no less scared but less uncertain.

A few days later at an all-morning assessment, Ben's neurological imperfections are on display. We have an appointment with a developmental pediatrician, a "brilliant" person according to Dr. Toms. For the first half hour, she asks all the same questions any new doctor seemingly *must* ask including, "What was your pregnancy like?" . . . "Did you experience this . . . Did you experience that . . . ?" I do my best to contain my exasperation.

When it comes time to examine Ben, she places him on his back and strips off most of his clothing. I really don't want him to be so exposed but that's the way this "genius" wants to see him. The office is very chilly and I'm sure he's frozen. Within a few minutes of being prodded and manipulated, Ben gets a look of fright on his face, outstretches his arms high in the air, turns red, and lets out a little cry. The doctor is unconcerned and turns him on his side. Within a few seconds, Ben comes out of it.

This is his first seizure in more than three months. I want to think that it was "induced," that it was too much stimulation too quickly. For the rest of the day, I'm on edge. Jan isn't bothered by it but my uneasiness won't leave me. There are countless medications that can control the disorder but none cure it. It is the mysterious neurological components behind these seizures that I fear the most. There are so many unknowns with them, it only takes a glimpse of them to rouse in me that awful feeling of my life spiraling out of control.

* * *

"Me" time

The next day Genevieve arrives in the late afternoon to show Tara all of Ben's passive stretching exercises. Tara has become comfortable with Ben so quickly that we are confident she can take on an even bigger role. Genevieve is never anything but pleasant and Tara is eager to learn—a perfect combination. Jan is able to participate before her evening shift even though she is well aware of the routine. It is more like a review but it does highlight a couple of things we were doing wrong and some things we were leaving out. Another reminder of how it's always beneficial to step back and self-evaluate once and a while.

When I arrive home from my usual 90-minute public transit adventure, all is calm. Tara tells me that Ben actually fell asleep in his high chair, perhaps a result of his MMR (measles/mumps/rubella) vaccination earlier in the week.

His late day nap means that he does not want to go to bed at the usual hour. After another long day, my stamina is waning for being on high alert for the last few days, in anticipating of some adverse reaction to the MMR shot. I am frustrated that he is still awake as the clock ticks past 10 p.m. I know that it serves no purpose to react this way but tonight, I am being swept up in a wave of self-pity of how I never get time just for myself. Most days, I don't need any "me" time—my kids are all I need—but tonight my mind starts racing and I feel very discouraged that I never get to do anything. This always happens when I'm tired, when I wind up losing my cool with Conor and Tori, and then nobody wins.

The next evening, I'm feeling guilty. Ben is "sitting" in front of the couch. On the floor. He looks quite natural with his arms and hands relaxed by his side. He really is sitting, upright, and is quite proud of himself. No straps, no side support, just the couch at his back! I start to convince myself that he will be sitting up on his own, all the time. Maybe even by Christmas! I can't wait to call Jan to share my elation.

I so much want him to sit up and crawl and start holding and grabbing toys all at once. But the rational voice inside my head is telling me to temper this jubilation because the scales can tip the other way with very little effort.

Such a simple, routine accomplishment is really what I enjoy most. Who needs "me" time, anyway, when I can have "Ben" time?

* * *

More guideposts

I am a little apprehensive about Ben's neurology appointment this morning. No question, he is improving but my confidence is fragile today. Some days are like that. Fatigue is always a big factor. Sitting in the clinic, surrounded by a dozen children who clearly have very serious issues, more serious than Ben's, makes me all the more nervous. This isn't going to be us, someday, is it? It's overwhelming me. A stranger retrieves us by calling out Ben's name. We're almost on schedule.

The EEG setup is different from that in Saint John. Here, we can stay in the same room as the technician and can watch the needles dance on the page. It's much less suspenseful and that's a good thing. As the test begins, Ben is alert and unbothered by the thousand cotton balls stuck to his scalp.

A strobe light flashes in front of him. When the flash intervals get quite short, Ben becomes interested. The technician tells us that he has good "driving" response at the different strobe speeds meaning his brain is processing the light at the same speed as the light is flashing. You mean he actually passed a test? Not much vision, eh?

The remainder of the test is painless. Ben cooperates by dozing throughout, a good combination to test a variety of brain wave patterns.

The follow-on appointment with Dr. McDonald a short time later focuses only on the good, beginning with praise for Conor and Tori's behaviour. I never get tired of hearing that. Sifting through hundreds of feet of graphical output, Dr. McDonald points out the good waves, the normal sleep waves, and some of the background seizure spikes that are still present on the left side of his brain.

She tells us the risk of Ben losing the ability to swallow or his head swelling due to enlarged ventricles is "less than 1% . . . ." When it comes to neurological disorders, it can never be 0%—that's the rule of thumb.

"It would be very rare for either of these things to occur," she exclaims.

I didn't think a neurologist could ever be this upbeat.

She recommends that Ben have his upcoming *Pertussis* vaccine since there have been some outbreaks of whooping cough in the city. In her view, the risk of any fever resulting from the vaccine is heavily outweighed by the trouble Ben could experience if he does contract the disease.

Before leaving, we chat briefly about Sandra's CMV hysteria. Dr. McDonald shakes her head in dismay and agrees that it is more likely that a person can "catch" CMV from another adult, even in the supermarket, than catching anything from Ben. People can become very paranoid about contracting every little thing.

And they do . . . but there's not a damn thing we can do about it.

* * *

Marathon sessions

Today is the big day. A full nine hours of appointments ahead of us—Sick Kids in the morning, the Hugh McMillan rehab centre in the afternoon. It all begins with Ben's 5:30 a.m. wake up call.

Up first is Audiology with a punctual audiologist. A rarity. The impedance equipment that is used to test a person's eardrums is not working today, and hasn't been since September 20th, according to a yellow sticky note that is attached to the main control. That's three weeks ago! The backup machine is much older and doesn't look like it could measure anything. This antique claims there is no eardrum movement on Ben's right side but registers negative pressure on the left.

A quick test of his hearing aids gets unusual results after they are popped into a small box that is lined with a thick, spongy foam. At first, the analyzer shows there is no increase in loudness (called "gain") at any frequency, but after a few pushes of buttons and twistings of dials, proper gain is shown on the adjacent monitor. This device reminds me of an old oscilloscope that I once used in a physics lab many years ago. Sometimes, I wonder if these specialists aren't just winging it.

An ABR test, which Ben had as an infant, can't be done today since that device also isn't working (c'mon, this is Sick Kids hospital, isn't it?). Our life is now full of acronyms, needless to say, and any previous **A**uditory **B**rainstem **R**esponse analyses have always proven to be a waste of time, so Jan and I are not disappointed that it can't be done today.

We proceed directly to a hearing test and position Ben in the soundproof booth. Part way through, the audiologist determines that he is showing some response to Jan's voice at 60 db (maybe even 50 db) and most definitely at 70 db. This is good. This is very good. If we can believe these numbers, Ben has reduced his hearing loss from a level of "profound" to one of "moderately severe." This is a good start to the day, although I still don't find these tests particularly scientific.

Our next appointment is with the ear, nose, and throat (ENT) department head, Dr. Crowley. ENT is a lot easier to remember than otolaryngology. He doesn't have Ben's chart and is a little embarrassed that he has to ask why we're here. He apologizes for the confusion.

Ben is exhausted from waking so early and begins to doze. Undeterred, Dr. Crowley gently scoops a great deal of wax from Ben's ear as he continues to drift off to sleep. He finds fluid in Ben's right ear—I guess the antique machine wasn't crazy after all—but the ear is not infected.

"If the fluid does not clear up within six weeks, something should be done to get rid of it. As long as there is no infection and Ben is not in any discomfort, there is no need for antibiotics."

Dr. Crowley asks to see him again in about a month and promises to be better prepared. His sincerity has come through today. It was time well spent.

Trekking two floors higher and manoeuvering through several winding corridors, we make our way to see a consultant to the Audiology department. Her name is Leslie and she is also a school teacher. Jan and I aren't quite sure what this person can tell us but we listen. She begins by describing the different services that we could have access to—ones we already have! She then proceeds to go into great detail about how we should be constantly stimulating his hearing. While we're knitting our brows, she tells us that we should give Ben things to hold, like a brush, and get him to brush a doll's hair.

"Whoa, what is she talking about?", my eyes communicate to Jan. I'm missing something here. My perplexed look must catch her off guard.

"Oh, it's all right for boys to play with dolls," she proclaims. "It's only while Ben is so young."

Play with dolls? Are you kidding me? Play with *anything* would be great. Did she miss the fact that Ben has multiple disabilities? The last thing on our minds are his sexual preferences! This discussion is going nowhere. Jan quickly interrupts her and says that we are late for our other appointments.

Our visit with Dr. Forester begins, as usual, with seeing one of her nurses, followed by one of her residents. Quite painless this time. The personality of her staff matches hers—warm, inviting, genuine. After a pleasant greeting, Dr. Forester focuses on Ben, remarking how healthy he appears to be. Her physical examination reveals that his liver and spleen are both normal size.

Her inquiry into our recent experiences with Sick Kids is our cue to open up about of the frustrations we have encountered, such as our first visit with Ophthalmology where the resident asked us a million questions, even ones like ". . . How was the pregnancy? . . ."

We tell her that we often talk about preparing a one- or two-page summary of Ben's history to limit the number of ridiculous questions that get asked. She agrees that more coordination with scheduling appointments is very much needed and that Ben should be handled as a single case, not simply a series of individual and separate visits with a number of different specialists. That would be wonderful if she could pull that off but it will require a big culture shift within the medical community.

We thank her for her concern and support before scurrying to see a paediatric dental specialist, our last appointment of the morning.

After a hurried lunch, we arrive for our seating clinic appointment at the Hugh McMillan rehab centre. Its aged brick-and-stone exterior is very institutional, a reminder of a previous era in medical care. A wall plaque confirms its creation in 1957 when it was called the Ontario Crippled Children's Centre.

The front foyer is crowded with reporters and photographers. We even spot Genevieve in the crowd. A diminutive woman approaches us to see if they could take pictures of Ben for an OT magazine. She places him in a customized chair called a "grow-a-seat." As the photographer flashes his camera a few times, Ben looks up at the ceiling and smiles. He gets it. Several on-lookers comment at how comfortable he looks with all this attention. This is the real Ben.

After this photo shoot, we begin our appointments. There are several strangers in the room including a therapist, the coordinator of the seating clinic, one of the orthopedic surgeons, and a few other note takers. We are unprepared for this large an audience along with the surgeon's examination of Ben. We discuss how Ben could benefit from this "grow-a-seat" that we just tried, since it is very adaptable and versatile. But the $3,200 price tag is a non-starter. You could furnish your living room for that amount of money.

The remainder of the day sees us shuffling between occupational therapy, physio, speech, and psychology specialists. We learn that the reason Ben keeps his mouth open all time is to make it easier for him to sit. This "locking" of his jaw actually can make him feel more secure. They point out that it is quite realistic to think that Ben will be able to sit up unaided one day. The team is encouraged by what they see, commenting on how pleasant Ben is to work with, emphasizing how flexible are his limbs, telling us that many children with Ben's scope of neurological involvement are so severely contracted that they need orthopaedic surgery to release the stiffness. Ben demonstrates none of this. I guess that's a good thing.

The day finally ends. We made it, crisis-free. But with each useless appointment, lost chart, and unprepared specialist, my patience dwindles. It can't be healthy but I have no idea how to fix it.

* * *

Amazing kids

The sights, scents, and sounds of the halls of Sick Kids are the furthest from our thoughts right now as we unload into the parking lot of Roy Thomson Hall. Raffi is on stage tonight. In concert! Live! Conor and Tori are bouncing with delight.

Shortly before the 7 p.m. start time, we are escorted to our seats at the front row of the balcony. A spectacular view of the stage and of the hall itself. And lots of room for Ben. He isn't overly interested in the affair and drifts off for a little nap after drinking his bottle. Conor and Tori sway to the rhythm of "Everything Grows" and "Baby Beluga" while Jan and I sing along. The melodies are simple but heart warming. Something we need. For a few hours, we are captivated in this ideal world, like being at the top of a mountain. It's so relaxing, so real, so uplifting. A "great" day in every sense of the word.

Watching the excitement in their eyes, I am caught up in the enormity of the last 18 months and realize just how lucky Ben is to have them as his brother and sister. For as long as they can remember, they have seen the inside of a hospital, from that watershed moment when Conor left his toy truck in Ben's incubator to our most recent marathon session at Sick Kids. That day was so tiring but Conor and Tori remained as even-keel as you could possibly expect . . . for an adult, that is. For 3- and 4-year-olds to sit through so many appointments in one day is truly amazing.

I had never seen the inside of a hospital until I was six years old. And when I did, I was actually the patient. I had had some fainting spells over a period of a few months and no one was quite sure why. Before these fainting spells, I would claim that I could see coloured lights circling in front of my eyes. It was scary. Scary that I felt out of control. Scary that I had been admitted to hospital. Scary as I underwent an EEG, a spinal tap, and a host of other tests. Shortly after Ben was born, I remember telling Dr. Norris that I had been placed on *Phenobarbital* for 10 years and his response was, "*Really?!,*" widening his eyes as if he had never heard of anyone being on that medication for so long.

As Raffi strums another tune, Conor and Tori continue their dancing. They are more than truly amazing. They are heaven sent.

*   *   *

A magical evening

Each November 9th, I revel in the fact that Jan is no longer younger than I am. For only 150 days each year can she lay claim to being more youthful. This year is her 30th. It requires a celebration. We take a big step and hire Tara for the evening. A place called Richlee's is recommended by Genevieve. We take her advice.

Approaching the quaint street-front in the early evening hours, we get lucky and snag a parking spot directly in front of the restaurant. Two large hardwood doors, sheltered by canvas awnings sporting the numerals "1959," make up the restaurant's façade. It is quite inconspicuous. A lone plate glass window is sandwiched between the two entrances and an out-of-place air conditioner hangs from the window of what appears to be an upstairs apartment. Not exactly representative of a fine dining establishment but we're confident Genevieve would not lead us astray.

Entering the building, we realize that Genevieve knows us well. It is an extraordinary place. With only 18 tables dressed in brilliant, white linen cloths and napkins, and graced with shimmering wine glasses, the dining area is textbook elegant. The lighting is low and very soft music is playing. The high, coffered ceiling with dark maple beams provides an air of sophistication while the back wall, with its embedded wine racks, enhances the level of style. I am beginning to wonder whether or not we can afford this place.

We are seated at a table for two along the left-hand side. This will become our table for the evening. Exclusively. No other reservations for this table have been made. The same is true for all of the other tables, we learn. There is only one sitting, a hallmark of what personalized service really means.

Scanning through the menu, we are somewhat in disbelief at what we're doing. Until tonight, I never would have thought we could actually go out for an evening and leave Ben, with someone so new as Tara, especially since we're a 30-minute drive away at best so if we had to get home quickly, we couldn't. We have found a way to break the chains—okay, loosen them—at least for a few hours.

As the magical evening unfolds, we realize that for the first time in nearly two years, we are actually relaxed. Somehow, we have let go all of our worries, our stress, and feel a deep sense of peace, comfort and a renewal of our relationship. It is more than magical and with each passing minute our desire grows for it to last forever.

After nearly three hours of unspoiled pampering, it is time to leave. I have never spent this much time at a restaurant nor have I experienced true relaxation until that night. Perhaps we're being told that we really haven't been abandoned. What I do know is that we both need to find a way to reach this tranquil state far more often.

*   *   *

One stupid intern after another

As the weekend draws to a close, we are back at Sick Kids for two appointments. Ben's mood has improved and so has his congestion. This must be cold number 4 or 5. Putting in multiple restless nights has left all of us exhausted. Whenever Ben is not feeling well, he cannot sleep. If he's miserable, we all are. We considered rescheduling the appointments but couldn't find the energy.

First up is Dr. Crowley. Actually, it's an intern. Like most neophytes we have seen, she has no idea about Ben's history. After introducing herself, she looks to Conor and says,

"OK, Ben, hop up on the chair".

I think to myself, "You've got to be kidding me. Ah, c'mon young med student, does Conor look like a 17-month old?" This is the worst case of stupidity yet.

Once the case of mistaken identity is solved, she checks Ben's ears only to tell us that the fluid has cleared up in the left ear but not in the right. She then begins to talk about antibiotics, but only to Jan. Jan tries to explain Ben's reactions to them but she just blinks at Jan. Obviously, this was not the answer she was expecting.

Once her brain resets, she tells us that Ben should definitely get tubes for his ear. Jan quickly counters that Dr. Crowley told us at our last visit that tubes should not be put in unless absolutely necessary since tubes and hearing aids do not mix. She seems quite befuddled by Jan's comments.

A few uncomfortable moments pass until Dr. Crowley enters the room. Before he can extend any sort of greeting, the intern jumps to her feet and proclaims quite forcefully, yet nervously, how reluctant Jan is to put Ben on any antibiotics or get tubes put in. I shake my head. That's not even close to being accurate. I'm starting to get angry now, especially with so little sleep. Before I can jump in, Dr. Crowley reconfirms his belief that no tubes are necessary and emphasizes that we can certainly wait another two months without any problems to see if the fluid clears up on its own. In fact, Ben would be better off if the fluid did disappear on its own.

Our second appointment is with a cardiologist, to quell our fears about any heart issues that have been hanging over us since August, following some grave concerns from a resident at North York. Again, it's impossible to speak with any specialist without first being tortured by a struggling intern, and this department is no different.

Watching this young apprentice attempt to take Ben's blood pressure is like something out of a Seinfeld episode. She's not sure what size cuff to use so she tries them all. Ben's arms are too small for all of them. After eight attempts, she finally gets a reading of 135 over 95. She is quite concerned and tells Jan (somehow, I seem to be invisible today) that this is much too high. No kidding. But do you really think that's an accurate reading? Isn't this Sick Kids hospital?

She tries Ben's left leg and gets a normal pressure. Following this success, she takes it on Ben's left arm only to discover a different reading. After pausing a few seconds, she informs Jan that this difference means Ben could have a very serious condition.

Okay, I surrender. Where did this person come from? Is there a hidden camera somewhere? Still not satisfied, she keeps trying Ben's arms until she finally gets a normal reading in both arms.

"I guess everything is fine," she says quite proudly. Unbelievable!

Once we get to see the cardiologist, his examination lasts all of five minutes to tell us that Ben's heart sounds normal—no murmur, no nothing—but he suggests having another X-ray just to be sure.

We dash off to Radiology and get seen right away. Ben remains in good spirits even though he has been at the hospital for over six hours. The X-ray tech helps Jan to hold Ben's arms over his head to get him in the proper position. Ben just laughs—he is so adaptable. The X-ray reveals nothing abnormal though it is not as clear as it could be. Everyone keeps saying that to us. Did it ever occur to anyone that it's impossible to keep a baby still with his arms stretched over his head?

Arriving home at 4:30 p.m., Jan has no time to rest and whirls around getting ready for work. Ben is starving after a long, long day, devouring his supper and inhaling his bottle. By 8:30 p.m., he is snuggled into his crib and has little trouble falling asleep. His breathing is much quieter than it has been these last few days and there is no sign of any congestion. Good thing. We all need the rest.

*   *   *

A great teacher we will surely miss

November is coming to a close and so is our time in Toronto. Genevieve arrives for one of her last few appointments but Ben is still sleeping. Jan takes the opportunity to tell her how grateful we are to have had her work with Ben over the last several months, and just how much we have learned. Genevieve responds how she is a little sad that she won't have the chance to see us any more and asks Jan if she could do anything for us before we leave. Imagine, offering to help. Such radical thinking!

Genevieve believes that it is positive that Ben's hands and fingers are quite loose, just like those of a newborn baby. We must continue to put objects in Ben's hands and "teach" him how to hold things. When asked about Ben having increased tone and what that really meant, Genevieve states that Ben actually has "mixed" tone, since sometimes his limbs are difficult to move and sometimes they're very loose. She expects that Ben will probably never be able to control his body neurologically like most people can so we have to focus on making it physiologically easier for him to develop the coordination to do different tasks. The range-of-motion exercises will certainly benefit him in that regard by enabling his arms and legs to not remain stiff so that he can be placed in different positions.

Her approach is so natural and gentle, and her breadth of knowledge is unlike anyone we have yet to encounter. Moving to Toronto was worth all of the stress and hassle just to have met her. I can't imagine how we will manage without her.

A week later, Genevieve returns for a final visit. Ben is content to go through his exercises with her, as usual. Today, he is making all of us forget the litany of problems he is facing.

She tells us of a recent meeting she had with Maggie, the coordinator of the preschool Ben attended, of how it was going to be their loss that we were leaving Toronto. They so enjoyed working with Ben these past several months. Maggie told Genevieve how comfortable we made everyone feel at the school, how we were so easy to talk to. Genevieve compliments us how we have adjusted extremely well to having a child with so many challenges. In her experience, it is those with a "lot of education" who have the hardest time dealing with these sorts of things. They tend to have very high expectations of their children and are devastated to find out that all is not well.

We certainly do have high expectations but only because we believe that Ben is a genius trapped inside a body that doesn't work. We can never stop until that genius is finally unleashed.

* * *

Final days in TO

Emotionally, we seem to be a state of limbo. We have almost completely detached ourselves from our Toronto life, which means we can't plan anything exciting or fun but yet we still have seven days staring at us before we re-establish our Saint John life. Nothing is ever simple.

Ben is miserable again. He is warm to the touch and not interested in drinking his bottle. Jan gets to see Dr. Toms who discovers that Ben has a bad infection in his right ear, his first one in a long time. His right ear seems to be problematic. We are both relieved and nervous to hear of this—relieved because this explains his recent "clutchiness" and restless nights, nervous because he never reacts well to antibiotics. I'm not sure why we didn't figure this out on our own since, over the past few days, he has winced each time we would place his right aid into his ear.

Dr. Toms prescribes *Suprax* which, he hopes, should be a little easier on Ben's tummy. Jan has a long talk with the pharmacist at North York General who believes that Ben could be bothered by the artificial flavouring in drugs like *Ceclor*. Who would think that such a commonplace additive would have so much effect on Ben?

His first morning dose is uneventful. He swallows it without much effort or resistance. A good start. By evening, he has boundless energy, happy, lively, and kicking a lot. His coughing is also noticeably less. I can't believe that one dose could produce such a dramatic change. The next day, he starts swinging his arms and kicking his legs while sitting in the high chair in a manner he hasn't done in quite some time. I'm beginning to believe that the *Suprax* must be loaded with caffeine.

The day before we are set to leave I am feeling quite melancholy. I certainly am looking forward to getting back to our own house, to our own bed, to our families, but I also want Ben to continue to learn from the wonderful care givers we have found. We just started to lay the groundwork especially with Hugh McMillan therapists, and, of course, Genevieve. I'm nervous just how little momentum will carry over with us back in Saint John.

Peering out of our kitchen window to the street below I am reminded of how it was really Susan Ward who went out of her way to meet us last year, knowing the anguish we were experiencing as Ben's new parents. She and her husband were so helpful and encouraging during that first year. I am perplexed why we haven't heard from them since the summer. Had something happened to their son? And Tony and Jen Haines, our other Ontario "CMV family." Perhaps we should be telling them we're leaving. They graciously welcomed us to their home and provided Conor and Tori with an exciting tractor ride at his parent's farm a few months ago. I want to be back there today and leave behind the stress of the move.

I should have made a better effort to stay in touch with them. I feel a little guilty that so much time has passed and now we're leaving. If I called them today, I'd feel uncomfortable saying, "Oh, by the way, we're moving back to the Maritimes tomorrow . . . ." How awkward would that sound? And yet, I shouldn't just leave without saying goodbye. The more I stare out of the window, the more unsettled I become.

Moving day arrives. I'm feeling empty. I try to reach beyond the emptiness but I can't. I don't really want to go home and restart old routines. Life is actually working here. As we pile into the cab destined for the airport, the light snow in the air turns to rain, making this day even more dreary.

*   *   *

9

A DOWNHILL SLIDE

Back home on our tiny, close-knit court, everyone is a friend. Although quite unusual for a city neighbourhood, the emotional and physical closeness of our neighbours in this community helped us through those awful first months of Ben's life.

A night out without any children can be accomplished by walking a mere 50 paces to the home of a neighbour for an evening of Trivial Pursuit. Tonight, it's Tom and Francine's turn to host the event. Their house faces our back door directly, which makes checking on things very easy. Just getting out for a few hours is so wonderful, even though we don't go far. It is the best of both worlds—we are away from our house, together escaping our world for a short time, but also taking comfort that we are just across the street, ready to respond.

Later in the evening, it is my turn to check on everyone and I come home to put Conor and Tori to bed. As I button my coat to return to the competition, a familiar noise blurts from the monitor. Ben has awakened and he is not happy. I dash upstairs and pick him up. He snorts several times and falls back to sleep on my shoulder. Leaning over the side of his crib, I gently place his cuddled body back onto the mattress. His mouth opens wide after feeling the release of my arms. After 10 seconds of silent crying, he begins to wail. I pick him up again, and within moments he is back to sleep. This repeats a half dozen times: my night out has come to an end.

An hour passes and Jan returns home, figuring that the fun is over. She relieves me and takes Ben downstairs to rock him for a while. I dim the lights, turn the TV down low, and we both help to console him.

Jan stirs him from her shoulder to make him more wakeful to swallow a dose of *Tylenol*. Within seconds, Ben turns his eyes upward and displays that heart-sinking look he has just before a seizure. The enjoyment of the evening disappears completely, flushed away by fear, anxiety, and the expectation of another sleepless night. His eyes return to normal after a brief blippy moment, and he gradually tunes in to where he is. We walk a fine line with Ben between nervousness and confusion, panic and outright terror.

By midnight, Ben is resting comfortably on Jan's shoulder. His breathing is regular and his skin colour is normal. If he is getting another cold, the first night, this night, will be the worst. Laying him in his crib produces no unwanted crying this time and no agitation, just restful sleep. We were lucky this time.

It had been a full day with our cross-border excursion to Calais. The weather was great and so was Ben. He ate and drank well in unfamiliar surroundings, even while in his stroller. A little shopping for me and Jan, a lot of fresh air for everyone. To think we could finish the day at a neighbour's house seemed now to have been too much to expect. We try to make the most out of every opportunity, no matter how small the time slice we are given. Sometimes that slice is a little too small, though.

*　　*　　*

Tori counts too

The issue of Tori's "kissing" tonsils was first identified by Dr. Toms back in the fall, just by observing her as she patiently sat waiting during one of Ben's appointments. He questioned whether or not she had sleep apnea. His comments felt strange at the time. He didn't know that her tonsils were actually touching each other, their size restricting her breathing, a fact we would only learn about months later. Simply the way she breathed was a warning sign to him.

Constantly distracted and often overwhelmed is a daily occurrence for us. At times, we don't notice the needs of Conor and Tori, and we are completely perplexed that Tori seems to run out of energy long before other kids her age do, even during basic activities. But it doesn't really concern us. It's probably just laziness, Tori's that is. Neglectful? Probably. Stunned? Most definitely!

A few days before her surgery to remove her enormous lymphoepithelial tissues, Tori awakens not long after going to bed. Her face is taut with worry, mindful of what the week will bring her. With little effort, her 3 ½-year-old body climbs into our bed, finding a spot between me and Jan. It doesn't take long for her to drift back to sleep. At 1:30 a.m., she wakes me up to take her to the bathroom. She hasn't needed me to do this since she could walk. She's clearly troubled.

As I head back to bed, I just have to check on Ben. He is breathing very fast, almost gasping, not able to draw a deep breath, but still asleep. He is curled up on his belly, bringing his arms into his chest. I pick him up and hold him in front of the small humidifier to slow his breathing. It works temporarily. Jan awakes soon thereafter and takes over. I carry up a rocker from the basement and place it in his bedroom. Jan rocks effortlessly for over an hour, holding him close to the humid mist with his compact body resting naturally on her shoulder. It's as if he was made to fit there. Struggling to stay awake as I sit in the darkness of the boys' bedroom, I feel a wave of panic wash over me when I realize I have completely forgotten about Tori and her anxious thoughts. Not only am I exhausted but I feel worthless as her father.

We pay a visit to our local ENT specialist, Dr. Garrison, a few days later to confirm that Tori is still fit for surgery. She has developed a head cold, as have the rest of us. Could fatigue be a factor? (You think?) Dr. Garrison tells us that only if the infection moves to Tori's chest would she cancel the surgery. She also takes the opportunity to examine Ben and reports that his ears are clear. (Hah! Take that, Sick Kids interns!)

I stay home with Ben so that Jan can accompany Tori for her surgery. I really can't let go of my chronic anxiety about Ben to be overly concerned about Tori. She is a very healthy child and the procedure is not only straightforward, it is very brief. It's still surgery, it's still cutting and bleeding and stitching. But it's not registering with me today.

Late in the afternoon, Jan calls to report that Tori is out of recovery but not before she scared everyone. There had been a problem with her breathing after surgery and they needed to keep her longer until she stabilized.

At that moment, a flood of fear rises inside of me, forcing me to realize how Tori is still a child, and our continuous focus on Ben has forced her to mature a little too quickly. The seriousness of what might have happened leaves me light-headed.

Jan senses my guilt and worry, and tries to lighten my feelings by telling me that when she arrived in Tori's hospital room *after* the procedure, she was whimpering and said, "I don't want to get my tonsils out!"

I just want to hold her forever but I'm stuck home with Ben.

*   *   *

Spending too much time with Ben

Painting our living room is taking forever and 10 days of having the house in a mess is beginning to wear on everyone. None of us can find anything, there's dust everywhere and the paint odours just won't leave us. Jan and I are running out of energy to finish the job. Scooping up some newspapers from the floor, I call out to Jan to grab a garbage bag. I wait a few seconds and call her name again. This is very strange. Perhaps she's outside, though her coat is still on the hook.

I walk into the backyard and hear *my* name being called. It is coming from inside our storage shed. What the . . . ? It's Jan! Both doors are closed and the outside latch is in its locked position. There's no handle inside so there's no way for her to get out. There is no light or heat inside either, and no way for anyone to have known that she was inside. I quickly open the doors to free her but she storms past me, furious that I didn't hear her screams.

A few hours later, while we're cleaning up more of our disastrous living room, she breaks her silence and asks if I think that our marriage would not be this bad if Ben had not been born. To be honest, I really didn't consider it to be that bad but I am not in the greatest of moods to talk about this topic, still frustrated that somehow it was my fault that she got locked outside. I respond, "I don't know."

She begins questioning whether it would have been better for Ben to have died. That's a knife through my heart. My stomach starts churning. I thought she had moved past those feelings. This is proof that unexpressed feelings never die. I tell her that we have to keep remembering how awful things used to be, dealing with frequent seizures and him not being able to sit in his high chair for very long. How he doesn't need his head held during mealtime anymore. How he can sit up without falling over for more than an hour at a time. How he can lean forward to suck on his fist and lift back up when he wants to. None of this matters to Jan. None of these "accomplishments" include walking, or talking or feeding himself, things a child his age should be doing. It reminds me with a sinking feeling of Dr. Norris's prophetic words.

I tell her how earlier in the day I had flipped through the logs that I have been keeping, and realized that it has been a year since Ben had that terrifying seizure. I confide in her that the words I had written were enough to hurry me back to that horrific day and, momentarily, stir up that sick feeling again. But that was okay . . . and I'm okay now.

Nothing more is said. To Jan, it seems that the storage-shed incident is a symbol of her captivity, of her being trapped with no time for herself, to just do what she wants, even if it's only for 20 minutes. She needs an outlet, a distraction, regular interaction with adults. She is spending too much time with Ben. I get to go to work every day and get a break from the stress. She needs to do the same. She needs to find a job.

Later in the evening, Ben is in his crib watching his mobile when I spy Conor fastening his Boston Celtics basketball hoop to the side of Ben's crib. It shakes for a few seconds as Conor ensures that it is secure while Ben turns his eyes momentarily to connect them with those of his big brother. Conor feels my gaze, looks towards me, and before I can say a word, he states quite proudly that he is putting the basketball hoop on Ben's crib in case he wants to play with it. With the same love and care he showed Ben when he lay in the neonatal unit during those early days, Conor is once again eager to share with his brother. His thoughts are not clouded with the least bit of doubt of what Ben can or cannot do nor are they muddled by the myriad of problems that Ben is facing. I wish my mind could be so certain.

A few minutes later, Jan finds her way upstairs. She greets Tori, who happily shows her the picture she is drawing. Tori is forever creative. Jan enters the boys' room and Conor is sitting on his bed. With the same enthusiasm and excitement he showed me, he tells Jan that he is letting Ben use his basketball hoop and eagerly points to it.

"I put it there in case he wants to stand up and throw the ball over the side of his crib."

Tears begin to form in our eyes and Conor is puzzled why we look so sad. Jan sits down beside him, hugs him tightly, and says it will be a glorious day when Ben stands and walks.

Ben is oblivious to the conversation and the emotions in the room. Quietly, he examines his surroundings but can't really see the basketball hoop from his lying position. It doesn't matter to Conor that Ben can't see it nor that he is not yet able to play with it. He is still giving him the opportunity.

*　　*　　*

Still don't get it . . .

Easter Sunday arrives early this year, the first weekend in April, and it is the first time in four years that I'm not involved at work in a big project that uses the long weekend to cut over to a new corporate computer system.

We decide to have dinner at our house, and invite my mother and father to spend the afternoon with us. My mother is not very pleasant today and is trying to pick a fight. Instead of enjoying her grandchildren, she is eager to find things wrong with them, especially Ben. Ten minutes into the visit, she comments on his high palette, wanting to read something into that. I ignore her. My father, who should know better, seems to enjoy pointing out that Ben is still not sitting up yet and asks repeatedly,

"Do you think he ever will? Will he ever get head control?"

Again, I just shake my head and try to remember that this is supposed to be a feast day. To myself, I am crying out inside, yelling,

> *"Listen, Dad! When he is able to sit up on his own, you will be the first to know!! It may not happen for six months, or 16 months, or ever. But his progress from month to month is there so don't keep asking the same questions over and over again."*

Today it doesn't stop at Ben. We are late eating and Tori is both tired and hungry (let's not forget that she is only a week away from her 4th birthday). Throughout dinner, she displays her sour mood quite noticeably which prompts my parents to generalize and say how she is always grumpy, how she rarely eats well, how she never grows, and that there must be something wrong with her. All of this while Tori is present. And then they wonder why she doesn't want to give them a hug when they leave.

I'm ready to let them have it but hold back. After all, it's Easter, isn't it, a time to be thankful and joyful? After they leave, Jan lets *me* have it and can't believe I didn't say anything to them after each wave of unkindness. She starts questioning herself about Ben and about Tori. But, really, there is nothing wrong with either of them.

My parents still don't get it. If they're forcing me to take sides, *my* family comes first. All of the good will has been spent. I can't remain neutral and sane at the same time.

For Tori's birthday party a week later, a dozen 3- and 4-year-olds descend on our basement. Even Ben stays awake for the afternoon, feeling the excitement on this warm spring day. In the evening, after the mélée has subsided, my mother and father drop in to visit and bring hats for Conor and Tori (they had given Tori her birthday present last week). There is no hat for Ben. When I ask, my mother fumbles her answer and tells me that she didn't know whether or not the one she saw for him would be the right size. I believe that what she is really trying to say is, "... *he wouldn't know the difference anyway!*"

"Size has never been an issue before; he can always grow into it." I respond.

Conor is clever and as my father is handing him his hat, he confidently asks, "Did you get one for Ben?"

*   *   *

A full IWK day

The day before leaving for our spring trip to the IWK, I visit Julie, Dr. Campbell's secretary, to borrow the patient file he has on Ben. The folder is bulging with documents—it's not designed to hold so many reports. A letter from Dr. Norris summarizes our recent appointment with him, describing how he enjoyed seeing us again, that taking Ben off of *Phenobarbital* is certainly an option, as long as he continues to be seizure-free, and that he is uncertain whether the incident we described last fall was really a seizure or just a result of Ben's spasticity. In a strange way, it is comforting to read.

An hour into our IWK trek, we turn onto the gravel driveway of Nana Brook to give us all a break. Hearing the slow crunching of the stones underneath our tires, she pushes open her storm door to welcome us, her feeble voice exclaiming an excited, "Hiiiii!", her voice still thick with the New England accent she acquired as a child.

Conor and Tori run to give her a hug. She returns the love to her great grandchildren. Inside, we assemble in her kitchen, which is always kept too warm by the large iron woodstove. Ben readily drinks his juice while I take Conor and Tori outside to watch the never-ending rush of the brook beside her house. We take a few minutes and walk to the head of the brook that comes out of the hillside and notice that it's still winter under the shade of the towering cedars.

Our visit is not nearly long enough for Nana Brook's liking but we tell her that we have to get to Truro by lunch time in order to feed Ben.

"Yeah", she responds disappointedly. For a woman of 87 years, she manoeuvers quite well, without any support, and shows us to the door. We make to it Truro for a late lunch and a little rest, and by 5 p.m., we arrive at our hotel in Halifax, needing a full day to travel 450 kilometers.

Our first appointment is with Dr. Gaudet, a paediatric immunologist who is also a family friend. His thoroughness and interest in Ben is refreshing, and he keeps us for two hours. He is eager to understand the complete history, the pregnancy, how we made out in Toronto, and about allergies in our families. He runs the gamut of allergy tests on Ben's back and observes the same reactions that were present last year.

During the conversation we mention the scare we had after giving Ben some milk and seeing welts form on his face and chin, and how Dr. Norris had said that food is meant to be eaten, not rubbed on your skin, so just because your skin reacts doesn't necessarily mean that you are truly allergic to it. He concurs and proceeds to tells us that drinking cow's milk is unique to North American culture and quite unnecessary since calcium can be gained from many other foods. In an almost preacher-like tone, he goes on to inform us that the presence of dairy products is simply a result of strong lobby groups to include them as part of *Canada's Food Guide* and the availability of alternatives to milk and dairy products is very sparse since mainstream grocers do a poor job. Jan and I wonder what this has to do with Ben.

Dr. Gaudet suggests that as we try new foods, we should first rub a small amount on the inside of Ben's lips to see if anything happens. Now that's useful information.

Before we leave, he tells us that he would like some blood work done because there are more reliable tests that can be done for allergies through the blood. He scribbles a requisition for this and asks us to visit the blood lab at the IWK. We hustle ourselves back into the car, late for our 11 a.m. appointment with an orthoptist, which is not to be confused with an ophthalmologist.

Orthoptics deals with eye movement and alignment and so, quite naturally, Ben is asked to track objects as they pass in front of him. This morning, Ben performs well, tracking a lighted Sesame Street figure that is moved about. The orthoptist tells that she is testing to see if Ben's eyes move together, in particular that his left eye moves with his right. She notes how she understands when kids are "tuned out", that just because a child does not follow on one particular day doesn't mean that his/her vision is bad.

There is a TV at the far end of the examination room and she shows short clips from the cartoon, Robin Hood. Ben is able to see it and responds well. Conor is also trying to get as close as possible to catch a glimpse but is very quiet about it. The session ends with a visual acuity test. Ben scores much better than he did a year ago, improving to that of a normal 22-month old. I never get tired of hearing the words "normal" and "Ben" used in the same sentence.

At 5 minutes to noon, we head to the cafeteria for a lunch break. Our appointment with Dr. Lavoie is for 12:15 p.m. but we know he is always overbooked and late, so we don't rush. Ben enjoys the cafeteria's buzz and chooses to eat a good portion of his lunch. Conor and Tori are very helpful in finding a place to sit. and in gathering cutlery with plenty of napkins.

By 1 p.m., Dr. Lavoie is ready to see us. He is quite abrupt this time as he informs us that Ben's eyes are functioning well but we will have to see if the cognitive part of his vision develops. Jan asks about Ben not seeing objects that are below "eye-level," wondering if there could be a problem with his visual field. Dr. Lavoie suggests that Ben likely has to be "taught" how to see. For example, if you have to hold an object up in front of him and then move it down for him to drop his eyes or head to see, then that's fine at this stage. He hopes that as Ben matures he will learn to see things that are not initially directly in front of him.

Dr. Lavoie focuses his attention on the "nasty scar" on the retina of Ben's left eye. I am fixated on that. We have known that it was there from early days and everyone, including Dr. Lavoie, has always downplayed its presence. But today he seems to be emphasizing the word "nasty". In the same breath, he also reassures us that it is not likely to worse. Which is it? Is it really nasty? Should I worry about? Stop playing head games with me.

He wants to see Ben in six months and mentions that he will send a letter to Dr. Goderich to keep him up to date. Why bother, I muse, we will never go back to *Dr. "I-don't-think-there's-much-vision."*

We have an hour before our next appointment and proceed to get Ben's bloods done. The tiny and somewhat inaccessible waiting room is empty and we are called before we can sit down. One nurse tries to find a vein in Ben's left arm but has a difficult time. She pokes the needle into him. He jumps but doesn't cry. She moves the needle around and around but cannot get it to puncture the vein, telling us that he has "rolling veins". She continues for about 30 seconds but is unsuccessful. Slowly, she pulls the needle out of his arm, places a little *Band-Aid* on him, and lets him rest for minute. Another nurse enters the room and they try his right arm. Ben jumps a second time as the needle punctures his skin but, again, doesn't cry. A vein is found this time but only after a similar search. There isn't a good flow of blood so they resort to "pumping" his arm to get enough blood. Despite all this, Ben doesn't seem to be troubled or upset.

With more than 30 minutes before the appointment with Orthopaedics, we venture a block and a half away to a small playground. It gives everyone a much needed break from the halls and smells of the hospital. For a short time, we're all free.

Minding the clock, we find ourselves under the bright lights of the orthopaedic clinic much too soon and are brought into an examination room almost immediately. Conor and Tori are content to remain in the waiting room since there are plenty of toys to keep their attention. Periodically, they come to assure us that they are fine. They are how old again? A full hour passes before one of the surgeons sees us. I hate when that happens. What's the purpose of bringing us into the room if we're only going to continue to wait.

Dr. Ramsay is very pleasant, quite young in fact, and examines Ben for a few short minutes, impressed by how well he moves his legs. She remarks that there is no curvature with his spine and, though his hips appear a little stiff, there is nothing to be concerned about at this stage. She tells us that she wants to get an X-ray of Ben to use as a baseline to compare in future years. Jan takes Ben to get an X-ray of his hips while I wait with Conor and Tori. This late in the day, she is gone only 10 minutes and returns with the films in her hand. After another short wait, Dr. Ramsay meets us and looks at the X-rays. She explains what she is looking for in the bones of his hips and, for now, everything is as it should be. Making a follow-up appointment in a year's time would be appropriate.

Another eight-hour day behind us. Everyone is glad it is over and happy that the reports were all very positive for a change. We pile into the car and head north to Truro for a few days.

* * *

Life changing

The phone rings late in the evening. I answer it and it's Marg, her voice weak and shaky. She tells me that Clem has been in a car accident, and she needs to speak to Jan. His car had left the highway and crashed into a small ravine. No other vehicles were involved and no one seems to know why he lost control.

The kids are asleep, including Ben, and Jan asks a neighbour to keep watch so we can head to the hospital to get a read on her father's condition. All our attention is turned to Clem with little worry about Ben. If this had happened a year ago, we would have been torn, and likely unable to cope. For a fleeting moment, I see that our daily routine has become just that—routine—and we can pick up and go if we really have to.

The drive to the hospital is miserable. The night is damp, rainy and foggy. Extra dark, it seems. As we burst through the ER doors, doors that are all too familiar to us, Jan's mom, sister Rita and brother Paul are huddled in a quiet room, noticeably upset and very worried. All they know is that he had a lot of internal bleeding, possibly from a ruptured aneurysm, and is in the operating room. We are told the procedure could take several hours and, with all the bleeding, the outcome is very uncertain.

We wait in disbelief, feeling sick to our stomachs, and we talk through a series of disconnected topics, including the condition of the used car that Clem had just purchased about a month ago. Was it to blame? And how one of Jan's uncles had died of a ruptured brain aneurysm 13 years ago. All of this chatter provides little comfort.

After a couple of hours of waiting, and not really learning much, Jan suggests I go home. She is going to stay until she finds out if he makes it through the surgery. Clem is such an important figure in Jan's life. I don't want to think that he could be taken away.

Not long after I get home, the phone rings. He made it. He's not awake but he's stable, resting in ICU. Jan's focus is on her dad. It can be only him right now. She can't worry about Ben.

*   *   *

Losing weight?

Jan has been at the hospital all week with her father and misses reading the report that has just arrived from Dr. Gaudet. It seems fitting to receive such a large, detailed report to go along with his detailed examination of Ben. A few sentences into this monstrous document the tone turns very gloomy, almost disturbing, especially his comment that Ben has dropped from 23 lbs to just slightly more than 21 lbs in less than a year. Why isn't Dr. Campbell concerned about this?

The document goes on to mention the risk of thyroid and other endocrine diseases developing in CMV kids, with weight loss as a possible indicator. What is he saying? Couldn't there not be some other explanation for Ben's apparent weight loss? Why does it have to be related to some nasty disease?

He's wrong. I know he's wrong. I begin to think of all kinds of reasons to justify Ben's low body weight—that he has a smaller head or that his muscles haven't developed properly since he doesn't crawl or walk. I tell myself that his bowel function has improved through the simple addition of natural wheat germ to his diet, and that he is now consuming regular foods (no more processed baby foods) with more taste, more calories, more vitamins; that we're doing all the right things for Ben and that Dr. Gaudet is focused too much on the numbers.

Then I think that perhaps Ben's low energy is related to his noisy breathing and recurring congestion similar to Tori's. Before she had her tonsils out, she was a noisy breather, who often slept during the day, and sat and ate snow on a winter's day while everyone else was running and jumping. What if a similar sort of problem existed with Ben? I know what happens in a normal child like Tori; what if that's the source of Ben's recent low energy and congestion problems? His facial structure is certainly not normal and we know he puts a lot of energy into just getting enough oxygen. Maybe if he breathed more efficiently he would start to do more physical things, burn more calories, want to eat more . . . What if it's not only the cognitive issues he is dealing with but also that he is not getting enough oxygen?

Perhaps his weight loss is a result of some poor mechanics and not because of some condition or disease. There are so many dependencies and complexities when it comes to Ben's growth but if we could get things into a better equilibrium, maybe that's all that's needed.

A lot of maybes and perhaps. I try to tell myself not to get upset but I'm not doing a very good job.

*   *   *

No-win situation

Today is not a special occasion but the gorgeous weather beckons us to take a Sunday drive somewhere—as far away from doctors and hospitals as possible. Even though Ben seems a little off this morning, we decide to take a short cross-border trip to get a change of scenery. A short visit to a Christmas craft store (in May!), an hour of playground time, a quick meal break and back home by 5 p.m. As we pull into our driveway at the end of the day, Ben is smiling: he needed the break too.

I place a call to my mother for no particular reason other than we haven't chatted in several days. What a mistake! She lashes into me for not having called in so long, emphasizing that it is my responsibility to call her on a regular basis. It's the same misguided mindset where I must call *her* on *my* birthday to thank her for her gift as opposed to her calling to wish me a happy birthday. But on *her* birthday, I must call her to wish her a happy birthday. It's impossible to reason with this warped logic but I try to continue the conversation. It only deteriorates with each spoken phrase.

She lambasts me for having taken Conor and Tori to the Monster Truck Show the day before, saying it was no place for her grandchildren to be. Before I can respond, she complains how she never sees Ben and how we never take him out. I want to tell her that we had just been to Calais for the afternoon but don't want to risk her saying "that I have more money than brains."

Instead, I say that that's old news, my tone becoming sharper and louder, that we tended to stay home *only* when he was a baby. Ignoring my answer, she proceeds to say that we never took him out for the year we were living in Toronto, even though she knows that we went to the playground nearly every evening. She tops off her verbal abuse by claiming that when she had visited us last summer in Toronto, she witnessed first hand how we didn't take Ben anywhere.

I am furious! My face gets tight, my head begins to pound. I scream back, "What the hell are you talking about? Do you not remember that Ben was sick for three days that week? Do you forgot that I spent a night in the hospital because he was so dehydrated?" It's a no-win situation. Any statement I make is refuted, regardless of how incorrect or insensitive her come-backs.

The conversation ends in anger. I am incensed by her words and frustrated by her repeated lack of support and empathy. She hasn't found a way to accept Ben, let alone love him, and is a world away from finding any means to help us. I'm not sure she ever will.

* * *

Another view

Ben is very congested this week and is coughing a lot. These symptoms have been hanging on for nearly a month and the previous dose of antibiotics has had little effect. An evening ER visit to see Dr. Campbell reveals that Ben's nasal areas are very irritated. His noisy breathing is coming from his upper airways, not his chest. No pneumonia. Thank God! He prescribes *Cephalexin*, a more potent antibiotic, and a nose spray called *Beconase*. Ben and a new drug is usually a bad combination but we're out of energy to worry about that today. We have to cure this congestion.

Three days later is Ben's appointment with Dr. Norris for an EEG. Somehow, I haven't written down this appointment and have booked myself with some work meetings. Jan isn't impressed and has to take Ben by herself.

The results are much better than the one he had had last fall at Sick Kids. The epilepsy is confined to the rear part of the left side of the brain, which is encouraging. Dr. Norris wants to keep Ben on *Phenobarbital* for now and will re-evaluate this in six months.

Jan tells him that we seemed to have solved Ben's constipation problem by simply giving him table food. He thinks it must be the increased fibre in the food and is glad that that was all we had to do. He is also appreciative that we had forwarded to him a copy of Dr. Gaudet's report. He remarks that Dr. Gaudet tends to be very detailed and thorough, even excessively so. He advises Jan not to worry too much about Dr. Gaudet's concerns. The thyroid issue is worth investigating and can be controlled if it becomes a problem. Of course, a hundred things can go wrong with Ben but we just don't keep them in the front of our minds on a daily basis. Dr. Norris believes that Ben's weight loss should not be a concern (yes, he said NOT to be concerned) and is quite certain that Ben will not require growth hormones or a significant increase to his diet. He tells Jan that compromised kids like Ben tend to be smaller than normal and it may be nature's way of keeping them small since they are not as mobile as other kids and don't need the extra weight. Jan learns that Dr. Norris always thought that Ben was rather big and had noted that his leg development is a good example of that.

Before wrapping up the appointment, Dr. Norris inquires on Ben's congestion and asks if he is usually this "snorty". She tells him that Ben has been unable to shake this problem for the past month and asks what he thinks about seeing Dr. Garrison to check into any facial/structural problems with Ben. He agrees and will call her office to get an appointment. He also gives Jan a requisition for blood work to look into the thyroid possibility.

Jan and I talk about the Dr. Norris appointment and, strangely, begin to feel good again about Ben. We didn't think we would ever see Dr. Norris in this light—we can still hear the words, "extensive calcifications," but we are learning that he has a very practical and conservative approach to things, especially with Ben's case. He doesn't panic or over-react easily and prefers to let nature take its course, relying on natural interventions whenever possible.

Perhaps we feel this way because that's what we want to feel. We want to believe that there's nothing else wrong with Ben, that Dr. Gaudet is way off-base. It's so difficult to determine who is right. One week we are fed one set of opinions and the next week, a very different set. It certainly highlights the imprecision of medicine. This conflict is really becoming a metaphor of our daily struggle to make the right choices for Ben. Every day there is more information, more complexity, more uncertainty. And the choices get harder and harder to make. I hate it.

*　*　*

Congestion won't go away

Ben's energy level continues to drop despite another round of drugs. He is finding it hard to breathe normally—even what's normal for him. For three consecutive nights, what seems like hourly, he has awakened abruptly, cried out, and coughed for several minutes. His eyes are still very green and look really sore. I'm unsure if they are the cause of his restlessness or if his gums are still bothering him. I'm never sure about anything.

He's extremely tired during the day since he can't get any decent rest, and has little desire to do anything. Feeding him is becoming a challenge and a worry, not from his lack of hunger but from his inability to hold his head up. We even convince ourselves that he's experiencing hay fever-like allergies and try *Seldane* for a few days.

His congestion is no better and my frustration is growing. We need help. Ben needs help. My persistence with Dr. Garrison's receptionist gains me a phone appointment with her.

Without stopping between sentences, I tell her how Ben has had a cold, a sore throat, an ear infection, an eye infection, all swirling for the last 2 months and how we are getting very concerned. I go on to emphasize that he seems to put all of his energy into breathing and his restless sleep has become a vicious cycle—he's too tired during the day to rid himself of the infection but can't get enough rest through the night to help him through the day.

I also draw a comparison to Tori and what a difference having her adenoids removed made in her. Dr. Garrison responds that removing enlarged adenoids can increase a child's activity but it's not always the case. I reply that I am not expecting miracles and begin to open up with her . . . perhaps too much.

My dissertation begins with my annoyance of how all too often, when no one can explain why Ben is this way or that, the default reason reverts to his neurological damage, and that includes why he mouth breathes. I follow up my claim with Ben's recent constipation issue. No one could really explain it other than to say that his lack of movement has a large impact on the efficiency of his bowels and his neurological irregularities, of course, most likely affect muscle coordination of his digestive system. While these may play a role, I tell her that all it took was switching Ben from junior foods to "real" food to make a significant difference, and how I find it strange that no one could suggest that simple solution.

Before hanging up, Dr. Garrison says that she will order an X-ray before our appointment with her next month. And for the interim, we should continue with the *Beconase* spray because, since it's a topical steroid, it needs several days to build up in his system.

I am not sure if she really understood what I was trying to say but it felt good just to tell someone. How many more sleepless nights lie ahead?

* * *

A period of observation

We decide to keep our appointment with Lisa, his PT, even though Ben has been feeling lousy. He has no energy for her exercises today, struggling through waves of noisy breathing. Ten minutes into the session, he appears to stop breathing for a moment, or at least give a long pause. Lisa thinks it may be a seizure (she's quick to say that, anyway). She stops her routine to express her belief that he looks thinner and, in fact, she will be calling Dr. Garrison this afternoon to express her concerns. In some ways, I am glad that she is concerned, too—a fresh voice may spark some action.

It doesn't take long for Dr. Garrison to call to inform us that after speaking with both Lisa and Dr. Campbell, she is going to admit Ben to the hospital for a one-to-two-day observation period to run a number of tests that will hopefully determine the reasons for his breathing irregularities. This would be less disruptive than dragging him back and forth to the hospital over several days. As well, they could watch him over a longer period of time to get a better sense of what is going on. She tells us that it may be a structural problem, a muscular problem, or a neurological problem but that she would be better able to find out if he were in hospital. We are in total agreement. We have to get to the bottom of this.

The next day we make our way to PICU to begin the observation period. Ben weighs in at only 20 ½ lbs—a full pound drop from our April visit to Dr. Gaudet and 3 lbs less in the last six months. Maybe Dr. Gaudet is right.

Dr. Garrison stops in the unit briefly and looks in his ears. She sees some wax but otherwise no concerns. She also looks in his throat and says that his tonsils are fine. During her examination, she hears him snorting for the first time, and inserts a stethoscope-like device with a rubber tube into his nose and listens for any air. She says that he probably isn't breathing at all through his nose, which is not surprising to us. It could be his adenoids, she suggests. Before leaving, she indicates that she will try to get an X-ray done some time that evening.

Dr. Norris arrives a short time later and chats briefly about the events of the past few months. He agrees that it is certainly possible that enlarged adenoids could affect his breathing and that an X-ray would show if there was any blockage. He wants Ben hooked up to an O$_2$ saturation device to record his oxygen levels through the night.

Jan decides to leave for a while to pick up some groceries and I give Ben his supper. Despite the sterile surroundings, he is quite hungry and eats well. As I am giving him his bottle with *phenobarb*, one of the nurses approaches us carrying a tray of food. She asks if he has had his supper, thinking the tray might be his. It has a big bowl of large *Jello* cubes along with a plate of macaroni, beef, tomatoes, and cheese plus some peas and carrots.

"Sure, sure, that's what he normally eats!" I say to myself.

Would someone really try to feed him this if we weren't here? Isn't it written down somewhere that Ben doesn't chew and has many food allergies? This is a hospital, right?

After the food incident, a team of nurses attempts to hook Ben up to one of the O$_2$ saturation monitors. They start by placing the large clip on one of his tiny fingers. The clip is twice the size of his finger yet they still try repeatedly to make it work. It doesn't. Surely this isn't the first small person to need his O$_2$ levels monitored. They appear to abandon all attempts to connect him to any monitor until I suggest that they try it on his foot.

Isn't one of the main reasons Ben is here is so that it can be determined how much oxygen he is getting?

Didn't Dr. Norris specifically order that he wanted a printout?

"Come on people, put a little effort into this!", I say under my breath.

Jan arrives a short time later to relieve me and to spend the night with Ben. There is a quiet room a short distance from the Unit where Jan chooses to get a few hours of sleep. The nurses tell her that they will come to get her whenever Ben awakens.

Jan has no trouble closing her eyes in the comfortable surroundings of the quiet room, which is equipped with a plush leather couch and soft, ambient lighting. She awakes with a start at 1:30 a.m., after being lost in a deep sleep. Calmly approaching the Unit to check on Ben, she is surprised to hear him sobbing loudly. She rushes in to discover the light over his crib is shining brightly into his eyes. Perplexed, Jan asks why no one came to wake her as they said they would. The night nurse tells Jan that she thought he might be hungry and need a bottle. (What 2-year old still wakes up for a middle-of-the-night feeding?) Jan remains by his side for the rest of the night. It is uneventful.

This becomes a watershed moment for us. We had expected that nurses in an intensive care unit would appreciate the complex needs of someone like Ben, someone who is developmentally challenged and cannot speak for himself,

In the morning, we chat with Dr. Norris who informs us that Ben had a few low oxygen incidents throughout the night but nothing life threatening. Life threatening? You mean there was a chance he could have stopped breathing, forever?

He thinks that Ben is a little young to have his adenoids removed but indicated that Dr. Garrison will speak with us about this after she has had a chance to view the X-rays.

A few hours later, Jan meets up with Dr. Campbell. He surmises that, perhaps, the first sore throat/cold Ben had in April might have constricted an already narrow breathing space with built-up tissues. And it is certainly possible that removing his adenoids might help. On the other hand, it might be cerebral meaning the brain might be changing breathing patterns now that he is two years old, and that it may be having trouble doing so. If Ben does require surgery, he says that his heart and lungs are strong enough that any concerns about additional risks because Ben is, well, "Ben," shouldn't exist.

Dr. Garrison doesn't get to the Unit until early evening. She tells us that Ben's adenoids are "humungous" and that they are completely blocking the airways in his nose. She asks if the antibiotics that he was on over the last several weeks had done any good. We respond that the *Cephlax* seemed to be the only one that helped him at all. She says that she wants to try him on it again for 14 days to see if that helps and then reassess him at that time. If nothing improves after that time, she will schedule him as an "urgent" case to remove his adenoids. Twenty-four hours in this place is enough for us and we are more than ready to accept her advice.

At home, Jan and I talk about what we have learned and decide that we really want to have his adenoids removed right away. In the middle of our conversation, the phone rings and it is Dr. Campbell. He is surprised that we had left the hospital. We relay the outcome of our conversation with Dr. Garrison but he questions why she would prescribe an antibiotic. He tells us that she is on call tonight and he will try to see her before he leaves on vacation.

I'm really agitated now.

* * *

What a system!

Our sleep doesn't last long. Ben wakes up crying quite forcefully as the clock ticks past 1:30 a.m. Perhaps there's something about this time of day. Perhaps he was dreaming of his PICU visit. It's so hard to know what he is thinking and how he really feels.

In the morning, while drinking his bottle, he cries hard again. The left side of his jaw, near his ear, seems very tender and I can't get him to calm down for quite a while. We connect with Dr. Campbell. Jan takes Ben to see him before he leaves for Italy on vacation. Diagnosis is a swollen lymph gland—not mumps—but swollen, nonetheless.

A call from Dr. Garrison's office a short time later tells us that Ben is being placed "on standby" for surgery tomorrow. Jan immediately calls me at work and I head home to get ready. Another hospital stay. Yuck! We convince ourselves that this time will be better. This one is planned. We've been through it many times before and we tell ourselves that we will be on top of things this time, and not allow dumb things to happen. Ben's breathing is going to get fixed this time.

We arrive back at the hospital not quite 24 hours after leaving it. We're not in PICU this time, but share a room with another child. It's much more relaxing. Jan chooses to stay with him for the night, not leaving his side.

In the morning, I take over, waiting for Dr. Garrison to come. Early afternoon comes and it's time for the nurse to start Ben's IV in preparation for the O/R. He is sleeping and I insist that she not wake him. He has had so little sleep over the past month, there's no one getting between me and him right now. I suggest she wait a half hour or so and he would probably be awake. She is not impressed.

By 4 p.m., Dr. Garrison makes an appearance and apologizes that Ben keeps getting bumped because of emergencies and that it might be 3 a.m. before she can do him. She was ready to do him at noon today but couldn't get an anesthesiologist. Rather than stand by any longer, she concludes that it would probably be better to discharge him and reschedule.

This is unbelievable. He's going to be sent home so he can continue to breathe like a freight train, continue to lose weight, continue to lose sleep, and everyone is okay with that? No wonder this health-care system is unaffordable. Ben has been admitted twice in one week—what does that cost? And simple things like meals. When we arrived Thursday evening we asked for some food for him but nothing came. On Friday, we were told that he was to fast from noon onward, and at lunch-time a huge tray of food was delivered!

Dr. Garrison really has no idea when the next surgery time will be. The person who needs the most help and is the most vulnerable is the one who has to suffer the most. This system is completely dysfunctional.

* * *

10

THE OPERATION

I am being torn apart. We need to fix his noisy breathing but I don't want to put him through surgery. The more I struggle with this dilemma, the more anxious I become even though I realize that this is our only option.

Why do we always need a doctor?

We never really know with Ben what will work and what will not. There's a chance this may not be the answer. What if the procedure doesn't go as planned; what if they find something else wrong? He has never had anaesthesia before. I'm not sure I can handle any more bad news.

Too many unknowns. Too many possibilities.

The hardest part for me is I have no way to explain to him what will take place. He can't ask me questions about will happen or tell me how he is feeling. I have no way to hold his hand through the surgery, and no way of knowing how he will react.

We seem to be sentenced to spending our lives in a hospital somewhere. I'm sure this impression is a result of our repeated admissions recently, waiting for this stupid surgery to happen. I'm sure it's because we really have spent so much of the last two years in one clinic or another for appointment after appointment with specialist after specialist.

Part of my anxiety is wishing we could just stay home. I hate hospitals.

A week passes before we get the call. Ben's surgery is scheduled for July 8, a Friday. Why are they always booked on Fridays? Enjoying the July long weekend is not possible; this seems to be a trend. Leading up to Surgery Day, we're both very nervous.

Does he speak English?

Conor and Tori are staying with Marg and Clem (who has made a full recovery). Jan and Ben pick me up from work and we proceed directly to the hospital. The lobby is devoid of activity at this time of day and Ben notices this. After the elevator doors open onto the 4th floor, we turn left towards the paediatric wing.

As we have done so many, many times before, we are required to describe Ben's medical history to the admitting nurse. I'm sure somewhere all of our answers from previous visits have been stored, and this time could be used simply for review, but not today. The nurse does not seem either interested or comfortable.

Before taking his vitals, she asks, "Does he speak English?"

I wrinkle my brow, not knowing quite how to answer. Perhaps because he is wearing hearing aids that she is wondering? Or that she has never seen a child with multiple disabilities? Or perhaps because she's just representative of a healthcare system in crisis? I probably should be more polite but I respond with a curt, "yes!"

All his vitals are normal and I notice that she writes down "rectal" for his temperature even though she took it in his ear (it should have been "tympanic"). Not sure why this hospital hired the bottom 10% of the graduating class!

Ben has only one roommate whose name is Nathan, a very pleasant eight-year old. He asks Ben's name and gives him a warm greeting. This warmth is chilled a few moments later as a stern-looking man enters the room. With a noticeable British accent, he introduces himself as "the anaesthetist".

I respond with, "Hi. And your name is?"

"Dempster," he replies.

His tone is somber as he describes what will take place. He is concerned about Ben's asymmetric facial structure and whether he will respond well to being put to sleep. No introduction, no explanation, no attempt to make us comfortable, just straight to his concerns. What is this man trying to say? Dr. Garrison had described it as a routine procedure but this guy makes it sound like it's open-heart surgery.

We later learn that Dr. Dempster is always concerned about everything. Bring on the happy people any time!

*   *   *

His first surgery

The halls are quiet as the sun begins to peek into the 4th floor windows. It is a few minutes before 6 a.m. when I gently push open the door to Ben's hospital room. He is still sleeping. Jan whispers that he had a reasonably peaceful sleep, waking up only a few times. A short time later, two nurses greet us and say that we need to start waking him. His surgery time is two hours away.

We first turn on a light over the bed next to him and softly tap his shoulder, introducing the world gradually to him. After 15 minutes of constant poking, he is fully awake and not pleased. Jan slowly gets him into his yellow-striped hospital jammies as one of the nurses arrives to spread a numbing cream on the backs of his hands.

It seems strange not to be feeding him and I can sense that he is wondering why. At 10 minutes to eight, a hunched, middle-aged woman with a deep, raspy voice enters the room. She is the porter who will be taking Ben down to the O/R.

"Where's Benjamin George?", she yells out, her voice piercing the morning stillness. As she gets closer to me, she is reeking of cigarette smoke. At this early hour, it is quite disgusting.

"Oh, he's sleeping!" are her next words. This place is amazing!

Jan and I shake our heads and tell her that he has been awake for a while. And with that she unlocks the wheels of his bed and whisks him out into the hall. No introduction, no telling him where he's going or what she is doing. She must have attended social skills classes with Dr. Dempster.

Hurriedly, I follow her down the hall, holding Ben's hand. I begin to get knots in my stomach. I have no way to explain to him what is going to happen. I wish I could know what is running through his mind.

As we get closer to the surgical suite, I feel worse. It is not that dreaded sick feeling but more one of helplessness, an aching of how much he means to me. How much I love him.

Without warning, the porter exclaims, "Far as you can go!", meaning I can't walk into the O/R with her. My anxiety meter goes through the roof. I feel awful that I can't be with him. I want to call it off. Too late—the doors swing closed and he is gone.

Jan and I sit in the cafeteria and wait. We are not really interested in eating but manage to choke down a bitter cup of coffee. Our silence is deafening. Neither has much to say to the other. We wish we knew what was happening.

We drag ourselves back to the paediatric wing and wait in the quiet room outside of PICU. The soft, ambient lighting means nothing right now. After a half hour of fidgeting, I leave for the bathroom. At the same time, the O/R calls to give us an update. Jan takes the call and rushes down the hall to find me, relieved that he is fine and telling me how she could hear him crying in the background.

Nearly two hours pass before he is wheeled up from the recovery room. Jan and I impatiently stand beside the elevator doors to greet him. Amidst the rumble and clatter of the opening of the doors, we finally get to see him. He is alert and, wow, is he angry, alternating between yelling and crying. The oxygen mask that is placed over his face is much too big and not really serving any purpose. Doesn't this place have anything that fits him? We can see gobs of fresh and dried blood trickling out of his nose. But it doesn't bother us. We are over-the-moon happy to see him and thankful that Dr. Dempster's fears did not come true.

He is escorted into PICU and placed in the same bed he had during his observation period. Jan just has to hold him close. He is still whimpering. A nurse comes near and gives him some *Tylenol* for the pain. The dose is only 80 mg. We mention that we give him twice that at home but the nurse retorts that that's what Dr. Garrison had ordered.

Jan tries to give him something to drink. He isn't interested so we don't push it. Having slept in her clothes all night, Jan leaves for home a short time later to get cleaned up. He takes a few naps but wakes up mid-afternoon, crying hard. I know it's time for another dose of *Tylenol* and I approach the nurses to inquire. They are so unhelpful and make me feel like I'm imposing.

One nurse asks, "Oh, he didn't have his *Phenobarbital* this morning. Would that help?" I tell her not to worry about that; I guess she thought it would have a calming effect.

"That's not the problem," I tell her. "He's in pain."

At that moment, I remember back to our Toronto days when we had to change giving his *Phenobarbital* from bedtime to earlier since it was making him quite wakeful, and Dr. McDonald mentioning how that's quite common but was actually a good sign. I don't tell the nurse any of that.

She says that she will page Dr. Garrison to see what Ben can have. That's not very helpful for him. I go back to his bedside and wait. After half an hour passes, I approach her again and she pages Dr. Garrison again.

"Do you think she is going to say NO to more *Tylenol?*", raising the volume of my voice in frustration.

She responds by telling me that those are the rules of the hospital, how she can't give anything unless the doctor orders it.

"You know, having him cry for an hour isn't good for him, either!", I snap back at her.

It is so frustrating. Here is a two-year-old fresh from surgery, in obvious discomfort, and all that can be done is page the doctor? My fatigue is taking over as I begin to see the PICU nursing staff as working against me. They have sat behind their station for more than two hours and done absolutely nothing to care for Ben. Then, one of them says,

"Oh, it's time for me to go on break".

"Break? You've just sat there while my child is crying his head off! You haven't done a thing—why would you need a break?", I scream inside myself.

Twenty minutes after the second page to Dr. Garrison, a nurse comes over. This time she gives Ben 120 mg, saying it's what Dr. Garrison has prescribed. I question her about the earlier dose, a smaller dose, but she claims ignorance. I am thinking to myself that they misread the order the first time, just like when "rectal" was written instead of "tympanic" for the method of taking his temperature, but no one wants to admit it. I was wrong, this is *the very bottom* of the graduating class.

The evening shift of nurses arrives at a quarter to seven and the two teams exchange news of the events of the day. After this briefing, a nurse sits down beside me to get my story of what Ben's day has been like. Clearly, she was the class leader, someone who understands her role, who is engaged in her work. An hour later, she returns with some *Codeine* and more *Tylenol*, this time with a dose of 145 mg (calculated for his weight). It's 8:45 p.m.—by 9:30 p.m., he is asleep.

* * *

Spending the night

My head begins to bob as I sit in the straight-back chair next to his crib. The lights are dim and the curtain is partially drawn. My 17-hour shift has taken its toll and I decide to get some sleep. I approach the nurse's station and tell them I'm going to the quiet room down the hall and ask them to please come and get me if he wakes up or starts to cry. This is the same quiet room in which Jan had slept a few weeks ago when they didn't come to get her. This nursing team seems much more capable and so I take a chance. Ben's nurse tells me that she will be checking his vitals at 1 a.m. and so I set my watch for 12:50 a.m.

Lying down in the quiet room, I can't hold my eyes open for very long.

The faint "beep-beep" of my watch startles me. It can't be one o'clock already. It is. I tear myself away from the comfort of the soft couch and back into the Unit. He is still asleep. His nurse is gentle but efficient at taking his vitals. No concerns. I shuffle back down the hall. Before lying down, I reset my watch for two hours later.

I oversleep by a half hour and jump up with a start. It's 3:45 a.m. and I feel like I've missed something. My anxiety is clearly evident as I re-enter the Unit. All six PICU beds are full now—they have had two new admissions while I was sleeping—but all is quiet. His nurse tells me he's had a very peaceful night.

My eyes are hurting and my head is fuzzy. Before drifting back to sleep, I reset my watch for 5 a.m. I am punctual this time and head back to Ben's side. His nurse has already checked his vitals which, again, are fine. She informs me he had desaturated to about 83 percent at one point but only because he had fallen off of his pillow. After straightening him up, he was fine.

I reset my watch a fourth time, for 7 a.m., to give me another 90 minutes. No such luck. At 6:30 a.m., his nurse knocks on the door to wake me because Ben is crying. I hurry back to his side and snuggle him into my shoulder. It's comforting for him and his crying quickly disappears. His eyes remain open to examine the surroundings. I realize that he is probably hungry so I get him set up for a drink. Not having eaten much in the last 36 hours, he is ready for his bottle. Two ounces of *Isomil* with his *Phenobarbital* disappear with ease. After another six ounces find their way to his belly, he is quite satisfied.

He doesn't drink any faster than before but this time there isn't as much of a struggle for him so there's very little mess. Saturday morning has arrived and is starting on an uptick. It looks like our stay will be short.

*   *   *

It's never simple

Ben still seems hungry after his 8 oz drink so I try him with some rice cereal. He isn't crazy about it but manages to eat half a bowl. As he is finishing, Jan arrives and Ben is happy to see her.

The clock creeps close to 11 a.m. as Dr. Garrison arrives. She asks how he is doing. She was pleased with the operation and says that we can go home any time. The swelling will probably last four or five days but within a week, the soreness should be gone.

Jan asks about seeing her next week for a regularly scheduled appointment in her clinic along with an audiogram. She says that it is worthwhile to do the audiogram but that there is no need to see her unless we have concerns. Jan also inquires about the surgery itself, whether there are any particular details that we should be aware of regarding the procedure or anaesthetic details that we could relay to future physicians. Dr. Garrison happily reports that there was nothing out of the ordinary, that Ben has a normal larynx and was intubated without any problems.

"Hmm", I mutter to myself.

Before Dr. Garrison leaves, Jan mentions that my sister and her two children arrived last night for a 10-day visit and they believe that at least one of them has contracted parvovirus. Given that Ben just had surgery, we are wondering if there are any precautions we should take. She has no specific information but advises that we should keep Ben isolated from them for the next week.

Never satisfied, I wander down a floor to the Neonatal Unit to find Dr. Smythe to get his opinion. The nurse I speak with informs me that he won't be in until noon but would pass my message along. She remembers Ben, and tells me that she was the one who admitted him to the Unit after he was born. She is glad to hear that he is doing well.

Having been given the green light to leave, Jan and I waste no time packing up Ben's things. He seems as eager to depart as we do. We make a quick stop to pick up Conor and Tori from Marg and Clem, who live quite close to the hospital. Making the turn onto their street, I notice two vehicles parked in Dr. Smythe's driveway (he lives in the same subdivision). He has not called yet so I take a chance and walk down the hill to try to speak with him.

His wife greets me in a very soft and pleasant manner. After introducing myself, I tell her of Ben (she has heard much about him) and the complication we are now facing. I mention how grateful we are for Dr. Smythe's care for Ben over the past two years and that I hope to get his advice now. She says that he is asleep but assures me that she will get him to phone us.

It doesn't take long for Dr. Smythe to call our house. On the subject of parvovirus, he tells us that it is very common and that it's also known as Fifth disease. Actually, Fifth is caused by parvovirus, he says, and is labeled as such because it is classified as the fifth one in the list of childhood rashes such as measles. It is typically contagious only in the early stages, before any rash has developed.

When I ask about complications to Ben if he contracts it, he says that it is virtually impossible to protect Ben from it since it is so widespread, much like CMV. To isolate the whole family is neither practical nor realistic so he advises that Ben stay out of direct contact with anyone suspected of it. He goes on to say that Conor and Tori need not limit their exposure to their cousins since they may already have this virus or others that Ben could contract just as easily. I thank him once again for his time and devotion to helping us. He is a rare breed, indeed.

Things are never simple with Ben. What are the chances of Ben having surgery, at the same time his cousins are visiting, at the same time they have contracted a virus? A hundred percent, obviously. Perhaps I should buy a lottery ticket.

*   *   *

A watery journey

A full three weeks from surgery day, we head for Halifax for the weekend, for a vacation.

Leaving late in the day, we stop at Nana Brook's to feed Ben his supper. An hour later we're back on the highway and make it to Amherst, about 120 kilometers from our final destination. We need to find a restaurant to feed the rest of us. It is nearly 8 p.m. by the time we are seated, time for Ben's evening bottle. He is more interested in looking around than drinking. Within a few minutes, a tour bus unloads and fills every last seat in the house. The onslaught of seniors overwhelms the tiny staff and they forget about our order. A half hour passes. We can't wait any longer. We flag a waitress to cancel everything and leave. She is not impressed.

Driving into Halifax the next morning is uneventful, though the air is dripping with humidity, close to 35°C. Our hotel room is perfect, though a little pricey. Ben's inability to eat take-out or restaurant food of any kind relegates us to a small suite of sorts, anything with a small kitchenette.

Conor is keen to purchase a Sega Game Gear and so we do some comparison shopping at a couple of stores. We start with Toys R Us: too much. Then Sears: not the model he's looking for. With a few phone calls, we learn that the best price is at Consumers Distributing. The store is closing in 20 minutes so we ignore a few traffic laws to get there. With only a few minutes to spare, we make the purchase. Conor is extremely happy and can't wait to try it out.

Our journey back home takes us over water. It's a 90-minute drive to the ferry, a one-hour wait to board, and a three-hour cruise. No faster than driving but a lot less stressful.

Jan boards on foot with Ben in his stroller while Conor, Tori and I drive on. Each car and each truck is sandwiched together in the vehicle bay with no room to spare. Making our way along the narrow and slippery path beside the vehicles is a little treacherous. The lighting is poor, and the mixture of seawater and exhaust fumes is not very pleasant. The stairs from the vehicle bay to the main deck are nearly vertical, an impossible task for anyone who can't walk. Did I say a cruise? Jan and Ben are waiting patiently for us at the top of the stairs.

Part way through the excursion, we stand outside and watch the water rush past. The breeze is constant and somewhat cool but refreshing nonetheless. A little recharge time for each of us. The motion of the ship doesn't bother Ben. I didn't think that that might be a problem until now, a little too late I guess. Thankfully, it seems like nothing is bothering him lately.

We place the kids in a semi-circle to take their picture. Ben and Conor are laughing from the dampness of the rushing wind, and Tori almost manages a smile. She stands between her brothers, holding on to the bottom of her orange and white summer dress, and waits for the camera's shutter to click.

For Jan and me, it's our first time on the Digby ferry, ever. Our children are taking us to new places—some exciting, some distressing—but always memorable.

*   *   *

11

"SCHOOL TIME, WORK TIME, PLAY TIME" . . . REPEAT

They arrive in the heat of the August sun, parking their Alberta-registered Chevy Astro in our driveway. We haven't seen them in years. As the five of them scramble out of the vehicle, it hits me that they have just driven 5,000 kilometers with three small children. They must have lost their minds! Conor and Tori have no knowledge of Mandy, Courtney and Nicholas but they introduce themselves as only young kids can and become instant friends.

Jeff and Cheryl give us each a big bear hug in front of the whole neighbourhood. That's one of their unique qualities, being unafraid to express their feelings. We step inside and introduce Ben to them. In his open and unabashed manner, Jeff comments at how pleasant Ben looks and says he didn't really know what to expect. It's all good, though, and we feel happy that they are so unafraid of him.

The evening isn't long enough to share everything we want to share but we do our best. The calmness of the summer sky and the surprisingly good-natured play of five kids under five are essential ingredients to a wonderful time together.

We tell them of some of the tough times, especially the first few months after Ben's birth. Cheryl contrasts our ability to deal with these shocking events by recalling a time when we were living in Edmonton shortly after Conor was born, and Jan had asked her to stay over night since I was working in Calgary for a few days.

With a gleam in her eye, Cheryl recounted that she got sidetracked, didn't come over, and Jan called her house a dozen times to see where she was. She had been rather amazed at the level of Jan's nervousness back then, when there really was little to be nervous about. Jeff recalled how Jan used to check on Conor "a thousand times" while he was sleeping, just to make sure he was breathing.

With this recollection of the beginning of our journey as parents, we are able to appreciate just how much we have accomplished, and how well we have been able to cope with appointments, surgeries and seizures, and still find the energy to care for two other children.

Our friends have helped us to pause and enjoy life again. We haven't enjoyed much of anything in the past two years. It is a perfect anniversary present.

A milestone trip

Ben is eager to get on the road. It seems that even *he* wants to take advantage of his string of good days and restful nights. The 1,500-km round-trip trek to Rhode Island is ambitious, no question, but we are trying to live as normal a life as possible. My parents have decided to take their habitual summer retreat to Maine at the same time, and we travel as a convoy of two vehicles, with Jan, Conor, Ben, and my mother in our car, and me, Tori and my father in his car.

As we cross the border into Calais in the blinding morning sun, Ben is ready for his breakfast. Sitting in McDonald's takes me back to the first day-trip we made to Calais when Ben was only nine months old, when a day-trip was all he could handle. Our stop lasts 45 minutes and we begin the second leg of the trip on Route 9. This 145 km stretch of road is the longest part of the trip, or so it seems, with its narrow, undulating, and winding path through largely uninhabited areas. The scenery is picturesque in spots, with large rolling hills and natural lakes, but the miles and miles of dense forest that line the patchy shoulders feel isolating.

By 2 p.m., we make it to Augusta for a lunch break; what should have been a three-and-a-half-hour trip has become six hours, typical of life on the road with Ben. About two hours later, we pull onto Freeport's Main Street, a shopping outlet Mecca. The town is packed with people, pets, and vehicles and it takes more than 20 minutes to inch our way into a side parking lot and another 15 to actually find a spot. Ben takes the stop-and-go action in stride. A short distance away is the flagship store of LL Bean and in its quaint courtyard, Ben and I find a comfortable bench to stretch, get some needed fresh air, and replenish ourselves. He is very comfortable in the open air, despite it dripping with humidity, and consumes his juice rapidly.

Gazing at the multitude of pedestrians crowding every side street as well as those walking past us, some needing to get a glimpse of Ben, I pause and realize that we are nearly 500 kilometers from home, with Ben, in another country, and everyone is enjoying themselves. Two summers ago we were in the throes of 2:30 a.m. feedings, nine weeks of colic, and Jan's gall bladder attacks. My life doesn't seem real some days.

Before leaving, we all get a very overpriced ice cream from the cramped, outdoor stall of Ben & Jerry's just outside LL Bean.

We check in to our Portland hotel at 5:30 p.m. Not bad. Only nine hours on the road. Smoking rooms are all that remain, even though we reserved a non-smoking one. It's a little small. Ben doesn't mind, and neither do Conor and Tori. They are just happy not to be driving any more. We feed Ben his supper in the room and then ride the elevator to the main-level restaurant to feed ourselves.

The toll of the day is showing on Ben's face. He begins to fuss and then cry. This is new for him. Believing that he is overtired, we take him back to the room. Conor and Tori stay with their grandparents while we try to get Ben to settle.

It doesn't take much. Once his little body hits the bed, his mood instantly changes. He just wanted to lie down, stretch out, get out of that chair for a while. He is happy, talking and kicking wildly. Jan decides to stay in the room with him so that I can go back to the restaurant.

Part way through the meal, I hear the phone at the desk of the *Maitre d'* ringing off the hook. I begin to wonder if that is Jan calling to tell me that Ben's in trouble. Nobody is answering the phone. My mind then races to a disturbing scene where she can't leave him alone and she's got no one to help her. After a few minutes of anxiety, I excuse myself and find a house phone to call the room. The line is busy. I try again. Still nothing. My heart is racing now. I immediately think Ben's having a seizure. I rush up to the room and . . .

Ben is fine. Surprised to see me, Jan tells me that she was calling the desk but only to tell me not to worry, that everything was fine. I am both relieved and exhausted, and return to the restaurant, feeling a little embarrassed. Everyone is finished by the time I sit down, but I have little interest in finishing my plate. As we leave, an older couple sitting next to our table goes out of their way to tell me that I have wonderful children and how well behaved Conor and Tori were.

"Thank you. They really are great kids", I reply and give them each a little hug. What a rush of feelings.

The next morning, everyone is well rested and ready to tackle the final legs of the trip. My parents meet us for breakfast and wish us well. Cruising on an eight-lane stretch of highway outside of Boston, Jan and I are still in disbelief that we have made it this far from home, that we can take such a long trip with Ben and everything be OK. We know it's because we have pushed him a little each day, and his response to us has been to bring on more. I am relieved to think this trip will be fun.

* * *

A new start

Jan starts training for her new job and Conor starts school. All on the same day. Summer is unofficially over!

We have hired Penny to look after Ben and Tori for the day. She is a woman in her mid-forties who has an 18-year-old son with multiple disabilities. We found her through a friend and decided to bring her in while Jan is on four weeks of training, before she begins a schedule of evening shifts. Our first conversation with Penny revealed a tough, wise and caring person, someone we hope to resemble 15 years from now.

After showing Penny where we keep Ben's food, bottles, spoons, bowls, clothes, diapers, and wet wipes, I whisk Conor into the car and drive him to the corner to catch his bus for the first time. It doesn't seem right to put a five-year-old on such a big bus for a half-hour ride. I feel like I have missed something. How did he get to this stage already? I think I am more anxious than he is.

Dwarfed by the bus's towering yellow metal frame, Conor eagerly climbs the oversized stairs of the noisy vehicle and finds a seat near the back. I follow the bus through its entire route, occasionally waving at him, until he disembarks in front of his new school. Less than a decade ago, this sprawling structure, with its six separate though inter-connected buildings, served as a high school. Today, it is still a public school but solely French Immersion from kindergarten to grade 8. Its hugeness is a little overwhelming for young children.

Bus after bus unloads hundreds of students as Conor and I make our way through the maze to reach his classroom. Conor is quite content to join the fray with the other students, most of whom are strangers to him so far. After briefly chatting with his teacher, Miss Hatcher, I return to my car and go to work.

I am not very productive at work that day, feeling I need to call home hourly. My worries are unfounded. Returning at lunch time to check in on things, I am relieved to see how natural Penny is with Ben. She has him constantly doing some activity, not just leaving him alone to sit and stare at the ceiling, and interacts with him appropriately.

On Day 3, Penny decides to try feeding Ben some Corn Flakes for breakfast, a new food that we wouldn't have considered. Ben seems to enjoy it. The next day, she takes all of the kids to the corner store to buy them a treat, as a reward for their stellar behaviour and how good they are to Ben. She has commented a number of times how helpful and playful Conor and Tori are with him. She believes that this is a key ingredient to Ben's pleasant mood and it's clear to her just how much he enjoys having them around.

By the end of the week, Ben awakens quite early. I bring him in with us, thinking that the comfort of two warm bodies might help him to get to sleep. Seconds before my 6:15 a.m. alarm rudely buzzes, he drifts off. As I finish my shower, Conor comes running in the downstairs bathroom to tell me that Ben is throwing up. I dash up the two levels, dripping wet, as Conor says, "I already got a towel for Mom."

When I get to our room, Ben's breathing is very shallow. I stick my finger in his mouth. He bites it, and starts to breathe more normally. Jan and I thank Conor for waking up and helping out so quickly.

"Any time!", he replies proudly.

When it comes to things that really matter, he knows exactly what to do, and does it!

These shallow breathing episodes are becoming a little disconcerting. Jan wonders whether or not they are really seizures because of how his body reacts. They are disruptive enough to wake him from a sleep and often make him gag and heave. It is so difficult to put it all together. Not knowing what these episodes really are and when they are going to happen effectively means we must be vigilant 24 hours a day. I hate this.

Penny arrives just as Ben is waking up. I finish getting myself ready for work. I can't imagine getting the adrenaline pumping so quickly and so early in the morning is good for me. As I walk out the door at 8:30 a.m., Ben is back to normal, drinking his bottle, talking, and smiling

My noontime call home finds that Penny has given him a bath . . . in the morning! A morning with one of those episodes! Whoa, whoa! I can't handle this! I remember when we would barely feel comfortable giving him a bath ourselves let alone let someone else do it. After only five days, I'm learning a tonne from her. I hope Ben is, too.

* * *

One year seizure-free

It comes from being a huge Bugs Bunny fan, I'm sure. As a youth (and an adult), I took every opportunity to view an episode or two. It didn't matter that I had seen each one dozens of times—it was always entertaining. And from these episodes I would often relate memorable lines to whatever situation I was experiencing, usually with my kids, usually mimicking the voices.

"Now, <u>drink</u> your juice!," in Yosemite Sam's raspy tone would be a common one I'd use to make sure Conor or Tori would finish drinking their orange juice in the morning.

When Ben turned one and it was clear he wasn't going to learn how to speak any time soon, I created a voice for him, guessing what he would say in each situation. Ben's "voice" became a fairly high-pitched one, like a toddler, but it also had some Bugs Bunny flair, with a bit of sarcasm just for fun.

Early one fall evening, when I am bathing Ben, Jan entered the bathroom, after a long day of training. In her version of "Ben's voice," she says,

> "Oh, Dad. I can only have a bath in the morning, and not on a full stomach. And you have to bathe me really quick 'cause I might have a seizure!"

With that, we realize that his last seizure had been exactly one year ago, while we were attending an assessment at the Hugh McMillian Rehab Centre in Toronto.

No seizures in a year!

No more noisy breathing!

Leaving him in the care of someone else for the whole day!

How liberating! What a great feeling!

A few days later, the autumn air slips back into summer, so much so that I leave the front door open to keep an eye on Ben while Conor, Tori and I play a game of baseball on our front lawn. Ben is on his belly in the living room, constantly lifting his body up on his forearms to get a glimpse of every pitch. The door separating him from the outside is screened from top to bottom, allowing him to easily have a good view. It's an attempt to include him and he is content to just watch.

This setup may not seem like much progress for a two-year-old, but for us, it's at least a handful of grains of sand.

*   *   *

Need a fresh approach

The morning is cold, damp, and drizzly—not great weather for Jan to take Ben to a combined physio and OT appointment. Approaching the lower-level parking lot, which is reserved for "handicapped" card holders, Jan discovers that it is full and must find a spot in the other lot, which is a considerable distance from the front entrance and situated above ground level. The "handicapped" parking spots in this lot are always available—I wonder why.

As Jan straps Ben into his wheelchair, the wind picks up and the rain is more steady. There are only stairs to allow pedestrians access from this lot to the entrance of the hospital so wheelchair users have little choice but to traverse the roadway next to the parking attendant's station and battle on-coming traffic.

Jan ducks under the wooden gate at the entrance of the parking lot since there is no room to squeeze beside it. Fortunately, Ben's chair is low enough to fit underneath. A car fast approaches them to enter the parking lot, splashing its way along. The driver is angered that Jan and Ben are in his way, sounding his horn a number of times to signal for them to get out his way.

Jan is not impressed but no one seems to notice this encounter. The parking attendant is completely clueless. Once inside the hospital, dripping wet, Jan and Ben wait an extra 20 minutes since Lisa is late for their appointment.

Ben is likely not impressed either and does not want to perform for her today. Lying on his belly, he lifts up to look around as Lisa remarks, "Oh, that's new!".

Jan chooses not to say anything but is thinking, "C'mon, Lisa. He's been doing that for over a year now. Don't you write anything down?"

For the rest of the appointment, he shows little energy. Lisa then tells Jan that she doesn't think he is progressing very much and wants to see him only once a month. Jan is furious. With a reserved tone, she says,

> "You know what Ben is like, Lisa. Some days he does nothing and some days he amazes you with his energy level. He just needs the right motivation."

It does little to change Lisa's mind. She never believes us when we tell her that he is doing this or that. Just because he doesn't perform during the 45-minute appointment doesn't mean he can't or won't. It is clear to Jan that today Lisa has little planned for the appointment and has no idea what the next steps should be.

Before the end of the appointment, Lisa tries stretching his legs and discovers that they are very tight,. Clearly the cold weather and his wet clothes aren't helping him achieve any level of relaxation. She then asks if Dr. Ramsay has mentioned surgery to us to release the tightness. In a controlled manner, Jan responds that both Dr. Ramsay and Dr. Norris have remarked on just the opposite, that they feel that Ben has very good range of motion. Ben must hear Lisa's skepticism and immediately relaxes. Lisa is surprised how loose his muscles have suddenly become. She's not new to the job but it's as if every day is her first day with Ben.

As she helps Jan get Ben back into his wheelchair, Lisa suggests that he should go back to wearing his hand splints since his fingers feel tight. Jan ignores her.

The appointment with Marsha, his OT, is in the room next to Lisa's. When Jan and Ben enter, she is standing in the middle of the room, looking a little out of place, like they caught her doing something she shouldn't. Jan opens the conversation by mentioning Lisa's remark regarding the splints. Marsha examines Ben's hands and quite calmly says that his hands and fingers are fine, that the splints are not necessary.

"C'mon folks, you're a team, aren't you? Get your act together!" Jan says to herself.

Then Marsha asks, "Is there anything else I can do for you?", making it quite obvious that she also has nothing planned for today's appointment. Jan is flabbergasted. Wait a minute. Who's the specialist here? How would Jan know what Marsha should do for Ben?

The appointment ends quickly. What a complete waste of time. Useless One and Useless Two! There's no accountability, no one to complain to. I guess that's why they're allowed to be useless.

* * *

A typical log entry

We're all a little sad that it has come to an end. Four weeks ago we didn't think we could leave Ben with a stranger but today we're not sure how we will manage without Penny. She has been so loving and caring to everyone, and it's exciting to see Ben respond to her in so many different ways. But Penny's time was only temporary. We knew that going in but we needed someone to help us this past month.

Ben is especially down, perhaps sensing that Penny will not be staying with him any more. He is quite irritable and doesn't settle into bed until 9:30 p.m. Jan and I quickly get to bed ourselves in anticipation of a long night.

Midnight: Ben cries out loudly and forcefully, awakening the household. His cries are rough and scratchy, an indication that his throat is very sore and his temperature is a scorching 39.5°C. Jan and I stay up with him for about an hour and watch some late-night television.

2:00 a.m.: He is still not settling so I decide to take him downstairs to walk and rock him, anything to help him find some comfort.

3:15 a.m.: His exhausted little body gives up and he falls asleep. Carefully, I climb the stairs to his bedroom and slowly lower him into his crib.

4:45 a.m.: His stinging cries mercilessly shake me awake. Too tired to get up again, I bring him into bed with me and Jan. He fusses for another hour or more before, again, he gives up and falls asleep.

7:45 a.m. Ben's worn-out, bloodshot eyes open but he does not cry. His body is still on fire and I desperately attempt to hydrate him with his morning bottle. Fortunate for us, Dr. Campbell is on-call this Thanksgiving weekend and asks us to meet him at the hospital to see what's bothering Ben. Oh, I love spending my Saturdays at the hospital.

10:30 a.m.: Dr. Campbell greets us in his usual, pleasant manner. He wants to get Ben's weight. It registers at 23.6 lbs, an increase of more than 3 lbs in three months—a record for Ben. And likely all attributed to the absence of his oversize adenoids. Despite my fuzzy head and almost sick feeling from lack of sleep, I am somewhat buoyed by this discovery. Through his examination and targeted questions, Dr. Campbell determines that Ben has swollen glands and an upper respiratory infection, but no ear infection this time. He comments that he took this long weekend to be on call because he thought a lot of people would be away. He was wrong. Before we leave, he calls in a prescription for *Suprax* and tells us that after a few days, Ben should begin to feel much better.

Noon: We are back home. A big turkey dinner has been planned for today at The Camp (Marg and Clem's summer place directly across the highway from Nana Brook) but Ben is in no shape to attend. Jan takes Conor and Tori while I stay home with Ben. I am unsuccessful in getting him to drink much of his bottle but do manage to get his *Suprax* into him, as well as some *Tylenol*. By early afternoon, he is back into piercing crying spells which continue for about 90 minutes.

3:30 p.m.: He is now content, lying on the basement couch feeling quite relaxed and showing an occasional tiny smile. The *Suprax* must be working.

4:00 p.m.: He is yawning repeatedly, obviously telling me he'd like to take a nap. Seconds after laying in his crib, he falls into a deep sleep.

5:30 p.m.: He wakes up quite happy. I attempt to give him his bottle but he cannot find a way to drink it. Each time I lie him back to get him to drink, he starts to cry, as if something is hurting him in that position. I can't figure it out.

7:00 p.m.: Jan returns home and Ben seems to be reasonably well but still not eating very much. We can't get him to swallow his dose of *Phenobarbital* but do manage to get his second dose of *Suprax* into him.

9:30 p.m.: Ben is in bed and is quite peaceful.

A complete day of my life has passed me by, consumed with no breaks and with little choice. I guess I should be thankful that it didn't involve much hospital time.

* * *

The annual IWK trip

Thanksgiving Monday begins as a fairly normal day but soon turns hectic as I compress three days of trip preparation into half a day. With Ben being sick and Jan having to work her usual 5-p.m.-to-1-a.m. shift this evening, I scurry about to get everything packed for tomorrow morning's train to Halifax. I'm still not sure how this is going to work. Ben doesn't run his life by the clock.

The next morning, Ben chooses to sleep in and wants to drink his bottle leisurely. Conor and Tori are doing their best to help Jan load the car as Clem and Marg arrive to take us to the station. At 8 a.m., I cut off Ben's breakfast. Our haste is for naught since the train is running 45 minutes late. During the reprieve, I let Ben finish his morning bottle in the noisy surroundings of the Departures Lounge.

Climbing onto the train is just as difficult as I thought it would be. As with most modes of transportation, accessibility is low priority. Conor and Tori climb the open, metal stairs from the concrete platform with excitement, speed, and agility but lifting Ben and his wheelchair generates a great deal of sweat. Staff seem to avoid us as we struggle to get on board. The narrow aisle is barely wide enough for Ben's chair and the carpeted floor provides some unwanted friction. We find a group of seats near the front of a car and spin them so they face each other. Conor and Tori are bouncing up and down as the wheels of the train unlock and a slow fluid, forward motion begins. Jan and I fall into our seats and simultaneously heave a powerful sigh.

The six-and-a-half-hour ride is uneventful and somewhat relaxing. Rocketing through the hills surrounding the Wentworth Valley of Nova Scotia, our senses are stimulated by the myriad of fall colours rushing by us. To witness this spectacular view, I take Conor and Tori into the Observation car which has a roof made entirely of windows. The seats are just high enough above the rest of the chain of rail cars for us to be able to see for miles.

After crossing the outer boundaries of Halifax's suburbs, the train slows to a crawl and continues at a jogging pace as we pass neighbourhood after neighbourhood. Our late departure and this painful last mile ensures that we will be late for Ben's first IWK appointment.

Our tardiness doesn't matter since his new dentist, Dr. Rundle, is busy with other patients. Such is the case with most doctors. The receptionist greets us with a nervous laugh as she shuffles through some folders looking for Ben's chart, attempting to register us. She tells us that the "regular girl" is on vacation in Cancun. I suppose she is trying to make us feel welcomed but I really don't care where the regular girl is, having just finished a very long train ride and Ben having been ill for the last three days.

Another hour passes before Dr. Rundle's hygienist escorts us to an examination room in order to transcribe some of Ben's medical history. Her manner of questioning is not nearly as irritating as others who have asked the same litany of questions. She seems genuinely interested. The lights are bright in this large room and Ben is fascinated by the overhead fixtures. Conor and Tori stay in the waiting room with "the new girl", entertaining themselves with colouring books and building blocks. Ten minutes later, a tiny woman, who couldn't have been more than a few years older than we are, enters the room. She introduces herself as Dr. Rundle and sits down beside us. Immediately, we can feel how suited she is to this occupation, especially for children with as many needs as Ben. Quite politely, she asks her own set of questions and is particularly interested in Jan's pregnancy. Such questions are easier to answer when they are asked by a person who cares.

She is able to examine Ben in his wheelchair, since the seat itself rests in a slight recline. She tells us that Ben's gums may be a little thicker than normal but we shouldn't worry about the rate at which his new teeth are coming in; they will come in when they are ready. Their slow rate is due to his slow development, in general, as well as a lack of regular chewing. She stresses that it is quite important to be diligent about brushing his teeth since he is still drinking from a bottle.

Continuing her examination, she notices a cut on his upper lip and his swollen glands. She also spots that the enamel is gone completely on his top two middle teeth and spotty on the bottom two. She taps them with her explorer instrument and is pleased that they are hard. Ben is unfazed by her probing. Dr. Rundle re-emphasizes that those teeth are more susceptible to decay without the enamel. We knew this but are more concerned about his second teeth, which, because they form around 7 or 8 months of age, would not be affected by CMV.

She finishes her routine by giving Ben a flouride treatment, brushing a brownish substance on his teeth. He is quite cooperative and doesn't seem to mind the intrusion; I think he is tired from his train excursion. She tells us that this substance will actually help to harden his teeth and give him a better chance of preventing decay.

As the appointment is wrapping up, Conor peeks into the room to see how much longer we will be. Dr. Rundle greets him with a warm smile and says that she is all finished, and that Ben was a great patient. Conor acknowledges her with a nod and dashes back to the waiting room to tell his sister that we are ready to go. We stop at the reception desk to sign the insurance forms and make our way to the front entrance of the hospital to catch a cab to our hotel.

The next morning arrives too early for Conor and Tori. We clumsily unload ourselves from the taxi in front of the IWK. Just inside the doors lies "The Gift Horse," a small gift shop staffed by volunteers but crammed with just the right things for a kid's attention. Though confined, the store is very bright, its large windows bordering the front entrance of the hospital allow large amounts of sunlight to add to its charm. The short and tiny aisles are packed with stuffed animals, balloons, cards, books and toys. It's difficult to manoeuver a wheelchair but is no effort for small people with tiny legs.

Immediately, Conor is drawn to the shelves with Lego. He carefully examines each box before showing Jan the one he wants. A little pricey but a small reward for spending his playtime in a hospital. Our creative Tori finds the crafts section of the store and wants to get a booklet full of tiny, shiny stickers. A few dollars will keep her happy. Always thinking of his brother, Conor chooses a brightly coloured book for Ben.

Our mood nicely boosted from this short pit stop, we shift our attention to Ben's appointment with Dr. Lavoie. This is not his regular clinic day so his waiting room has only a few people. As usual, Ben's visual acuity is tested by flashing Teller cards in front of him. Today, the nurse records a response somewhere near 20/150, which is somewhat worse than before. Several moments later, Dr. Lavoie enters the room, and is quite pleasant and talkative. He explains that he is going to conduct some tests to determine the extent of Ben's visual field. Checking his notes from our last appointment, he finds that Ben was unable to see in his lower visual field. Today he indicates that his visual field is fine.

Dr. Lavoie dims the lights in the room and holds a small pen light above Ben's head. This is entertaining for Ben, as he tracks the light's movement with ease. The lights are turned back to an annoying brightness and Dr. Lavoie wheels his stool quickly to the other side of the room to pick up some eye drops. One by one, they are deposited into Ben's open eyes. Ben blinks forcefully as he feels the pressure of each drop.

A half hour later, Dr. Lavoie is ready to examine Ben's retinas. He tells us that Ben is definitely trying to focus on things which means he is obviously seeing them, that the image is being formed on the retina. To what degree this information is getting through to his brain remains an open question, however. In his usual matter-of-fact self, Dr. Lavoie states that while Ben will never have the vision to fly an F-18 fighter jet, he is certainly not blind, and the key for us is to help to develop and optimize the vision that he does possess through constant stimulation of various kinds, especially with high-contrast things. Ben can still do a lot of things with the vision he has as long as he is encouraged to use and improve it. The doctor also recommends that when we are getting Ben to follow things, not to do it too fast. Give Ben the time he needs to focus on an image, determine that he likes it, realize it has moved, and try to focus on it again. We mention that Ben enjoys pulling off his glasses and Dr. Lavoie tells us that it is certainly fine to give him a break once in a while but suggests that we should focus whatever reward system we use to get him to keep his glasses on and, again, to get him to exercise his vision. He ends the appointment by welcoming us back in a year's time.

Ben's pupils are still hugely dilated. To avoid the brightness of the afternoon sun, we decide to wander down to the first floor Orthopaedic Clinic and take advantage of their well-equipped play area. Jan attempts to register Tori for her next-day appointment with Dr. Ramsay but the receptionist replies,

"Oh, the system won't let me do that."

I love it. Her answer is brilliant. It's the computer's fault. You can't lodge a complaint about a computer. That should just about shut down the conversation but Jan is unfazed. She asks if Dr. Ramsay might be able to see Ben right after Tori's appointment so that we wouldn't need to come down in April. Eager to pack it in for the day, the receptionist leaves us with a faint hope that this might be possible but stops short of trying to make this happen. For once, it would be refreshing to find someone with a deep sense of serving patients, especially kids like Ben (and their parents) who have traveled a lengthy distance just to make the appointment, and who would rather be any place else than at a hospital. There are plenty of opportunities for this level of service to be displayed but most are squandered.

The day is finally over. We need the rest.

The third day has another early start so that we can be on time for Tori's 8:30 a.m. appointment with Dr. Ramsay. Unlike yesterday, the clinic's waiting room is very active and filled with kids of all ages, some with casts and a few with wheelchairs. It hits me that not many of the patients are like Ben—most are here with limb fractures or for foot inserts for flat feet, like Tori.

Tori makes out fine with Dr. Ramsay, who tells us that Tori is "over-flexible," and that she has flat feet but no skeletal problems. If we go for long walks, she would benefit greatly from wearing inserts in her shoes. Very likely, the reason Tori asks to be carried often is that she is in discomfort and doesn't really know how to express it.

Jan asks Dr. Ramsay if she could examine Ben in place of his appointment next spring. Without hesitation, she accommodates our request and

Jan signals for me to bring Ben into the boxy examination room. I place Ben on his back on the noisy paper of the exam table as Dr. Ramsay greets him. She is thorough in her assessment and discovers that Ben's legs, specifically, his hamstrings, are quite tight; showing us how she can bend them only half the normal range. She recommends continuing with our regular stretching routine since it may help to increase his range of motion. However, as he grows, it's very possible that his muscles will further contract and then the only option would be surgery.

Jan helps to sit Ben up with his legs dangling over the side of the table so that Dr. Ramsay can examine his back. "It's perfect," she comments happily. Because Ben tends to sit in a frog-like manner, with his legs pushing into his hips, there is less of a chance that his hips will become dislocated, at least for now. She cautions us that if he begins to cross his legs, it might force his legs to migrate out of their hip sockets. Overall, she is pleased with Ben's progress and tells us that she would also see us in a year's time, so that we can coordinate all of his appointments over a few days.

What a great experience: another physician who is focused on her patients, devoted to serving and making things as straightforward and efficient as possible, who can appreciate the anxiety and complexity of traveling with Ben, and who actually takes the opportunity to build a healthy relationship.

*   *   *

Another fall cold

Ben does not seem annoyed by the arrival of another infection despite becoming increasingly congested over the past few days and his airways emitting an intermittent gurgling sound as if they are completely blocked. With the absence of a fever and little irritability, it is simply a bad head cold. We are determined to let him fight this one on his own.

Two evenings later, hundreds of trick-or-treaters descend on our street, stimulated by the mild air and calmness of breeze. In most years, October 31st gives us a glimpse of the biting winds of winter but tonight we are spared this discomfort. Ben is upbeat with the activity and the constant ringing of the doorbell, eager to be part of the action. Ignoring his cold, we take him into the night air so that he can collect his share of treats.

Over the next few days, however, his cold doesn't budge. With each sneeze, he is able to clear his nose of the greenish mucous and seems to have things under control. This weekend Jan has to work the overnight shift and we are a little anxious about how we will manage it all.

At 2:30 a.m. on the weekend's first night, Ben awakes, laughing, talking, and coughing. He still has a lot of junk in his throat and nose but isn't too annoyed by its weeklong presence. Alone, I gather the strength to carry him into bed with me. His eyes remain open for two straight hours despite my gentle rubbing of his back and hair. Occasionally, I drift off but prevent myself from falling asleep for too long.

He repeats his early rising the next morning, disturbed by more coughing and sneezing. It's 6 a.m. Standing over him, I realize that he is having trouble breathing, having that look he gets when he's trying to swallow and catch his breath. I pat him on the back a few times, remembering what Penny said about clasping. He coughs a few more times and begins breathing more easily. Within a few minutes, he nestles his head back into his hands and falls asleep easily.

Jan arrives home an hour later and asks how Ben's night was. She is exhausted and drops herself into bed as quickly as she can. Moments later, Ben's voice streams through the monitor, happy and contented sounds.

Somehow, we find a way to get through this weekend and Ben has fought a cold on his own.

* * *

Planning ahead

As Ben grows, we find that we are forced to make difficult decisions sooner than most young couples, forced to choose before we are ready, both emotionally and financially. If we assume that Ben will take a while longer to learn how to walk, it will become increasingly difficult and dangerous to traverse stairs with him, which means our split-level home is actually an obstacle to Ben's care; it's certainly not wheelchair accessible. Moving or building is the kind of decision that has to be made well in advance. The steps to make it a reality take months, and once you start down that road, it is nearly impossible to turn back.

After discussing this for a few weeks, Jan and I sit down one evening to browse through some magazines of home plans. I ask if we should have four bedrooms instead of three to accommodate an older Ben and an older Conor, wondering whether Conor will still want to share a bedroom with his brother when he's a teenager. Jan's eyes widen as the words spill from my mouth and her shoulders drop. Her voice quivering slightly, she asks me if I don't think that Ben will ever do very much. She tells me that she looks to me as the optimistic one and if *I* feel this way, our future with Ben is very dim.

I am blindsided that my simple question could have such an impact. All the enthusiasm has been sucked out of the room. My pragmatic, analytical self has risen to the surface, perhaps in a cold manner. But it's an important decision since it would be very difficult to add a bedroom once the house is built.

I try to pull her back to a better place by saying that I really don't know what the future holds so rather than let it pass us by, we can make plans and choose to make it better. These words are empty ones to Jan. We close the magazines in silence. No progress has been made.

The next morning is November 11th, Remembrance Day, and true to form, it is a dark and dreary day. The symbolism of the weather is eerily apt year after year, a reminder of war time, I suppose, and a harbinger of winter's quiet fury. Last evening's conversation replaying over and over in our heads does little to lighten our mood. Ben is quite tired this morning, really not interested in doing very much. I have to wonder how much of our moods he feels every day.

Jan and I consult our lawyer later in the morning about our wills. Driving to his office, we ponder whether we should reschedule when we are feeling more upbeat. We keep the appointment. It is too important. Our lives are so unpredictable.

Following this appointment, we go across the street to view some proofs of the kids from a recent photo shoot. A middle-aged woman, dressed to the nines and plastered in makeup, is our guide to help us evaluate each pose. Her remarks drip with superlatives, much like her physical appearance, complimenting us on how good our kids look, how striking their clothes are and how she really loves all the poses. The pictures are far better than I think they are going to be: Conor's red turtle neck is as bright as his smile; Ben's navy turtle neck is as subdued as his mood; and Tori's gentle arm supporting Ben's head as she kneels very comfortably beside him in her teal and blue dress, helps to join them together showing what loving siblings they are. Our mood gets a much needed boost. Perhaps *this* is a more accurate glimpse of our future.

* * *

12

CHRISTMAS TIME, REFLECTION TIME . . .

Both of us NOT leaving the city at the same time is an unwritten rule that we follow. It is based solely on our insecurity and Ben's unpredictability. We have a Christmas party to attend in Fredericton, an hour's drive away. A company event, similar to the one I longed for the day Ben was born. Tonight, it's different. The longing isn't there, the feeling of having my freedom taken away is not there. Just a desire to have a little fun. Just me and Jan. We think we've earned it. We think we've earned enough credits to temporarily suspend the rule, at least for a few hours[1].

Travelling the dark, narrow highway to the party, we are feeling upbeat and energized, looking forward to spending some relaxing time, some adult interaction time. We arrive as only the second couple, ironic since we have likely traveled the farthest. The company I work for is small, only a dozen people, and so the gathering will be more intimate and less party-like.

After some quick introductions, I call home to tell of our arrival and to check on Ben—not Conor and Tori, just Ben. They seem so capable even though they're only four and five years old. Checking on him being a hour's drive away is a bit foolhardy in a way. If he is doing fine, then that's great. If there is a problem, then there's nothing we can do to help.

---

[1]   It wasn't until Ben was 16 years old that Jan and I were able to take a
      vacation, 3,000 kilometres from home, just the two of us, our first in 22
      years of marriage.

If there is a problem, we will be trapped in an extended state of worry and stress until we get back home. So it's almost better to not even ask the question but to wait to be told only when something is wrong.

Four hours of mingling and eating allows us a small break from the lunacy of our lives. As each hour passes, I feel more and more confident, more and more relaxed (must be the wine). So what if we're 120 kilometres away. It's Christmas. A time to celebrate. Maybe we'll make a weekend out of it? What do you think, Jan? Of course, I'm kidding.

As midnight approaches, we realize that the fairy godmother's spell will be wearing off soon. Climbing into our frigid car, I suddenly feel very tired. The return trek seems longer, darker and colder. In a few weeks it will be Christmas, Ben's third, and another winter will be upon us. For a moment, I wish myself back at the party, wanting to put this free time on pause.

As the days wear on, they are becoming more and more magical. Conor's excitement is over the top and everyone can feel it. His feelings are so energizing, so exhilarating, almost 3-dimensional, a pure joy to experience. Ben is picking up on this *woo-hoo* energy level, certain that this day, Christmas Eve, is a special time.

Going to bed early is easy but falling asleep early is about as likely as being struck by lightning . . . twice! Jan and I keep their upstairs bedroom doors closed so that Santa can have some privacy. Conor and Ben's bedroom door stands directly at the end of the hall and provides a perfect line of sight to the Christmas tree on the main level living room. Tori's door is closer but being on the side of the hall it is more difficult to sneak a peak.

After getting things ready for Santa, Jan and I head to bed knowing the morning will come early. It's a such a perfect feeling; we love our lives again.

At 4:30 a.m., Conor is awake, wanting so badly to run downstairs to see what goodies are awaiting him. Sensing Conor's energy, Ben wakes up, and stays talking and laughing for a full hour. Though the early hour, Jan and I welcome Ben's excitement. It's different this time; he's not waking because he isn't feeling well or needs to be changed. This is a natural response for any toddler on Christmas Day.

All of us fall back to sleep but Conor can't wait any longer after his eyes reopen at 6:15 a.m. We let him get up and he dashes for Tori's bedroom, knocking feverishly on her door, telling her to get up. Ben is still sleeping and we let him catch a few more winks.

When Conor and Tori reach the top of the stairs, they stop abruptly. The entrance to the living room is covered in a huge roll of Christmas wrapping paper, from floor to ceiling, from one wall to the other, at least 10 feet across. They are perplexed and turn to us for an explanation. We shrug our shoulders and tell them that Santa must have done that to keep them from peeking. They are in awe that Santa would do something that cool.

They approach the paper wall with caution, not quite knowing what would be an appropriate way to open it. With her tiny fingers, Tori begins to gently pull a corner of the paper, just as she would a wrapped present. Conor mimics her but quickly grows impatient and punches a hole in the shiny gift-wrapped wall. Tori isn't impressed that he would do such a barbaric thing until she gets a glimpse of what's behind the paper. Her eyes wide with glee, she helps Conor break through to get to the tree.

Ben begins to stir as Conor and Tori cross the "Santa Threshold". I wander up to his bedroom and he is lying fully awake, his eyes gleaming, wanting to be a part of the action. The unwrapping of gifts is a great time for everyone.

By early afternoon, we arrive at my parents' house for Christmas dinner. They are happy to see everyone today, including Ben. The usual midday nap he takes is pushed aside today as his energy level runs high. Only during supper, sitting in his high chair after eating, does he begin to doze, his eyelids dropping and his head bobbing. Returning home in the early evening, Ben is still excited to be with his siblings. Even with no naps and awaking so early, he can't fall asleep until well after 10 p.m.

Boxing Day is the same—up early, no naps, vocal all day, in bed after 10 p.m.

This is the Christmas I was hoping for.

* * *

The all-too-often fallback reason

Ben's few days of boundless energy have come to a grinding halt. The congestion he was battling before Christmas, which seemed to retreat temporarily, has rebounded. This morning, he doesn't have a lot of desire to do very much.

We are able to see Dr. Campbell at the last minute, with no scheduled appointment, no doubt because he always goes out of his way to help us. We don't want to run into another holiday weekend without having Ben checked out. He is somewhat concerned by Ben's lingering cold and isn't quite sure where to begin.

After his regular examination, which really didn't provide him much in the way of clues, Dr. Campbell wants to rule out a blockage in Ben's nasal cavity and proceeds to insert a long tube into both of Ben's nostrils. We really don't know what Dr. Campbell is trying to do and can't tell Ben what to expect. Dr. Campbell just mumbles to himself and proceeds. Squirming and opening his eyes wide, Ben shows that he is in a lot of discomfort and does not like this procedure at all. Being the fighter that he is, Ben holds back any tears. Dr. Campbell can be quite rough during his examinations; this is another example.

The test is negative which does little to help reach a firm diagnosis. Seeming a bit stumped, he suggests that his latest breathing difficulties could be related to his general, compromised condition, that somehow his neurological abnormalities may be causing this. He comments that Ben's high palate may be linked, as well.

This is a bit of a downer. We are so thankful that Dr. Campbell will see us any time of day or night but it's frustrating to hear him fall back to the default reason that it's a result of CMV. Just tell us that he's not sure what the cause is. Ben's disabilities can't be the reason all of the time.

When Ben was having problems with constipation, and all he really needed was a change in his diet, Dr. Campbell thought his sluggish bowel was due to his developmentally compromised condition. And earlier this year, when Ben was losing weight and was putting all of energy into breathing, Dr. Campbell thought these were a result of his poorly developed neurological systems. In fact, this was caused by his humungous adenoids.

This time it's a lingering cold and persistent congestion. While our confidence in and respect for Dr. Campbell is unconditional, we're going to keep looking for an answer. I (hope) know he's wrong.

*   *   *

Cautious ambition

It's New Year's Eve and, after a restful sleep, Ben seems more like himself. He is interested in his morning bottle for a change, though it takes him a long time to finish it. Several times he raises his head and tries to sit up while drinking. I begin to wonder if he is tired of drinking in a reclined position after two and a half years and needs a change. Or does he need to come up for air because he is having a hard time breathing? It's so hard to know.

We have planned a holiday brunch at our house for about 30 people. Not something that Ben would get much out of so he spends a few hours with Nana while we entertain. Conor and Tori have spent the night there and are happy to see their brother.

The brunch is well attended and very invigorating. Several people ask the whereabouts of our kids. I begin feeling a little guilty for not having included them. By 2 p.m., everyone clears out and I jump back in our car to pick them up. Arriving home, Ben is quite alert, more than he has been in several days. Jan sits down on the couch to take off his jacket. He looks immediately at her, smiles, and begins to kick with excitement. I love days like today when he has so much life in his eyes.

Shortly before 4 p.m., he falls asleep just as Jan is leaving for her evening shift. He coughs off and on throughout his nap but his eyes remain closed. A little more than an hour later he awakes, though it appears that he could have slept an hour more. Picking him up, I sense that he wants to snuggle so I rock him in the living room until he is fully awake. After 15 minutes of rocking, he lifts his head, smiles at me and goos.

He plays with Conor and Tori while I clean up the kitchen and get things ready for our supper and his. They dart back and forth, playing an indoor version of tag, and each time they approach, he sits erect, smiles happily and gets increasingly excited. He really is in tune with their activity and wants to join in.

Sitting up well through his meal, Ben looks at me intently as I talk to him throughout and he seems to answer me at the appropriate times. I sign, "*My name is Daddy*" and "*Your name is Ben*" touching him when I say the word "*Your*". Hearing his name, he smiles.

The remainder of the evening is just as enjoyable and it gives me a chance to pause, to reflect, and to unwind. I guess that's a New Year's Eve thing to do. My mind races through the last year, highlighting Ben's weight loss, his breathing problems, and, of course, his first operation. I realize that the biggest achievement, by far, is the absence of seizures for the entire year. If not the toughest for me, seizures are certainly near the top of the list of things that cause me the most stress. I hope these are gone forever. Ben's anticonvulsant dosage is now less than half of what it was at the beginning of the year and, in a few months, he will be completely weaned off it. I want to keep this trend going.

After everyone is tucked in for the night, I start dreaming a little. Having him seizure-free has lifted a paralyzing burden. So many options seem available now. I jot down a few thoughts:

- Help him gain some independent movement;
- Get serious about developing a MOVE programme for him since they tell us that mobility is essential for learning;
- Get him standing every day;
- Teach him how to sit unaided, if even for only a small period of time;
- Allow Conor and Tori more opportunities to play with him;
- Never return to the dark days of that dreadful, first year!!!

* * *

The MOVE Programme

A man stands on a gravel road, in the middle of a gorgeous summer day, supporting the arms of his teenage son. The boy is standing close to his father, a huge smile on his face as he takes a step with his left leg. Ten feet behind them is his walker, steered off the road onto the grassy shoulder.

"Walking with his father is now a daily joy for Duane Bazeley," says the full-page ad in this month's *Exceptional Parent* magazine.

> "*The MOVE curriculum teaches standing, walking, and functional sitting skills to children with disabilities . . . [where] . . . appropriate movement, not static positioning, is the key to improved health and independence.*"

The imagery and its message are so uplifting, so energizing to me that I become obsessed with learning more about MOVE. I track down the publisher of this curriculum and order a copy.

Reading the first 10 pages of the large, spiral-bound text, I feel like I've died and gone to heaven. Finally, a programme that is structured, practical, and can be measured. Its underlying tenet, that mobility is essential for learning, is an awakening. It confidently describes a top-down approach to learning these skills, an approach that is counter to the common belief that one has to learn to crawl before being able to walk.

> *". . . We, in special education, are very creative and determined. We devised everything imaginable from upside-down bicycles to crawling machines. Unfortunately, none produced the desired effects of learning to crawl much less learning to walk . . . ."*

The more I read, the greater my passion grows. The words resonate so perfectly that I *know* that this is the right approach for Ben. We have to find a way to adopt its principles to his every day care and get Ben's therapists and specialists on board. We start by asking Lisa to look at the video that has accompanied the curriculum. She is willing.

Two weeks later, Ben has an appointment with Lisa. Perhaps he has been overhearing my excitement for the past month about MOVE because today he performs very well for her. She displays a curiosity about the programme, and she and Jan dive into a lengthy and open discussion about what to do for Ben. She has watched the video and shown it to a number of other therapists. She tells Jan that she believes that a number of kids could benefit from the special equipment that is described, such as a Mobile Stander, and agrees, for the most part, with the programme's philosophy. The appointment ends with a rare commitment from her to pursue this further.

We are pleasantly surprised and hopeful that we can begin a useful and successful rehabilitation path with Ben. We are somewhat dismayed that we seem to be left to discover things on our own and are puzzled that no professional seems to know much about this programme. I stumbled across it quite by chance, on the inside back cover of a magazine. Surely the professionals in the field should be aware of such programmes. I probably shouldn't care who found it, but I fear that I might be setting myself up for a fall if we're the only champions of it in our community.

Quality of life

Everything in life is relative, we are learning. What is classified as "normal" or "acceptable" or "reasonable" is done so in relation to some baseline. We have been challenged repeatedly to re-evaluate baselines, to see if they make sense. A recent tragic, headline-grabbing story has done just that.

A couple lived in Saskatchewan with their 12-year-old daughter who had multiple disabilities including cerebral palsy and epilepsy. Her 40-pound, quadriplegic frame had been operated on repeatedly over the years. She could not walk, talk or feed herself but did respond to affection and could display a smile from time to time. She was having seizures continuously and was in constant, excruciating pain. For six years straight, her parents did not get a peaceful night sleep. In October 1993, her father sat her in the cab of his truck, ran a hose from the exhaust pipe to the cab, climbed into the back of the truck and watched her die of carbon-monoxide poisoning. Today, a jury convicted the father, Robert Latimer, of second-degree murder, sentencing him to the maximum of life in prison with no chance for parole for 10 years.

Hearing this story has really disturbed me and begins to challenge my baseline for what is acceptable. Until we have experienced what Robert Latimer has experienced, we cannot begin to understand his pain. The unending weeks of colic we endured when Ben was young provides me with only a glimpse of that kind of stress and pain but it also gives me an understanding how it can leave you in an altered state. I had to deal with my child's pain for only nine weeks. Robert Latimer had to bear his child's screams for more than *six tortuous years.*

The question remains: does the father's suffering through his daughter's obviously excruciating suffering leave him the only option of ending her suffering? Though many medical and psychological experts would tell me I'm dreaming, I believe that one can never be 100% sure that his daughter would always be the way she was. Only two years into the journey of raising Ben, I have come to believe that you have to do whatever it takes, that you should never give up, no matter how difficult the journey. Something was lacking to leave the father in such a hopeless situation. Perhaps his family let him down. You certainly can't do this alone. Perhaps the community let him down. I say this as a person who has never faced his dilemma but also as a person who has the responsibility to raise a child with many, many challenges.

I cannot accept that he had the right to take the life of his child, no matter how much he or his daughter suffered, and he should be held accountable for his decision. However, looking at the harshness of his punishment, I feel even more disturbed.

Any sentence handed out should be relative to the severity of the crime. One must take into consideration how much of a threat to society Mr. Latimer is (probably none) and the likelihood that he would commit the same crime again (profoundly unlikely). I don't agree that a more lenient sentence would undermine the rights of "disabled people", as some groups have suggested. The fact that she was "disabled", whatever that means, is a red herring in this case. Mr. Latimer didn't see her as disabled but rather as his child who was suffering terribly day after day. He is "not a murdering thug", as his lawyer vehemently stated, but a person who, himself, has suffered a great deal. Is life in prison a just sentence for his actions when these same courts have handed Karla Homolka less time for the heinous, sexual offences she committed? She got 12 years for the rape and murder of three teenage girls, including her own sister, and Mr. Latimer gets a life sentence?

No one should be allowed to terminate another person's life no matter what their perceived quality of life. In my mind, it is not possible to draw the line between what is acceptable and what is not.

Relative to what?

If a person is born with a hearing loss, does that make his/her quality of life unacceptable?

Or the rare condition of being born without eyes? Is that where the line should be drawn?

The Latimers are convinced they did the right thing and have said that they believe that Tracy is now at peace.

After the sentencing, Mrs. Latimer talked to reporters and stated how loving a father Robert was, how he held Tracy for endless hours on his knee, rocking her, while she convulsed and cried and screamed and vomited, and said that no one thought that was a crime. She went on to say that when her daughter was born, she was without oxygen for a short period of time, causing all the brain damage, and no one said that was a crime.

Ben could be like Tracy, having seizures all day long. That would probably do me in.

But he isn't like her. He has so much life in his eyes—many therapists have commented on this. Some, like Genevieve, have emphasized how important it is to keep working with Ben, to repeat things many, many times. We know of children who cry all day long while others have blank stares. Not our Ben.

So how can we evaluate Ben's quality of life, a two-year-old who can't walk, talk or feed himself? It's all relative.

*   *   *

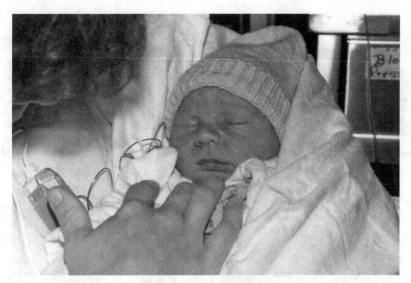

Day 2 in Mom's arms

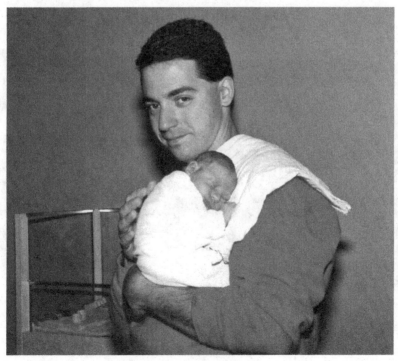

Day 4 in Dad's arms

Day 14 with big bro and sis

My new baby brother

Ben turns one

Reading Tailspin

Who says I can't lift my head

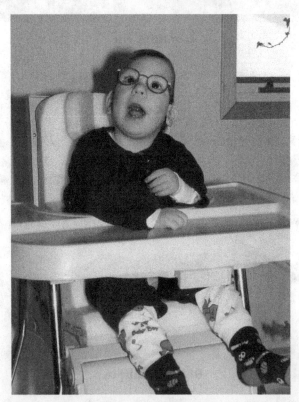

I love my ethafoam insert

Splashing at the Aquatic Centre

Sailing on the Digby Ferry

A day by the sea

A break from photo shoot (Ben at 5 yrs old)

13

THE THIRD WINTER

All night long the wind howls and the raindrops relentlessly pound every window in our house. At times, I think they're going to break through. By early morning, the intensity of this "mild" winter storm is cranked up a notch. Against the wind's ferocity, the two trees in our yard are bending uncomfortably, almost touching the snow-covered ground. The Weather Network is nothing but a red flashing screen on our TV, warning of a miserable day ahead with heavy rain and winds that could gust in excess of 100 km per hour. Looking out on our front walkway, I see that it is submerged in at least a half foot of water. The snow-cover here has melted in the above-freezing temperatures but with the ground still very frozen, the water has nowhere to drain.

A huge birthday party for Conor is scheduled at the neighbourhood bowling complex today but the sight of the weather is leaving us wondering about rescheduling it. The weather is no impediment for a six-year-old and Conor doesn't want us to cancel; he is so excited about spending the afternoon with his friends.

After Ben has had his lunch, the five Georges brave the winter whirlwinds and wade through the river of melted snow to our car. We can't use our back door because we are afraid that the lashing easterly winds would rip the storm door from its hinges. Wind is usually bothersome to Ben, sometimes taking his breath away, but remarkably it has no effect today.

Walking through the two glass doors of the bowling complex, the noise and the heaviness of the smoke-filled air are a shock to the system. Conor spies a few of his friends who have arrived early and he runs to greet them. Over the next 15 minutes, the rest of his invitees meet us, including JT, a rather tall 5-year-old. Conor has told us a few stories about JT and his behaviour problems at school, even though they are only in first grade, but Conor insisted that he be included.

Jan takes Ben into the Party Room, where later we'll be having pizza and cake, while I help to get the teams organized. I ask JT his shoe size. He responds,

"A three."

He certainly is a big boy for his age, at least a head taller than his classmates, but there is no way that his feet are that big.

"Are you sure? I think they would be too big.", I ask.

His eyes widen and, leaning towards me, he declares very emphatically,

"I said a THREE!"

Realizing that he is only five years old, I yield to his aggressive tone and calmly pass him a size three. A few minutes later, he tells Conor that his shoes are too big and I exchange them for a child's size 12.

The kindergarten teacher has told us how Conor befriended JT while many other kids have not. She is happy he did because he has had a calming affect on JT to the point where JT seems to follow Conor's example and keeps his temper in check (Such a temper at 5 years old?)

As I am relating the shoe-size story to Jan, Ben begins to get that terrified look on his face and throws out his arms. He inhales 3 short breaths very quickly and then starts coughing forcefully. Instantly, I pick him up from his wheelchair and he proceeds to throw up most of his lunch, some covering my pants but most of it splattering the soil-laden carpet of the Party Room. The pounding music and the toxic air close in around me. That sick feeling starts surging inside. I want all the noise to stop and everyone to be quiet. I just want to get out of this place.

For those few, awful minutes, I forget the importance of this day to Conor. I have no idea where Tori is. I'm consumed by Ben's episode. As my panic subsides, I glance at the bowlers and see Conor enjoying himself immensely. He is oblivious to his brother's distress and the stress level of his parents. This is *his* day, a time for him to be in the spotlight. The party carries on and Conor is making memories. Only on the drive home does he sense that Ben didn't seem to enjoy himself. We tell him that Ben was sick and he feels a little guilty that he wasn't able to help. We reassure him that it wasn't a big deal and that it was okay for him to enjoy his friends.

As Jan helps everyone remove their rain-soaked outerwear, I notice that the "message waiting" lamp is flashing on our kitchen phone. The message is from Dr. Campbell who wants to talk to us about Tori. We had taken her to see him last evening because of a recurring rash she had had on different parts of her body. Later in the afternoon, Jan is able to reach Dr. Campbell who informs her that Tori has mono, and probably has had it for the past several weeks, though she has shown no signs of the usual symptoms—fever or sore throat. He tells us that at this stage her body's defences will dissipate it on its own.

Jan asks if Ben could have contracted it last month, which might explain his behaviour in December. He did have a sore throat and was miserable for a few days. Dr. Campbell responds,

"Yeah, well, it's certainly possible. The symptoms can disappear within a few days but the virus can affect the sinuses and can last for three or four weeks. Usually, kids with mono are more tired than normal."

Yeah, it's certainly possible!

*   *   *

The frequency of these episodes

I decide to spend a Sunday afternoon with my parents since Jan is holding a baby shower for a friend. It's really more for my parents to spend some time with their grandchildren. I never know how the day will go, whether my mother will be pleasant or whether I will be made out to be the loser of the family.

With Ben and his siblings already inside, I begin my ascent up the stately sandstone steps that adorn their front entrance, carrying Ben's wheelchair and his usual gear. Living in a home that was built in the late 19ᵗʰ century, my parents are sentenced to climbing stairs. The black wrought iron railings that border the steps blend naturally with the home's architecture but are not very practical for Ben's gear. Halfway up, I see Tori on the run to tell me that Ben has ". . . spit-up." Groaning under the weight of my load, I think to myself, "Who cares?" But then I realize that she wouldn't be telling this if Ben had just spit up a little. I rush inside to discover that he has covered most of his jacket as well as a good portion of the afghan cover on the adjacent couch. He even had enough to "share" with his Grandmother.

"I was just trying to take his jacket off when he heaved and let 'er go!", my mother responds to the question I hadn't asked.

She isn't concerned about the mess. Her pretentious side must be in hiding today.

I carry Ben upstairs to my old bedroom to change his clothes. As I lay him down, he has a sad look on his face and starts to cry. I suspect his throat is irritated from throwing up and his lack of sleep from a(nother) restless night isn't helping. In what used to be my sisters' bedroom, up a third small flight of stairs, I find a rocking chair and hold him in my arms to help him fall to sleep. It takes about a half hour. During this time, Conor and Tori dart up the stairs to check on us. Though interested in their baby brother, they are still having a fun time with toys they don't get to play with very often.

Rocking mindlessly, I look around the room and begin to think back to when I was only 10 years old. Both my brother and oldest sister had moved out to attend university by that time and I think about how a lot of time spent at my parents' house was time spent by myself. It's not unlike today.

Even though I'm really not alone, I am forced to stay with Ben, separated from the happenings downstairs. I begin to think that I'm losing control again, that Ben can have an episode at any time and I am held hostage, having to suspend any planned activities and help Ben for some undetermined length of time before I get back to whatever it was I started. Sometimes a day passes me by, the many hours I could have spent with Conor and Tori, or just Jan by ourselves, are gone forever, stolen from me with no reason, no justification, and no warning.

After a good hour's nap, Ben is fine again and ready to be spoiled by my mother. She is enjoying his company today. Perhaps she's realizing that he desires to be loved like any child. I'm glad. I need the rest.

A few days later, my four favourite people pick me up from work. Conor and Tori are nestled in their usual spots on either side of Ben. He has his usual middle car-seat position that gives him an unobstructed view of the traffic in front of us. Not far from home, Jan happens to peer at him in the rearview mirror and realizes he is not right—he doesn't seem to be breathing normally and his right arm is outstretched. She pulls off into a nearby parking lot. I bump Conor out of his seat to carry Ben into the front seat with me, since there is more room. Ben is still struggling, almost panicking, and his color is poor. He coughs a few times and spits up a bit. I roll down the window to let some fresh air in, hoping its coolness will help Ben to come around. The air is very damp and heavy today, aggravated by slushy and sloppy roads.

My heart is racing not really knowing what to do. I try to listen to see how deep is his breathing but it is drowned out by a tractor trailer that has pulled up behind us, its headlights blinding us, its brakes piercing our ears, and the annoying rumble of its huge engine vibrating our seats. Ben seems to ignore this abrupt intrusion and returns to his normal complexion. Flabbergasted, I return Ben to his seat though my heart is still racing.

I hate this. I hate everything about this. That's two episodes in one week. It's stressful enough to respond to another episode but it's too much for me to have it happen on the drive home. Without warning or consideration, it just happens.

What if we were on a trip, miles from the nearest town, and he didn't come around? What would we do? Can we even consider taking another trip? Just as I was trapped upstairs at my parents' home on Sunday waiting for him to be all right, am I now trapped within the city limits? For how long?

*   *   *

A frightening weekend

The alarm buzzes at 5 a.m., waking most of us. Jan is heading to Rhode Island for a late-winter, four-day getaway with Conor and Tori, and they want to get an early start. I really can't believe how awake they are at such an early hour. After pulling on their snow suits and boots, they eagerly dart outside and jump on their swing set. Our backyard is still a winter wonderland, still enveloped in a deep blanket of snow. The sky is as dark as night and a northerly wind is producing quite a chill. The swing seats nearly touch the snowy floor but that doesn't stop them from swinging as high as they can.

By 5:45 a.m., they back out of the driveway and head stateside. Ben and I will stay home this time. It's too far a journey for only a few days. Ben is very peaceful, unaware of the departure of his siblings at this pre-dawn hour. I climb back into bed for another hour of sleep.

Lying there hearing nothing but the ticking clock and Ben's rhythmic breathing in the monitor, I remember two years ago when Jan went to Rhode Island with her sister, her mother, Tori, and Trish, a neighbour and good friend. Jan needed the break. But I remember having to take

Ben by myself to see Dr. Campbell and how terrible Ben really was that weekend. Closing my eyes, I pray for an quiet weekend this time but I can't seem to relax.

Not long after falling asleep, I hear Ben cry out. Rushing into his room, I discover that he is wide awake, his arms outstretched. He has *the clutches* and a scared look on his face. I quickly pick him up and he calms down. My mind starts to race. With every event like this, I still think about when will be his next seizure. These anxious thoughts are always just below the surface—I can't seem to get rid of them. I don't think I could deal with a seizure by myself. How would I get him to the hospital?

As the day wears on, Ben is reasonably happy, though a little tired. Me too. When darkness falls, a wave of anxiety begins to build even though Ben isn't acting up. There are days when I wish I could be alone and have time to myself. But when I am alone, I wish I weren't. I realize that I cannot enjoy being by myself. I need my family. I am missing Jan, Conor and Tori, even though they only left this morning. I don't know what I want.

Ben enjoys his bath in the evening but doesn't have the energy to kick or try to squirm out of my arms as he usually does. A year ago, I would have said that this lack of activity was normal for him. Not now. My heart aches with so much desire to keep him learning and progressing. Some days I feel like I can make a real contribution toward that and some days, like today, I feel completely powerless to do anything. The more he achieves, the more achievements I want him to reach and the faster I want them to become real. But never far away is a sick feeling that he could completely regress in an instant, that we're just one seizure away from him losing all skills and we'll be back in PICU forever. Tonight, these fears are bubbling over and I can't contain them. I have the log nearby, just in case. My premonitions turn out to be true:

> **3:10 a.m.:** Friday. Ben wakes suddenly and cries. Up until then, his sleep has been peaceful. To avoid having to get up every few minutes, I bring him in bed with me and he settles.

5:00 a.m.: He wakes again with a start and throws his arms out. I calm him by rubbing his back and talking softly. He settles only briefly and does it again. This continues in 10-minute intervals for the next two hours.

6:55 a.m.: With only a few hours sleep, my head is really hurting, my eyes are hard to open and my gut is not right. Without warning, Ben screams out—not crying, but screaming—and starts throwing up. The small towel beside his pillow is not large enough to catch the volumes of yellow bile spewing from him. His eyes are watery, red and terrified, and his face is blotchy. My panic rushes back.

7:45 a.m.: After settling for about 20 minutes, Ben wakes abruptly again and throws up. There's not much to come up but his helpless body continues to retch. I'm really concerned about his screaming: he's making sounds that I have never heard him make before. I want to cry myself. I am worried that I will need to take him to the hospital if he doesn't stop throwing up, fearful that he is quickly becoming dehydrated. In an instant, I am returned to our North York hospital visit of two years ago. The difference today is that I am alone. How would I be able to get him to the hospital by myself? He would have no energy to sit in his car seat. I don't want Jan to know how awful things are and how messed up I am but I'm not sure I can deal with this by myself.

8:45 a.m.: Lonnie arrives for her morning routine. She is a new person in Ben's life, a human-services counselor who works with him a few hours a week. I use the opportunity to run out to get some *Gravol* for Ben.

9:10 a.m.: I'm back home and call Dr. Campbell. The pharmacy didn't have children's *Gravol* and I need to know how much Ben can have of the adult product. Within 15 minutes, Dr. Campbell calls back—thank you, Dr. Campbell! He tells that Ben can have the entire 25 mg suppository: the worst that could happen is it will make him sleepy.

9:45 a.m.: Ben is able to drink two ounces of juice and keep it down. My fears ease a bit. With Lonnie still here, I jump in the shower to be ready for the rest of the day.

10:55 a.m.: He falls asleep.

12:15 p.m.: He awakes suddenly and once again has *the clutches*. I pick him up and he calms easily. A few minutes later, he lets out some very deep and painful burps. His lips are dry and thirsty, and he willingly drinks a little more than 6 ounces of juice. For the next two hours, he continues to show his discomfort from the waves of pain, alternating between crunching his torso and outstretching his arms.

2:15 p.m.: He is becoming vocal, almost telling me that he is hungry. Obviously, apple juice isn't cutting it for him; he wants something more despite his pains. I take a chance and give him a bottle of Isomil, unsure whether he will heave it. He welcomes the whole bottle.

3:00 p.m.: He hasn't wet in several hours. I try to reason with my anxious self not to be concerned about dehydration as long as he continues to drink and keep it down.

3:30 p.m.: He is squirming in his seat. As I get closer, I can see that he has soaked through his clothes. His diaper has overflowed. For the next hour, I sit him between my legs on the floor and we watch some cartoons. It is more for my benefit than his. I can't remember if I've had anything to eat today. Before I get his supper ready, I make myself a peanut butter and jam sandwich—comfort food.

5:15 p.m.: No naps for either of us today. The stress of the past 36 hours is making me a little fuzzy. I feel grungy from fatigue and my eyes feel like they're crusting over. Without thinking, I feed Ben a full serving of sweet potatoes and apple sauce for his supper. He readily consumes it and his energy level jumps noticeably.

6:45 p.m.: I change him into his jammies and give him his evening bottle of *Isomil* (the one that used to contain *phenobarb*). He seems to hit the wall half an hour later. I rock him until he falls asleep.

8:00 p.m.: He is sleeping in his crib. I tiptoe downstairs, hoping we can both get some sleep.

9:00 p.m.: I climb into bed myself, totally exhausted. Tonight is Michael Jordan's homecoming and I tune in to take my mind to a better place. I can't get there.

9:15 p.m.: Ben cries out in pain and continues to have *the clutches*. A short time later, our realtor calls to tell me that someone wants to view our house tomorrow. I gather what little strength I have not to unleash my anger and tell him off. Of course, he would have no idea, not even a whiff of the stress I'm going through, so I simply tell him that Monday would be better. Right now, I don't care if we ever sell our house.

1:00 a.m., Saturday: After tending to him twice an hour, I decide to sleep in Conor's bed. I'm not sure why I didn't think of this earlier. I pass out. Thinking I've been asleep for hours, I fling open my eyes and jump to my feet with my heart thumping through my chest. It's only 2 a.m. I wander back to my own bed, hoping that Ben will continue to sleep. Before I can close my eyes though, he wakes up, cries and clutches. How did he know I wasn't there? I bring him in with me and try to cuddle him.

3:00 a.m.: I give him another *Gravol* suppository since it had worked earlier in the day. Each time he rolls onto his back, the pain returns and *the clutches* begin. I prop myself up in bed into a half sitting position with him resting on my shoulder. It seems to work. It's nearly impossible for me to fall asleep in this contorted position but Ben is comfortable. As I try to sleep, I am startled by a weird sensation of falling. It's kind of exhilarating and scary at the same time. This sensation jerks my wiped-out body and wakes Ben. I last in this way for about an hour and give up.

4:30 a.m.: I put him back into his crib, just about at my wits' end. I'm not going to make it. He continues to wake up every 20 minutes and I feel my body shutting down.

5:35 a.m.: He cries out and throws up some yellow bile, but no gut wrenching screams and outstretched arms.

6:40 a.m.: He wakes for the day and appears to be quite happy. I'm not sure I can take another day like yesterday. My mouth tastes foul and my fiery red eyes are burning like never before. I have reached my limit.

I can't write any more in the log.

Late morning, I get some relief from a neighbour. Despite my exhaustion, I just have to get out of the house for an hour. I have to see other people, feel the winter air, anything for a distraction, anything to help me recharge.

The day progresses well: no more heaving; no more crying; no naps; just a hint of *the clutches*; a little smiling; a little kicking. I talk to Jan and tell her to stay until tomorrow. It will take her nine hours to get home no matter when she leaves so staying another night won't make a difference to me. I tell her the worst is over.

Ben is in bed by 9 p.m., just in time for me to catch the opening period of *Hockey Night in Canada*. An hour passes before he calls out to me. The *clutches* are still there but tonight he is consoled by a few minutes of gentle back rubbing.

The night is not peaceful. He wakes every hour but without the intensity of distress of the past few days. A simple stroking of his hair or changing of his position helps him settle.

By Sunday afternoon the Rhode Island travelers are home. Ben is having his best day of the past four. He is very excited to see everyone and so am I. My anxiety disappears. My relief is intense. Everything is intense these days. The terror of Friday and Saturday seems like a million miles away.

I wonder, though, what long-term damage these past 80 hours might have done to me.

* * *

14

A GOOD SUMMER TO COME

Like a couple of reckless teenagers, Jan and I bound out of bed at 4 in the morning. Marg has offered to stay for the day with the kids so Jan and I can take a crazy 18-hour excursion to Freeport, Maine. As long as we're back for bedtime, it shouldn't make any difference where we are.

We get on the road with haste, crossing into the U.S. at 5:10 a.m. local time. There's not much activity at this time of the day and the border guard is quite jovial—this is a first. After needing a "bio break," we find ourselves on Main Street in downtown Freeport, in front of LL Bean. Right where we were last summer, in the same spot that Ben and I stopped for a drink. I miss him right now.

It doesn't seem real that Jan and I are alone, in another city, in another country, with no kids, not even Ben. Aren't we just asking for trouble? But really, haven't we earned some much needed time away? I think we're quite clever, actually.

We eagerly take in as much shopping and eating as we can afford. The six-and-a-half hours we spend in this tranquil state seem like six-and-a-half minutes. I feel like all burdens have been lifted. I like this feeling. It's intoxicating. Is that what life would be like without kids? Without Ben?

The drive back is not nearly as much fun as the one early in the morning. There is no anticipation, no childlike excitement. I wish we had a Freeport just around the corner. We are both ready for bed as we cross back into Canada at a few minutes past 9 p.m. Jan checks in with her mother who tells us that Ben was sick just after supper. Her description sounds all too familiar of his recent episodes. The exhilaration of the day comes crashing down around us, like somehow we have been punished for enjoying ourselves so much. The dark evening sky turns even darker.

Jan starts talking about how these episodes are happening more often, that she thinks they really are seizures. I shake my head: I don't want to hear that. I want to be back in Freeport, right now. Forever. What is most troubling is that no one can say that they definitely are seizures or they definitely are not seizures. Someone needs to figure this out.

Fatigue is rapidly taking over. Jan asks me if I ever think about what things will be like for us and Ben 20 years from now. I don't respond. I can't. It doesn't matter what I think. I just want to get home. She says that we will eventually have to get someone to look after Ben. Ten years from now, when he's 12 years old, Marg won't be able to look after him, as she can now, unless he is able to do more. It's a rhetorical statement and one I can't deal with at the moment.

Tonight, we are reminded that we are still on call 24 hours a day, every day. There are no breaks, no one to take over, only those to "mind the store" temporarily. We are held captive. Anything can happen.

*   *   *

Unconditional support

Sitting in an uptown restaurant, I hear the dissonant warble of a pager. I don't recognize that it's really mine making that sound and am a bit confused in the midst of placing my lunch order. I keep a pager strapped to me whenever I'm out, in case I'm needed for Ben. Few people are aware of the number so it's not often used. Realizing that it's my call, I snap it out of its holster and see the burning numbers "**911**-692-4140." This isn't an errant caller since we use the 911 prefix to indicate that there's something wrong with Ben but I don't recognize the call-back number.

It turns out to be my neighbour Vanessa. She and her husband, Ken, along with their collie Sydney, live across the street from us. They have two grown daughters who have since started their own families. Our kids love to play with Sydney, and Vanessa and Ken are always welcoming for us to stop by and chat. My conversation, today, is a much different story. In one run-on sentence, Vanessa tells me that Ken has rushed Jan and Ben to the hospital, that Ben wasn't breathing well, that he has vomited and there was some blood in it. The color drains from my face and I am overcome with that all too familiar helpless feeling. Once again, my day's plans are postponed, my life has been put on hold.

Since I am without a vehicle, Rod, my lunch partner, offers to drive me to the hospital. He cancels his lunch plans as well, and wants to help in any way he can. Even though he is technically my boss, our relationship goes well beyond that. Rod tries to carry on a conversation during the drive but I don't feel much like talking. "*Blood in his vomit,*" is all I can hear.

Pulling up in front of the ER entrance, I see Ken waiting in his car. I wave to him and rush through the doors to find Jan. She is sitting on a chair near the back of the ER, talking to an intern. The ER is very busy, very full for a weekday afternoon, packed with elderly patients. Ben is asleep in Jan's arms. I return to find Ken and Rod to tell them they don't have to wait. Ken insists that I call him when we are ready to come home and he will come out to get us. Rod interjects, quite proudly in fact, emphasizing how great a neighbour Ken is to us. Believe me, I know!

Back inside, I find Jan and Ben in an examination room. The intern wants Ben to have a chest X-ray. Jan responds that she isn't keen on doing this, that Ben has done this before and never had any problems breathing. We have no hesitation in stating our opinion. A year or two ago we would have submitted to the X-ray. Since Dr. Campbell is at his clinic in Sussex, we tell the intern that if Dr. Norris is in the hospital, we would like to speak with him. Without much resistance, he pages Dr. Norris.

I ask Jan what had happened. She says that he was having a nap on the basement floor and woke up with that awful look and his eyes bouncing but this time, he didn't come round. She asked Tori to run over to Ken and Vanessa's house for help. Our five-year-old acting like an adult! Ken hurried back with Tori and asked if he should call 911. Jan said that she thought it would be better if they just went to the hospital.

I ask her about the blood in his vomit and she realized it was from his gums where he is cutting a huge back molar. "Of course," I reply. "It bled the night before while I was brushing his teeth." Instant relief!

As we are finishing our conversation. Dr. Norris enters the room. After listening to our story, he tells us that it's difficult to know what is happening. It may be that if we try something the episodes would stop but there's no way to know for sure whether or not the incidents will stop on their own without any treatment. He tries to reassure us that while these can be quite disruptive, they're likely not serious. Applying his conservative, non-invasive philosophy, he recommends that we wait it out a little while longer and keep monitoring the incidents, as we have been doing. He explains that if it's reflux-related and a small piece of food gets stuck, the larynx constricts and blocks off the air, which causes the person to panic. Once they relax, the larynx expands and the food may slide back down on its own, although you don't want to just wait around while he is gasping for air, either.

By 2:15 p.m., we climb into a cab and head home. I hate the ER, I hate having to stop everything, but today the overwhelming feelings don't linger.

In the evening, I speak with my sister, the family doc, about these episodes. She suggests that we monitor how long it is after he eats that the episodes occur, and whether or not what he brings up is recognizable even in terms of color. She thinks that his stomach may not be emptying as well as it should, which is not unusual for kids with cerebral palsy. The increase in these incidents over the last month may be a result of the flu he had in March. Even though the bug is gone, it may have left some irritability that could take several months to settle down. This conversation mildly helps to quell my fears but it's still full of "maybe" and "perhaps" and "could be" . . .

Thinking about how Tori reacted today is another reminder just how special our kids are. Imagine, having the courage to run over to a neighbour's house to find Ken, and then being comfortable enough to stay with Vanessa while Jan is at the hospital. And the support and kindness of our neighbours: it's unconditional. I learned later in the day that Ken was preparing for his daughter's wedding at the time, which is only two days away, and yet he was willing to drop everything, take Jan to the hospital, and wait for as long as necessary. Having such an incredible network of support is the only way we survive.

*   *   *

Counting my blessings

Springtime is music festival time in our part of the world and today is Conor's first foray into this annual competition. A year ago, his piano teacher was reluctant to take him on as a student since he was only five, but today she is quite proud of his talent.

After sitting through 32 renditions of the same piece, after seeing 32 six- and seven-year-olds march up on stage to perform, Jan and I are becoming a little stir crazy and so is Conor. I can see him crawling in and out of his seat in the front row of the large auditorium, in plain view of everyone, acting like a puppy in the "Dalmatians" song each child has just played.

The adjudicator seems oblivious that these young children have remained in their seats for the past 75 minutes and takes her time speaking and praising most. None of these budding artists are the least bit interested in what she has to say . . . until she begins reading the marks. Somehow they know that's what everyone has been waiting for . . .

". . . Teresa Gallant, 82, Conor George, 90 . . ."

What? A 90? No one gets a 90. I played in the festival for years and the highest I could muster was 83. This is his first time. He's the youngest in his class and gets the highest mark. Jan and I are stunned. I get goose bumps. The positive energy rushing through us is spine-tingling. All of Ben's problems don't matter right now. I want to freeze this moment forever, bottle it somehow so I can take a little drink the next time we feel overwhelmed.

A few days later, Conor's picture is in the newspaper, his oversized clip-on tie slightly askew and tucked under his smiling face. Some of my co-workers mention seeing the photo and I beam. They sense my pride. I am thankful that I can still enjoy Conor's achievements.

*   *   *

"Just like that!"

Walking through our back door, I instantly know something is wrong. Jan had just received a phone call from Faith, the specialist who is looking after Ben's seating needs. She has told Jan that she would not be looking after Ben anymore since she is pregnant and doesn't want to put herself at risk of catching CMV.

Here we go again. We would have thought that Faith would be the kind of person to get informed before making such a decision. This is pure emotion talking.

It's unfair; it's discriminatory; and it's misguided. Ben stopped shedding the virus more than two years ago and she *knows* that. It's no different than saying since you had the flu two years ago, I can no longer be your care-giver because I might somehow catch it. It is complete nonsense.

I want to scream.

How can this be allowed to happen . . . again?

What about Ben? Is no one concerned about his care and development? Or feel an obligation to help him?

Is accountability completely absent from the system? Is her organization not accountable for anything? Can you just show up for work and collect your pay every two weeks regardless of whether or not you are helpful? Someone needs to answer for this. The public health system is so bloated and so complex that no one really knows what's going on. It would do no good to speak with Faith's supervisor, if we could even find out who that person is. Faith has checked out, just like Sandra did in Toronto, so there's no point in forcing her to help Ben.

How is it possible that we can be left hanging? Just like that!? Again!

My gut is churning. My frustration level is off the scale. I have to find a way to cool down and channel my energy into something productive. Like an obsessed madman, I search frantically for the phone number of Dr. Forester, the infectious-disease specialist at Sick Kids. I get through to her on the first try. In a very angry and rapid tone, I ramble on about what had just happened and ask her to fax me some material about CMV and how it is spread.

She sympathizes with me and offers to call the head of the hospital, if I thought that would help. I tell her that I'm not sure if her efforts would go very far.

I feel like driving over to Faith's office to telling her exactly what I think. She, like so many others, have this false sense of security that if they choose to NOT work with Ben, they won't catch CMV. Doesn't she realize that it's pointless to avoid Ben since nearly 80% of toddlers could be carrying the virus at any time? That for every child like Ben who has shown symptoms, there are 10 more who are also carrying the virus but do NOT exhibit any symptoms? Didn't I go through this same rationalization when Sandra quit?

How does Faith think Jan contracted it? It wasn't from working with kids like Ben! What am I saying? What are ". . . kids like Ben . . ."?

Let's go right back to the 1960s and throw everyone with a disability into an institution, and let them lie around in beanbag chairs, staring at the ceiling, with no social interaction, and then wonder why they don't develop. Everyone is so backward in this town!

I still haven't found an outlet for my frustration.

* * *

The "chicken pucks"

Tori runs into our bedroom, both excited and a little worried, as she exclaims, "*I got the chicken pucks!*" It was just a matter of time since Conor first brought them home two weeks ago. She has witnessed his itching, scratching and general misery so she's not quite sure how to feel. The only thing running through my mind is, when will it be Ben's turn? He has been on a streak of very good, very energetic days. Make that very good *weeks*. Perhaps the virus is taking over our household at the right time.

Just days before the first few pox appeared on Conor's chest, we were enjoying a wonderful weekend at the Camp. It was Ben's first visit since he was very young and the first time he had ever stayed overnight. We all enjoyed the freedom of the natural, wide-open spaces, the grassy fields that roll in all directions, the fast moving brook that rushes past at the bottom of a small embankment, and the evening air that was still free of blackflies and mosquitos. Ben especially enjoyed sitting under the Centennial maple tree (planted in 1967, Canada's centennial year). He enjoyed taking in the expansive blue skies overhead while occasionally watching me practice my chip shots onto a makeshift green. It was unusually relaxing. That was then. The chicken pox are now!

The day after Tori made her discovery, I notice a small, raised, red blemish on Ben's neck. Great! That didn't take long! It makes itself known as he battles through one of his episodes. So now we have reflux (or is it a seizure?) plus the chicken pox.

Throughout the night, he is very restless, waking up every other hour, and his body is very warm, a sure sign of the virus. By morning, he is displaying more marks and the one on his neck is starting to blister. During the day, he isn't too irritable, though quite listless. By evening, he has them everywhere, even in his ears, and can wear only one hearing aid. Before bed, we give him a "baking soda" bath to help with the itch. It seems to work.

The second night is as disruptive as the first, with Ben waking up several times and burning up. I'm sure he must be itchy and can't relieve himself.

Day 3, he is not very irritable through the day and eats quite well. Bath-time is another baking-soda soak. But bedtime is a whole different story. He doesn't sleep much at all, crying out every 10 minutes. His fever is little higher tonight, over 39°C. Rather than get up a thousand times, I let him sleep with us but it doesn't stop his crying. Only picking him up provides any sort of comfort. He finally closes his eyes at 4:30 a.m. but only for an hour.

By Thursday, Day 4, we realize that it's not going to be the disaster that we feared. It has been exhausting but nothing we haven't done before. We know this achy, chronically tired feeling all too well. Our minds are blurry and slow to react, small events and our emotions become over-exaggerated, but there are no spirals of worry or heart-stopping events. Perhaps it is because we have had time to prepare. We know the cause this time and we know the timeline.

Despite having so little sleep, Ben is measurably more energetic today but his little body is plastered with the pock marks. During the afternoon, he begins to show his irritability once again. I am home early from work so that Jan can take Tori to her dance rehearsal. At supper, his appetite is reasonable but he doesn't want to be left alone for very long. Each time I leave the room, he whines or moans or cries. As soon as I return, the whines turn to smiles and tiny laughs.

Day 5, his body is still a mess but some of the pox are actually starting to dry up. Tonight is Tori's dance show and we can't miss it. Jan takes her early and I get Ben fed, bathed, and in his jammies by 7 p.m. Lonnie has offered to stay with Ben so that we can see the show. The show is wonderful, Tori is a natural, and Ben is starting to feel better.

* * *

These are the moments

The end of May brings the end to the chicken pox, the end of Tori's pre-school year, and the end of Conor's first spectacular piano season. The morning sunshine is warm and summer-like as Tori and I walk through our yard towards the neighbourhood pre-school she has attended for the past nine months. Today is graduation day.

The pre-school is in the basement of a neighbour's home. Mary, the school's owner and only employee, eagerly greets the graduating class of 1995, all 15 of them. It's really not something Ben would enjoy, and it would be nearly impossible to get him down the basement stairs.

The room is a bit crowded but all the parents manage to fit in the audience chairs while the students, outfitted in cap and tassel, neatly file into their respective seats. Jan and I are really enjoying this moment. Conor is at school, Ben is with Lonnie, and we can focus on Tori, revelling in her achievement, even though it is only pre-school. To her, it's a big deal and she holds herself very proudly through it all. When the ceremony is complete, Tori dashes up the basement stairs and waves a final goodbye to Sebastian the porcelain gnome who stands outside the basement door. She's growing up much too fast.

As evening approaches, so does Conor's piano concert. Actually, it's not *his* concert, it's a year-end celebration hosted by his music teacher at a local elementary school. The main foyer is packed with people, some standing, some chatting, and others heading to the gym to get a good seat. Kids of all ages are constantly moving about. The only access to the gym is down a dozen stairs. In fact, the building's only means of access at the front is up more stairs. Such was the norm of public structures built in the 1960s. Fortunately, Ben is still small so that carrying him is manageable. If we had brought his wheelchair, we would have been stuck in the parking lot.

Once inside the gym, Ben's eyes are wide as he gazes at the extremely high ceilings. The gym floor is glistening as the evening sun carefully illuminates the back wall, blazing through the large windows that seem to touch the sky. As the start time nears, everyone quickly gathers in their seats, like a large game of musical chairs, and the chatter settles to a few whispers. Conor's piano teacher briefly welcomes everyone and introduces the first soloist.

Each piece is short and very well done. The range of ages and grade levels provides a unique variety of melodies and moods. Ben really behaves himself tonight, too. When it comes time for Conor to play, I lean over to Ben and whisper to him to get ready for his brother's song. His rendition is as perfect as his music festival performance.

This is a proud moment for everyone, even my parents, who managed to make it on time. It is a normal event that our whole family is able to attend, just as we would have done had Ben not been "Ben."

*   *   *

No real commitment

After yesterday's exhilarating celebration of Tori's and Conor's achievements, I am eager to meet with Lisa today to talk about the MOVE Programme, to begin paving the way for Ben's achievements. Lisa is bit preoccupied today, turning our discussion about milestones and assessments into one about a specialized stander she has brought in to try with Ben. This *Giraffe Stander* is not one of the pieces of equipment recommended by MOVE but we go along with her line of thinking.

Looking at it from the side, I notice that the straps don't appear to be attached properly and the frame is leaning backwards. It doesn't look right. We try Ben in it but the prompts and the tray are much too high. He is clearly not very comfortable. Lisa looks lost, unable to figure out what to do next. She mentions that it is made by *Snug Seat*, a manufacturer that she is already familiar with, and thought it would be an appropriate piece of equipment.

Without any instruction manual, I try to figure out how to adjust the collection of knobs, levers, and pads. It is obvious that she doesn't know how to put it together, and I am getting a little annoyed that I'm using up Ben's appointment time to adjust this deficient piece of equipment.

With the hour nearly over, there is little time to talk about the MOVE Programme. Lisa very clearly displays her reluctance to use the equipment it recommends, listing a number of concerns that sound rehearsed. Repeatedly, she tells us that she doesn't really want to spend money on the programme's equipment because it may not work.

Even more frustrated, I get defensive and ask, "What do you mean by ' . . . *it may not work* . . . '? How do you measure whether or not something works or not?"

She is clearly not liking my question or my tone. Too bad, I say to myself.

Not realizing that Jan isn't liking my tone either, I continue down this path. I explain that, from my point of view, if we set some clear objectives up front, only then can we say whether there has been progress or not.

"If Ben advances only one step in one category of the Programme, I would say that he has made progress and that it worked." I tell her quite emphatically.

I want to say that if nothing else, it is a structured programme with a beginning and an end, unlike what we've been doing for the last three years. I catch myself before becoming completely rude.

We agree to write up a list of questions and she will contact the Programme's school board in California to find out more, and hopefully that will alleviate her concerns.

On the ride home, Jan tells me how rude I was to Lisa, and that if I think that she's going to help us after that approach and attitude, then I'm sadly mistaken.

Angrily, I respond, "Why *can't* we follow the programme? Why *can't* we find someone to help us, support us, encourage us? Someone who is engaged?"

No response.

"We've spent three years with nothing in place. She doesn't have a creative bone in her body and is obviously set in her ways. I don't need a 9-to-5 person, who puts no extra effort into her job. She should have known how to put that stander together. She is always looking for us to bring in interesting toys. What is she getting paid to do? There's never any structure, never a plan!"

I'm getting angry with the wrong person.

Lisa's behaviour is representative of an outdated way of thinking that just doesn't produce results, the very reason why MOVE was developed. I am dying to find someone who would take an interest in helping Ben achieve some real, measureable, physical milestones. I would have thought that, as a physiotherapist, she would have at least been aware of MOVE.

It shouldn't be up to the parents to recommend what treatment should be done. We have enough things to worry about with Ben. And I shouldn't be the one to tiptoe around people's feelings or personalities.

We seem to be stuck in this land of mediocrity where no one strives for excellence. No one has to, no one is paid to do so, and so it doesn't happen.

*   *   *

A day "by the sea"

I am still fuming about that ridiculous appointment with Lisa. Jan has mellowed a bit and wants to do something fun with the kids. I follow along. We decide to take an hour's drive to the seaside resort of St. Andrew's. It is a true tourist attraction with a population that swells dramatically in the summer months. With its relatively inexpensive properties and a favourable currency exchange, the coastal town is an ideal vacation destination for our American neighbours.

We search for an accessible parking spot, winding our way down Main Street and scanning the dozen side-streets that are bursting with tiny "shoppes." The weather is cliché picture-perfect, the temperature topping 25 degrees with a high heat index, way above seasonal for the 4th of June.

Ben needs to be fed and we find a wonderful playground near an elementary school to park ourselves. There is not a soul around, which suits Conor and Tori just fine. Dotted with large maples, the playground provides some welcome shade and Ben eagerly devours his lunch.

As Ben is digesting, Conor and Tori find a huge tire swing and take turns spinning each other and rocking wildly together, at times their bodies nearly parallel to the ground. The adjacent jungle-gym, well-constructed with large railway ties, has them climbing, crawling and hanging when they're not swinging. At the other end of the playground is a set of baby swings. Jan carefully seats Ben in one of them. With only the straps of the swing to secure him, Ben dangles without holding on. A few gentle pushes and he is swinging by himself, smiling and giggling with each flow of the pendulum-like motion. The day is a huge contrast to only a few days ago, but that's become the pattern of our life—Ben's back-and-forth motion is an uncanny metaphor.

Conor tells me he's thirsty. Time to leave. We gather our things and walk towards the main shopping area. I take Conor and Ben to find a drink while Jan and Tori find a craft store, located near one of the wharves. We catch up with them looking at winter items! There are three tables full of hand-made hats, mitts and scarves. We find a hat for Ben that is a perfect fit and pounce on the lucky find. It's just about impossible to find age-appropriate hats for his smaller-than-normal head. Good find, Tori!

With our shopping complete, we explore the wharf, sauntering along its wide and uneven wooden planks. The day is gorgeous. Conor peeks over the edge of the wharf, watching the small waves lick against the wharf's support beams. He is intrigued how the beams seem to disappear into the water.

Approaching the end of the wharf, we line up the kids to take a few pictures against a backdrop of small sailing vessels and cozy seaside cottages. The sun, radiating from the brilliant blue cloudless sky, is bright, bright, bright, in Ben's eyes. He turns his head so his cap can act as a shield. Quite clever. He gets it! No one can tell me that he doesn't understand everything that goes on around him!

Both Conor and Tori stand on either side of his wheelchair, with Tori pulling up her right leg, holding it with her hand, and balancing against Ben. She stands there confidently in her white blossom hat, dotted with raspberries and headlined with a pink bow, together with matching overalls and a hot pink short-sleeved cotton tee. Standing proudly beside his brother, Conor smiles widely, donning a fluorescent, lime green hat that is one size too big and a not quite matching teal tee. A picture-perfect pose.

Making our way back to the car, Jan and I ponder the possibility of coming down here for a weekend in the summer and staying in one of the inns with waterfront balconies. On this unspoiled afternoon, we feel like we can do almost anything, go almost anywhere with Ben. A year ago, Ben was putting all of his energy into breathing because of his adenoids, and now he is putting his energy into enjoying a day trip to St. Andrew's.

I wish every day were like this one.

* * *

Do we need to refocus?

The following weekend, Conor is not himself. His intermittent cough of recent days has grown worse and it appears he has developed a wicked cold. Jan asks Conor to pick up his dirty clothes in his room. He blurts out something unintelligible and then says,

"I can't do anything right. When I was trying to sell Uncle Walter a box of almonds and asked him for the money before I gave it to him, Nana made a big deal out of it and then everyone laughed at me."

What? Uncle Walter? That was back in the fall when he was fundraising for school. I know he is feeling lousy tonight but what brought that on? Jan and I calm him, and ask what is bothering him. He doesn't want to talk about it. As he leaves the room, Jan and I talk about the bad dreams he has been having lately and the scary thoughts about monsters, and about people taking me and Jan away from him. Perhaps the unseen stress that has grown over the last few years is taking a toll on him.

We certainly have never "babied" our kids, partly because we haven't had the time. But we also talk about a lot of adult things in front of them, perhaps too much. In the paper today, there was a story about an eight-year-old girl in Fredericton getting on an all-terrain vehicle with a stranger who later raped and killed her. And last week, Conor told of a classmate who wasn't at school for several weeks and was found on the west coast with his recently divorced father. In the mind of a six-year-old, these stories can be overwhelming.

Were we cheating them of their childhood? Were we spending too much time with Ben and expecting too much from the other two? In many ways, it's as if we have had a newborn for the last three years because we have to do so much for Ben. Maybe this is a bit of a wakeup call. Ben's care is important but it can't come at the expense of Conor and Tori.

Conor needs our attention tonight. He needs to be at the front of the line, now.

The next morning, Conor is miserable and, perhaps, even a little worse. Getting ready to leave to meet Dr. Campbell, Conor is overcome with nausea but has the presence of mind to run upstairs to the bathroom. His face is flushed and he is burning up. Several minutes later, we arrive in the hospital's parking lot. He lets go again and throws up on the ground. He is in rough shape and begins to sob off and on. This is such an unusual state for him. He's not supposed to get sick—only Ben is.

Once inside, the triage nurse takes his vitals—he has a fever of 40.5°C! My God, it can't be that high! She gives him some Tylenol. After having his blood taken and a chest X-ray, we get to see Dr. Campbell. Conor is not in the mood to be examined and cries a lot. He isn't his typical self. The insides of his ear canals are a fiery red, indicating a very bad infection. Dr. Campbell gives us a prescription for *Ceclor* and tells us not to worry—Conor is a strong kid. You got that right, Dr. Campbell. He pats Conor on the shoulder and gives him a big smile. Conor smiles back.

*　*　*

They continue to interrupt

A few days later, Conor is feeling much better, which allows us to make s brief visit to his grandparents. When we arrive home, Ben begins gagging and coughing without warning, and then vomits his lunch, retching and straining with much intensity. Everything was fine up until now. He hasn't been moany or warm to the touch, and this wasn't like his other episodes. I carry him upstairs to change his clothes. His cries are those of obvious pain.

Lying him on his back is a poor choice and he begins throwing up again. He continues to heave intermittently for over an hour, though nothing is left, until he falls asleep on my shoulder, exhausted. I am mystified by these sudden events, ones that have hijacked a fairly normal afternoon. Perhaps Conor's sickness has spread.

By late evening, he finally settles and has a peaceful night.

The dawning of a new week begins without much fanfare. Tori is carefully crafting a drawing in her room and Conor is in his final week of school. Ben is happily propped on the couch in the family room, focused on the TV. Suddenly, like the switching of a channel, Ben is transformed: arms outstretched, lips curled up, head turned to the side, and grey-like complexion on his face. Rushing to pick him up, Jan gives him some pats on the back and he comes around fairly quickly. Again, without warning, in a heartbeat.

Jan and the kids come into town to meet me for lunch the next day. I greet them in the Parkade and help to get Ben into his wheelchair while Conor and Tori scurry to get inside the mall. As we approach the ground level, Ben gets "the look," clutches a little, and turns mildly off colour, eyes bouncing slightly to the left. He doesn't bring anything up, nor does he even cough or gag. After his eyes return to normal, he is quite limp and lethargic, with a "far-away" look. We trudge on to the outdoor square to get a hot dog from one of the street vendors. Conor and Tori are having a great time but I feel like I was just mugged.

What is causing these episodes? It seems as if they're more frequent but what is reality these days? They seem to happen at any time and they drain the life from me in an instant. I want to think that they are only gastrointestinal-related and not some form of seizure but how will we ever know? No one ever sees them happen except us, no one with any medical training, that is.

For the rest of the day, Ben is great. Happy, alert, as if nothing had happened at lunch. In the early evening, Conor and Tori have a baseball game and we all attend. The walk to the ball field is very pleasant and Ben enjoys the summer breezes tousling his whisper-fine hair.

Not far into the game, I glance at Ben. His arms suddenly outstretch, as if my gaze suddenly triggered something. He's going to have another episode—I'm by myself, nowhere near a phone and a 20-minute walk from home. I pick him up and pat his back as he is doing the usual "not breathing" thing. He quickly comes around without coughing or gagging. As I put him back in his seat, he lets out two huge burps. No one can tell me that these incidents aren't caused by his gut. This episode does not bother him and he returns to his normal state rather quickly.

The game finishes in a matter of minutes, or at least it seems that way, since I have no recollection of the past half hour. Conor is excited about their victory but Tori could care less. To celebrate this feat, we stop at our corner convenience store on the walk back. Ben is fine but I'm feeling blurry again. These episodes are really playing with my head. We get through them but we can't seem to make any gains or plan anything too far in the future. I have a wisp of that trapped feeling again.

The next evening we are back at the ball field for another game and Ben is completely in tune and focused this time. Conor and Tori want to stay at the adjacent playground following the game and Ben is quite willing. I have forgotten my wallet at home so we're forced to make a detour on our way to the store in order to pick up a little cash. We're back to our neighbourhood by 8 p.m. with Ben still full of energy.

What's so different about today? Why no episode?

* * *

Celebrations ruined

After nearly 40 years in practice, my father is calling it quits. Not because he wants to or doesn't enjoy it anymore. It has been his life, his passion, and is, quite frankly, the only thing he truly loves to do. But his 75-year-old body isn't cooperating anymore and the pain from his right knee is becoming too much of a burden. Being the only child living in the city, I help to organize a retirement reception for him at our home. Actually, Jan does much of the preparation after many consultations and confrontations with my mother.

More than 50 people descend on our tiny three-level split. Fortunately, the gorgeous Sunday afternoon weather allows the overflow to mill about in the yard.

Ben spends most of the two-hour reception in his room, trying to fall asleep. The buzz of the well-wishers keeps him awake and, though he does need a nap, he wants to be a part of the activity like everyone else. After an hour of having him lie awake in his room, Jan brings him downstairs to greet the crowd. His eyes are quite heavy and he starts to whine softly. He can't decide what to do.

Walking past the living room, I hear my mother mention my name. Unsure of who she is talking to, I try to get involved in the conversation.

"Yes, Michael has two normal, very smart children and one who is mentally retarded", my mother tells the visitor, her voice trailing off near the end of the sentence.

I can't believe my ears. I don't know for whom I should be embarrassed! I quickly interject to correct her statement but the damage is done.

I want to scream and tell everyone the party's over. Ben doesn't exist, in my mother's mind. He's not really a person, just someone who is "mentally retarded," someone who should be left abandoned to rot in an institution, someone you don't talk about, whom you keep hidden. People can't know that he is "not normal." That's shameful and embarrassing. People wouldn't want to associate with you if they knew that.

My mother's comment is so hurtful and, on a day like today, into which we have put so much effort planning and hosting this event, where none of my siblings have offered any support or help, her comments seem to be even malicious.

I can't handle much more of this. I want her to be a loving, accepting grandmother to all of my kids, or she can forget all of it.

A few days pass and I'm a little calmer. Whether my mother realizes or not, I cannot easily forget her total disregard for my feelings. Still, I have to press on. Today is June 29, a special day for Ben, a special day for all us. He turns three.

We choose to have a noon-time BBQ party since Jan is working in the evening and the weekend is tied up. Ben is in good spirits and loves the attention. It is a bit rushed, though, since most have to get back to work.

As usual, my parents arrive late, almost a half hour late, compared to the rest of the guests, who have arrived before noon. There are no presents to open and the whole event is a little anti-climactic—we had ordered a canopy for his stroller which hasn't arrived, last evening my parents had contributed some money towards his new $1,500 stroller (no wonder I'm broke), and a month ago, Jan's parents had given Ben sheets for his new big-boy bed. A gift from one of my sisters is on its way and my other sister, who tends to put things off, hasn't gotten around to buying anything yet.

After lighting the three candles on the birthday cake, we join in a pitiful chorus of "Happy Birthday." Of course, Ben can't blow out the candles but his siblings are right there to help. As I'm cutting the cake, I decide to give Ben a lick of the icing. He loves it. Seeing this, my father asks, "Doesn't he have allergies?"

I whirl my eyes over to him. What a dumb thing to say in front of everyone. I mumble to myself, "Of course, Dad, you know he's allergic to milk and eggs. Why would you ask that question?"

Before I can respond, he rambles on, preaching how rubbing it on his lip was a bad thing to do, how that would allow the proteins to go right into his blood stream and on . . . and on . . . which is completely counter to what Dr. Gaudet had recommended when we saw him last.

There's a momentary silence that is quite uncomfortable. I decide *not* to respond. I so want to tell him to get real, that it's Ben's birthday, and a little taste the size of a pea will likely not send him into toxic shock. My celebratory mood is washed away once again. My father is still as awkward as ever around Ben, with no sensitivity that today is his birthday. Who cares!

The next day, Ben has his three-year checkup with Dr. Campbell. It's a great appointment. His progress is amazing: he weighs in at nearly 27 pounds and measures 3 feet in height. We're on a roll.

* * *

Closer to a solution

July is in full swing. We are entering the dog days of summer. I love it. I love the heat and I love the fact that the sun is still shining at 9 p.m. The long days are both energizing and relaxing.

Our drive to the Camp today is very routine. Conor and Tori are eager to see Nana and Grampy as much as they are to go into Fundy Park for a swim. Preparing to exit the highway, I glance in my rearview mirror. Ben's eyes aren't right and my calm demeanour is flushed away. I pull into a nearby gas station and rush to get him out of his car seat. He is having one of his episodes. I put him on my shoulder and walk around the car. The sun is scorching and the heat index is in the mid thirties. Right now, I hate the heat. It's an extra burden as I try to help Ben come back to normal.

After a few minutes, he heaves a sigh and starts moving his legs up and down. There is no crying, gagging, choking or vomiting this time, and he didn't lose any colour in his face. But the eyes, oh they're so unsettling to watch. We continue to the Camp, only a mile away. Ben is quite tired—he often is after an episode—and quickly falls asleep.

Every week there seems to be one of these unpredictable pauses. The day moves along smoothly until . . . BOOM . . . everything is suspended and we must wait to see if Ben is going to be all right. This build-up has wiped me out today. It has sucked the life out of me. I feel I'm one episode away from losing it. I can't deal with being on the edge of my seat anymore.

I don't want to think that they're seizures because seizures scare me to death. Lying on the couch inside the Camp, I begin to think back to his first seizure. That was three years ago. It was so unnerving and frightening to me. We wound up staying in PICU for a few days to try to figure out what had happened. I remember Dr. Smythe suggesting that the episode may have been a reflux attack, and the agony of that had sent Ben into distress, overwhelming his fragile nervous system. Kids with CP often have tummy and digestion problems due to spasticity and generally uncoordinated muscles . . . and the gut is a muscle, of course.

When I think about that day, Ben's reaction had similar characteristics to what we are seeing now: head turning, eyes bouncing, shallow breathing, off-colour, followed by gagging, and vomiting. Then a period of crying—no doubt because of the irritation of vomiting—but he always seemed to be "fine" in the hospital a short time later. I also remember a visit to the Hugh MacMilllan Centre in Toronto and Ben had an episode in front of a number of people. The doctor present declared that Ben was having a seizure. So maybe all these episodes are seizures or maybe they are not, but I'm sure they're all stomach-related, too. Could they be both?

After churning through these conflicting thoughts, tying myself in knots, I see that Ben is starting to wake up from his nap and is in a good mood. There is no inkling that a short while ago he was stuck in that altered state. Conor and Tori are eager to enjoy the weekend and I must not hold them back.

*   *   *

More and more in tune

Work got in the way of listening to the supper time stories tonight. With Jan fulfilling her usual evening shift, Nana has come over to get everyone ready for bed. And returning home from work at 8:30 p.m., I discover that everyone is already in bed.

It's a little earlier than normal so I hurry upstairs to say goodnight before they fall asleep. No one is, of course, but all are in bed. Tori waves hello as I walk past her room to check on Ben. He is lying quietly in his new bed with his back towards me. I reach over and kiss him on the top of the ear. Though he is "hearing aid-less", I talk to him anyway and tell him why I am late. He looks at me and smiles. As I leave the room, he rolls onto his back to try to find me and begins to answer me. Without hesitation, I come back to his side. He smiles again as if to say that he is glad I am home. I am glad to be home, too, and glad to witness this very normal, very natural response. It's times like these that I'm convinced he's a genius trapped in a body that doesn't work.

After thanking Nana for helping out, I return to Tori's room. She is just beginning to say her nightly prayers when Conor enters. I ask them both how their days were and they tell me about the fun they had at their swimming lessons. Out of the blue, Conor says,

"I think we should change our bedtime prayer from '*God, please make Benjamin all better*' to something like '*Please make his brain all better*' and '*Make it so he doesn't have to go to any more appointments.*'"

Not to be outdone, Tori chimes in with, "And '*Please make his head not flop any more.*'"

Wow. They continue to amaze me. They truly love their brother and want to do anything they can to help him.

Later in the evening, Jan calls to check in. She tells me about the great time everyone had at the Aquatic Centre today, including Ben. How he was very curled up and very tight at the beginning but as he got into the water, he relaxed to the point where he was lying on his back in the water surrounded by dozens of kids splashing about and bouncing balls. And he was enjoying every minute of it.

Despite these awful episodes that are killing me, Ben is maturing and becoming more connected to his world and ours. Why can't every day be like this one?

*   *   *

It's reflux!

Making the turn towards the long steep hill that leads to Jan's sister and brother-in-law's house, I sink in my seat as Jan calls out that Ben is having an episode. In the rear view mirror, I can see that he has his head turned, he looks frightened, and he is not breathing well. This image is permanently etched in my brain. I was feeling quite good all week but, like all the other times, the good feelings vanished in an instant. Again, the episode lasts but a few minutes, just long enough to zap the energy from me. Ben is wiped out and just wants to be held as he whimpers off and on.

Val and Terry are not home this weekend and so we are by ourselves. Conor and Tori help to carry our many bags and supplies into the house while Jan tries to settle Ben. Everyone is hungry, except for Ben, and I go in search of some fast food.

As we are eating, Jan talks about trying to get in touch with Dr. Gaudet, the over-the-top-detail immunologist we are visiting next month, to see if he can provide some direction for us. Though he just about killed us with his suggestion that Ben has some sort of endocrine disease, he is a great listener and quite helpful—Jan's sure he'd take our call even on a weekend.

I track down his home phone number and eventually get to speak to him. I can't seem to organize my thoughts very well to describe these episodes and start with how they have never happened in the morning, how they have become less severe over the past several months but much more frequent. How Ben will sometimes turn very pale or grey-like, how he sometimes vomits, sometimes gets very tired, sometimes very irritable.

My rambling is interrupted several times with very probing questions from Dr. Gaudet. Within a few minutes, he is able to play back a more detailed picture of the episodes to me, describing characteristics that I hadn't thought of and yet are "bang on." It is as if he had seen Ben having an episode. I am a bit spellbound. Have I actually found someone who knows exactly what we're seeing? Suddenly, I don't feel so alone.

His conclusion is that it definitely sounds like reflux and explains that Ben could be turning his head to cut off the regurgitation from entering his lungs. But, by doing so, he could also cut off his breathing somewhat. And the pain from the burning reflux could be so intense that a seizure could be brought on.

He agrees about seeing a gastroenterologist when we see him next and will make a referral to Dr. Sanderson at the IWK. Before hanging up, I ask why Ben would be so tired after these incidents. He says it's quite likely it's from the pain he experiences, and pain will tire anyone out.

A common sense answer. And a good one.

All too often we look for some complicated explanation, usually related to his lack of normal development. It's so refreshing to have Ben actually seen as a person, and to hear that anyone would be tired after these episodes, that it could happen to "normal" people. Okay, maybe this wouldn't happen to "normal" people but if it did, their reaction would be similar. It really makes me wonder how many times when he was younger he had had a reflux incident and we confused it with a seizure.

By early evening, Ben is settling for the night and we are starting to unwind. The conversation with Dr. Gaudet has helped us a lot. Now we might actually be able to come up with a plan to help Ben. It's always better to know than not. Uncertainty kills.

*   *   *

15

ACTIVE LEARNING

It's not a big deal anymore. We make the semi-annual journey without thinking, without hesitation. Even our car seems to drive itself, as if it knows the way. We turn each excursion into a mini-vacation, trying to glean the most enjoyment from each visit and to capture some positive memories for each of us—a task that isn't always successful since these visits are really all about hospitals and surgeons and therapists and X-rays and . . . Not really anyone's definition of a vacation but it's truly the only time we get to travel and stay in a hotel.

We plan a multi-day adventure in Halifax to attend a slew of IWK appointments and to take part in a half-day session to learn about an advanced approach to teaching kids with multiple disabilities. Yeah, it's a stretch to call it a vacation but it's all we've got.

It starts off vacation-like when we check into the Cambridge Suites on Sunday afternoon. It's summer, after all: sunny and warm. The room is spacious, comfy and equipped to help us relax. We even find time to tour the Tall Ships that have docked in the harbour near Historic Properties. Despite the lengthy car ride and the oppressive humidity, Ben enjoys himself and is content to be dragged from one venue to another.

The vacation illusion begins to break down a bit the next day as we arrive at the IWK for our appointment with Dr. Lavoie. We are actually seen on time for a change. He has moved his office. No longer are his patients subjected to the cramped corridors of the first floor. Instead, we are treated to all new facilities five floors higher, complete with a huge variety of new toys and brain-teaser activities. For Conor and Tori, it's hitting the jackpot.

Like many previous appointments, we are first seen by a resident who asks the usual questions, painful but expected. Dr. Lavoie's examination of Ben is efficient and thorough, this time without eye-drops. Ben is very alert, sitting in his stroller as the lights are dimmed and a flashy-like circle sticker is moved about in front of him. Ben tracks it well and Dr. Lavoie comments that he has excellent peripheral vision. Enduring this hour-long appointment is certainly no vacation but it was also the best one Ben has ever had with this doctor.

An inspiration

We all rise early the next day to get ready to attend the presentations. The hotel's continental breakfast doesn't seem as good this time, not as much variety. Perhaps we're getting bored with it.

Shortly before 9 a.m., we park our car next to the APSEA School in the south end of Halifax. The School is the Atlantic provinces' headquarters for visually impaired students and it is soon to be also for students with a hearing impairment, when the Amherst location closes in a few months. The closure is an attempt to reduce costs and promote inclusion, which means moving away from separate schools for students with disabilities. Unlike the Amherst school, there is no residence at which the students can live in Halifax and the two low-rise buildings that make up the campus separate the offices and staff from the school's classrooms, pool and gym.

As we approach the gym's front doors, we discover several hundred people sandwiched between the four walls. I'm sure the fire marshall wouldn't be impressed. This noisy gathering of people is made up of teachers, special educators, physical and occupational therapists, and parents like us. The venue is bright and near the rear doors a small stage and podium is assembled, along with video and audio equipment. Only standing-room spots are left and our last-minute arrival ensures that standing is what we must do.

From some of the itinerant teachers who have seen Ben over the last few years, we have been told much about the keynote speaker, Lilli Nielsen.

Born in Denmark in 1926, she is the second of seven children, four of whom were born blind. At the age of seven, she was tasked with taking care of her blind, younger brother. No one told her parents how to care for their four blind children so she developed her own techniques, mostly from trial and error.

She began her working life as a preschool teacher, became a psychologist, and later worked as a special advisor for the Refsnaesskolen National Institute for Blind and Partially Sighted Children and Youth in Denmark. At this Institute she encountered children who had multiple disabilities in addition to blindness. Discovering that virtually no research had been done on how these children could learn, she quickly realized that she had to figure this out herself. Less than 10 years ago, at the age of 62, she earned her Ph.D from the University of Aarhus on the topic of congenitally blind children's spatial relations, and in the last 15 years she has published nine books and countless papers.

She developed what is termed an *Active Learning* theory based on the concept that for a child to learn, he/she must understand that he/she can affect his/her environment, can be active in this environment, and can do so on his/her own without direct adult supervision. It focuses on what the child can do, not what he/she cannot do.

At five minutes past 9, the crowd begins to buzz as someone spots a tall woman with shoulder length, curly blond hair making her way down the walkway outside of the gym. As this stranger enters, escorted by two APSEA staff members, the seated crowd rises to its feet applauding. I am somewhat in awe and disbelief that such a world-renowned expert is standing within reach. Such an expert might be able to bring out the best in Ben. Here is someone who demonstrates excellence, in stark contrast to the mediocrity of therapists that we have to dealt with at home.

The more I look at this well-traveled 68-year-old, who has visited more than 20 countries and over 200 educational facilities, the more she seems to me to resemble my mother! Also of Danish descent, my mother's facial features and gait are very similar to Dr. Nielsen's. I find it all rather interesting.

Following a brief introduction where the audience is told how this brilliant lady has worked with children with multiple, severe disabilities for nearly 30 years, Lilli wastes no time in getting down to business.

She begins by recalling a 17-month-old blind child with whom she had recently met. The child's parents were lost as to how to deal with their daughter. Lilli tells us how the child curled up into her neck as she held her, as if to get away from everyone. Lilli then describes how she placed the child on her back on top of a resonance board. This is a 4-foot by 4-foot piece of thin, flexible plywood supported by a one-inch border. The gap between the board and the floor amplifies all movement on the board.

Over top of the child, Lilli places a piece of equipment called a "Little Room." It is an open-ended "box", for lack of a better word, that is composed of three thin wooden walls, supported by a light tubular frame, with a transparent plexiglass ceiling to allow light to enter the space. From this ceiling and all the walls are suspended ordinary objects such as plastic plates, kitchen utensils, metal keys, an electric tooth brush, belt buckles, and shoe laces. These objects are designed to provide the participant with a variety of tactile and auditory experiences, including the ability to understand the concept of numbers.

Once placed inside, this 17-month-old lies still for a few moments, and then moves to a corner in the Little Room where there are no objects she can touch. Lilli assumes that she has purposefully moved to that location. She recounts that a short time later, she doubles the number of objects hanging in the Little Room so that there is no place the child can move to without touching an object. After about 15 minutes of lying quietly, the child begins to bat at a few objects, kicks her legs and appears to be enjoying herself. Her parents are dumbfounded that their daughter is actually exploring on her own. This simple invention is intended to develop independent play, object manipulation, spatial relationships, motor and cognitive skills, sensory integration, vocal play, and self-esteem.

Lilli tells the captivated crowd that this is a perfect example of humans needing to learn by doing, no matter what their disabilities. This is one of the key principles of her *Active Learning* approach and was borne out of a lifetime of improving the learning environments for children with disabilities and by studying how so-called "normal" people learn. She expounds on her proven research, which demonstrates how playing, doing and exploring are pre-requisites for the development of the four basic human needs: physical, social, intellectual and emotional. And although these children have huge obstacles on their path to learning, including blindness, mental retardation, cerebral palsy, severe developmental delays, hearing loss, or speech disabilities, the way in which they learn is the same as that of normal children, it is just delayed, and their stages of development are no different.

She describes another encounter in which she had met a blind child who had severe cerebral palsy and was asked how this child could possibly learn to do anything when she couldn't see or sit or walk. The first question she asked the parents was, "Can she breathe?" It seemed like a strange question since the answer was obvious. Lilli then placed the child on her back in the Little Room. Initially, the child lay perfectly still, not moving at all. After a few minutes, her breathing, amplified in the enclosed space, became a stimulus, its rhythmic sounds grabbing the child's attention. After another few minutes, the child raised a hand a few inches and touched one of the objects. The child spent more than 30 minutes inside the Little Room and discovered that her arms had a purpose. All of this learning started from one of the most basic things the child could do—*breathe!*

Dr. Nielsen's words are music to my ears. Finally I have found someone who gets it, who understands Ben's world and, by extension, mine. She is a beacon of hope in a fog of anxiety, despair and oppression.

So far removed from ". . . he may never walk or talk or go to school . . ." and ". . . I'm not convinced there's much vision . . .".

Every syllable she utters feeds my hunger for knowledge about how to help Ben. For the last hour, I have forgotten where I am until Conor and Tori start getting restless. For four- and five-year-olds, that's amazing. I come out of my trance and take them outside to the adjacent playground. It is fenced and in plain view from the gym doors so I leave them and scurry back inside to catch the last half hour of Lilli's presentation.

Lilli instructs the audience to be patient and wait for the children to explore on their own. They will learn from repetitions as well as from their own attempts, their own successes and their own failures. Don't correct the child or suggest strategies, she tells everyone, but provide the right environment, the right choices, proper safety and the right level of challenges to continuously stimulate.

Hearing this reminds me of management guru Ken Blanchard's "One Minute Manager" where he tells managers to give their employees "the final exam" at the start. In other words, set them up for success and everyone will win. Just as important is to never punish learning since it will immobilize the team. Or to paraphrase Lilli, "Never correct the child. They are smarter than you think and they will surprise you . . ."

She goes on to explain how she rarely talks to a child while he/she is exploring. Emphatically, she drives home how important it is to remain quiet since any intervention interrupts the learning experience and "fizzles the neurons". Not even to praise the child. Only after the child is "done" should you talk about the great accomplishments and exciting things that have happened.

Lilli closes her lecture by summing up:

1) I never teach a child. I let him learn. I let him find 'the right way' to do things.
2) Let him experiment. Let him fail! Let him learn how *not* to do it.
3) This *Active Learning* will let the child acquire skills that become part of his personality and will then be natural for him to use . . . .

Through these 90 minutes of pure inspiration, Ben has been content just to relax in his stroller, doze occasionally, and satisfy his periodic thirst with a few sips of juice. It's as if even he is happy to have been listening to Lilli.

Turning up the vacation dial, we head back to our hotel to have lunch and unwind. My mind is still whirling from what I have heard: motivational things for a change instead of the usual dread, doom and gloom; energizing things, hopeful things, refreshing things.

Once their lunch is mostly digested, Conor and Tori convince Jan to take them to the pool. They have earned it and Ben has earned a much needed nap.

*   *   *

Looking back

Everything seems to be coming together—the reflux diagnosis, Lilli's lectures, the MOVE programme . . . For once, I actually believe that there is a real chance that Ben can learn to do many, many things, including walking, talking and going to school . . . and prove Dr. Norris wrong!

Having endured the worst day of my life and put it behind me, I understand that there is no easy way to tell you that your child is "*not OK*", that you and your child may be faced with a mountain of obstacles. But on the other hand, I am not sure whether Dr. Dunphy's direct, matter-of-fact, "*Mrs. George, we have a problem,*" approach is a good way either.

What I have learned, though, is that it is better to know the facts, no matter how bad the consequences may seem, than to face uncertainty. Though it took several days to determine that CMV was the culprit, it was important to know so early. We were fortunate that Ben showed symptoms within the first hour of his birth so that we could begin to understand the problems that might be encountered and figure out ways to overcome them.

When the facts are known, there can be intervention and, heaven forbid, a strategy, a plan! If you are unaware of the facts or are simply wandering in the dark, you are wasting valuable time. Sooner or later you will be faced with the cold, hard issues and whether you know at birth or when the child is two years old that something is wrong, the hurting will not be any less severe. It will hurt, no matter when. So, better to know early.

Our number one goal for Ben is to help him be as independent as possible but it took me three years to really understand what that meant. The every day things that are taken for granted, such as feeding, dressing, walking, talking, playing, are not things a parent typically has to teach a child. He will not learn to do these things by typical approaches but he will be successful given the *right* approach. To paraphrase Dr. Nielsen,

> "If the child is not learning, there is something wrong with
> the approach and nothing wrong with the child. All children
> can learn given the right environment."

She didn't say it was going to be easy.

* * *

16

HITTING BOTTOM

The weekend is wrapping up quite nicely. Jan has taken Conor and Tori to my parent's house ("Wentworth Street" we sometimes call it) so that they can visit with their cousins. I remain home with Ben so that he can have his usual afternoon nap. Rather normal. Rather peaceful.

July is nearly complete and the steady breeze from the Bay is keeping the air humid but tolerable. It wants to be a scorcher, and I expect that 40 km or more inland it is, but the coastal landscape won't allow it. I have all the windows open to take in the summer freshness. A perfect beach day for some. Just a time to unwind for me.

The baby monitor is transmitting the sounds of Ben's bedroom into the kitchen as I tackle the dishes from earlier in the day. My focus is cleaning not listening to the stirrings a level above me. In between the harsh splashing of the tap water and the clinking of drinking glasses I pause to hear a faint rhythm streaming over the monitor. For a moment, I turn my head, fixate my eyes on the speaker, wrinkle my brow and try to concentrate on the audio signal.

Something inside me doesn't feel right. I throw the dish cloth into the soapy water and dash upstairs. Ben is partially on his side, throwing his arms out wildly in rhythmic, pulsating motions, his eyes are terrifying me and are non-responsive, and he has vomited in his crib. At first, all I see are those eyes and I feel sick myself. Then I clue in. I rush to grab a hand towel to clean up the mess and then I reach into the crib to put him on my shoulder.

How long has he been like this? How could I not have heard him? I take my eye off the ball for what seemed like only a few minutes and this happens? Is this just a bad reflux attack or is it a seizure?

Ben is incoherent but his body has calmed itself. I call Jan. She tells me to call 9-1-1 and she'll meet us at the hospital. Within minutes, he raises his head from my shoulder, looks right through me with those killer eyes and starts convulsing again. This is not like before. This is serious. I don't have time to crumble with fear. I've got to get him to the ER.

Frightened!

After getting Ben stabilized by pumping *Valium* and *Dilantin* into his helpless body, the physician in charge contacts Dr. Campbell and admits Ben to the Unit. Did I say "beach day" or "a time to unwind"? Who am I kidding? My life is none of this nor will it ever be.

We are escorted to bed #1 in the unit, the same bed in which Ben recovered from his adenoid surgery. This place is becoming much too familiar for me. As the crew of nurses gets Ben connected to monitor his vitals, he lies there lifeless, eyes closed, with only the rising and falling of his barrel-like chest to indicate he's still with us. Seeing Ben like this, Conor is taken aback and whispers to me repeatedly,

"I don't want Ben to die!"

Until this point, I had not thought of this day in those terms but his six-year old insight is waking me up to the notion of just how serious the situation is. The sick feeling that has been building inside me for the past two hours rages like never before.

We begin to settle ourselves around his bed as Dr. Campbell walks in. With his usual thick accent, he asks to replay the events of the day. I tell how all was well and then discovered him convulsing in his crib. A puzzled and somewhat worried look engulfs his face and he tells us that he is going to keep Ben for a few days for observation.

Before Dr. Campbell can finish his sentence, a nurse exclaims, "Dr. Campbell! He's seizing!"

Ben is convulsing again. His eyes are closed but his arms are outstretched. Dr. Campbell calls over to another nurse and wants to get more drugs for Ben. Within a few minutes, Ben's complexion is looking poor, his face graying, the oxygen draining from the capillaries. I don't like what I'm seeing and neither does Dr. Campbell.

After administering more *Valium* (I think that's what was given), Dr. Campbell calls over the other nurses. The seizure has stopped but Ben is turning blue. He doesn't seem to be breathing. Like a scene out the TV series, "ER", there are now five adults standing around Ben with Dr. Campbell inserting some sort of metal device into Ben's mouth.

I've experienced intense sadness and anger before but this is new for me. I am really frightened. What if they can't revive him? I break down crying, holding onto Jan for support. Conor and Tori are hugging our legs, not knowing what is happening. Ben is now a million shades of blue and as limp as a rag doll. The voices of those working on Ben are becoming inaudible as they blend together. Dr. Campbell, whose usual demeanour is quite calm and methodical, has transformed into a fast-moving, life-saving paramedic. My heart is heavy and I'm feeling weak.

After what seems like forever, Ben's skin regains its pinkish hue and the team of life savers begins to walk away. Sweating and panting, Dr. Campbell says that the nurses will keep a very close watch on Ben over the next few days as he tries to figure things out.

I am emotionally drained. I can't get out of my own way. Jan suggests I take Conor and Tori back to Wentworth Street and try to clear my head. She will remain with Ben and will call me if anything happens. Reluctantly, I agree; Conor and Tori don't need to stay in this wretched place.

After ringing the doorbell, my brother greets me with his usual sarcastic tone, smiling as he often does.

"Mickel Miiichael", he exclaims, making reference to what and how our Aunt would sometimes call me. "How are you then?", he asks, thinking I'll play right along with him. I know he knows what has just happened but for some reason he has chosen to carry on like it's just a regular day.

"Yeah, hi", I respond, as Conor and Tori rush past me to reconvene with their cousins.

Somber and sullen, I carry my wiped-out body into the dining room where everyone is just finishing a meal. My brother's wife flashes a smile my way, which, right now, doesn't seem sincere. Almost annoying.

"Oh, hi Michael," she remarks. I can't believe she's ignoring things, too.

At least my father has the God-given sense to ask how Ben is, what had happened, and was Dr. Campbell there to see him. With everyone gathered around the dining table, I am in no mood to have any sort of conversation. My mother senses my stress and brooding mood. In the time since Jan took Conor and Tori to the hospital, she has been to the mall and purchased a new Toronto Raptors hat for Conor, something to help him not be bothered by the condition of his brother. I don't ask if she has anything for Tori. At this point, I haven't the energy. She understands at least, I think, that we are need of some support.

What's even more welcoming is her offer to take Conor and Tori for as long as we need. If we have to spend several days at the hospital, we won't have to worry about them. Given all of the grief she has delivered my way about how I don't know how to raise my children, my mother is now having a compassionate moment and her true motherly instincts are rising to the surface. Amidst this horrific day, I am thankful for this one bright event.

In sharp contrast, I am more and more dismayed that my brother seems not the least bit interested in the condition of his nephew. You'd think it would be natural to at least ask. Why is he rejecting Ben? Is it because he thinks Ben wouldn't know the difference if he cared or not? Is it because Ben is less of a person in his mind as a result of his disabilities?

Is it because he is afraid of Ben? Or is it because he doesn't want to ruin his vacation by talking about this crisis in my life? My mood is rapidly progressing through disappointment to discouragement to outright anger.

I am not getting any rest or comfort from my visit and decide to return to Ben's bedside. Before I leave, I bring Conor and Tori close, squeeze them for all they're worth and tell them to have fun but behave themselves. They each give me a wonderful, energizing kiss and dash back to their games.

Arriving back at the hospital, I make a quick detour to the ATM since I don't have a dime on me. I never do, of course, because in our world there is no such thing as a savings account, or a rainy day fund, or discretionary spending budget. We are a classic case of "living from paycheque to paycheque." Not because we want to live this way or because we are unable to manage our finances but from the simple fact that managing our life around Ben's care and needs is stretching us beyond our means. At 32, Jan and I don't have a lot of equity built into anything. No one would understand this if we tried to explain it and, really, it's no one's business.

The ATM screen reveals that we have $27 left in our account. It's so frustrating. What little money we have always seems to be wasted in hospital cafeterias.

As I enter the Unit, I am greeted by Jan's sister Val, who is keeping watch over Ben so that Jan can get away for 20 minutes, to clear her head, if nothing else. Val, too, is on vacation, visiting her parents. But after hearing about Ben, she has decided to suspend her family fun and support us in whatever way she can, subordinating her own interests for her family!

Sitting near the foot of Ben's bed, listening only to the dissonance of the beeps and warbles of the stacks of monitors, I can't believe that my brother has no desire to even want to help. I still can't explain why and find it all very disheartening.

It takes five days for Ben to return to his normal self. For us, that's five sleepless nights, five head-banging days in the Unit, and five days of my life taken from me . . . again!

The litany of tests that were conducted produce little new information. We leave the uncomfortable confines of the Unit beaten, exhausted, and even more unsure of what tomorrow will bring.

*   *   *

17

AN IMPORTANT IWK VISIT

The drive to Halifax this time is not going to be fun. Ben's dental surgery and long list of appointments will leave no time for play. Needless to say, Jan and I are both nervous. We would love for Conor and Tori to come with us but we don't want them to miss four days of school so early in the year.

Minutes before we leave our driveway, the mail arrives. I can't resist the urge to see what has been delivered. I'm sure it's not Ed McMahon telling me I've just won the Publisher's Clearing House draw but I just have to rifle through the pile of letters before I can leave. One of the envelopes bears the provincial government logo. With eyes wide, I tear it open and quickly scan the enclosures for the word "Approved". There . . . at the end of the second paragraph . . . Ben's mobile stander, a $2,200 stander, is being covered under the programme for children with special needs. I am over the moon. Maybe we'll get to follow the MOVE programme after all. "Are you listening, Lisa?" I mutter to myself.

My euphoria over this news cannot be dampened today by Ben's impending surgery. The drive to Truro passes by easily this time and we arrive at Val and Terry's in the late afternoon. As evening approaches, I start thinking less about our windfall and more about Ben's surgery. It becomes another restless night.

Our first appointment the next morning is with the Remedial Seating Clinic at the IWK, our first time in the Clinic since Faith dumped us. Our drive into Halifax is rushed. Crossing the MacKay Bridge into downtown, Jan and I joke that our worst nightmare would be if my mother arrived at the clinic before we did. She is in Halifax, herself, for her own dental appointment. We pull into the Parkade only 15 minutes late this time. Jan takes Ben into the clinic to get started while I gather Ben's insert, stroller and car seat. As I struggle to pile everything into the elevator, I see a man who looks very familiar. I can't place him but I sense I should know him.

The birth of new relationships

At the clinic's reception desk, Jan checks in.

"Oh, you must be Anna George!" exclaims a voice.

Jan's eyes widen and she hears from down the hall,

"They must have had a flat tire!".

The nightmare has come true. My mother *is* here! A few minutes later I walk in and see Jan and my mother together. There's another woman with them and it's not a hospital staff member. It's Rosalee, a friend of my mother's. And it was her husband I had seen get off the elevator a few minutes ago. This isn't happening. Why is she here? And why is she with Rosalee? I don't even know her.

I am not very friendly to them. I just want them to leave. Before I can find the words to ask them to do so, two people walk into the room where we're waiting.

"Hi. I'm Judy and this is Dan."

Sporting attractive glasses and short dark hair, Judy is the head OT in the clinic and Dan, who appears very energetic, is one of the technicians who will work on Ben's seat. As we talk to Judy about Ben and our frustrations with the clinic in Saint John, my mother and Rosalee make no attempt to leave. I am getting really uncomfortable discussing Ben in this setting.

Judy and Dan look over Ben's Avanti customized chair. She tells us that it is a very good system but it is not something she too often recommends because it is very expensive. The same goes for his *Convaid Cruiser* stroller. Hmm, very interesting. I certainly want Ben to have good quality equipment but if I don't have to spend a fortune . . .

Dan mentions that even though he has never worked with this particular seating system, his team is very experienced and comfortable with child equipment. Looking it over, Judy comments that the headrest has been installed upside-down (nice goin', Faith!). She will be able to raise the seat and move the padding that is under his thighs outward to give Ben a little more room. Though there is no way to make the seat wider, he does have another two inches, or so, in length remaining. Once we get to the end point, they could customize an insert that could fit this system.

She tells us that Ben's seating requirements will be constantly changing until he's finished growing. Unfortunately, seating configurations are quite static, being a snapshot of how his body is shaped at a particular point in time. Because of that, she prefers systems that have the most flexibility and relies on her techs to build inserts that are easily adaptable.

I'm going to like coming here, I can tell.

Before the appointment ends, Judy has Dan carve out a piece of ethafoam for Ben's new Cruiser to give him more lumbar support. Dan also makes a small piece for the headrest to keep Ben's head from hyperextending and offers some suggestions so that his car seat is safer and better fitting. She is making us feel more and more comfortable. Why can't the clinic at home be this knowledgeable and helpful?

The appointment lasts until noon. My mother has stayed for the whole thing. She informs us that she has to leave to get ready to go home. Thank God!

Our afternoon appointment is with Russ, a very knowledgeable audiologist with APSEA. The last time we met with him was when the school was still located in Amherst. Our previous interactions were very pleasant and we could tell that he really loves his job.

After meeting us at the front desk and leading us through a maze of hallways and a short elevator ride, he takes us to his office—a large room with lots of windows but filled with clutter. Boxes and packing material and parts for equipment are lying everywhere. He apologizes for the mess and explains that he is not quite finished unpacking from the move a few months ago.

Since this is Ben's first appointment with him, he gathers some history to familiarize himself with Ben's personality and overall health. He asks about the feedback the hearing aids are exhibiting and gives us some tips on what can be done to reduce that. As we talk more, Russ suggests getting an FM device, not only to help with feedback, but also as an effective solution for the classroom. The device would eliminate most background noise and the sound level produced is as if the source is only a few inches away. This might be an option for playschool.

Russ wants to tests Ben's aids to ensure they're functioning properly. Gently, he removes them from Ben's ears and pulls off the ear molds, leaving only the crescent-shaped hearing aid itself. He places them separately inside a small black box. Before closing the lid of the box, he connects the base of the hearing aid to a little plastic boot that is wired to the box. A series of high pitched noises is heard as the tests are conducted. The small printout of thermal paper shows that they are both in excellent working order but he notes that the tube on the left hearing aid is filtered but the other is not. Of course, we have no idea why they're configured this way. He tells us that the filter helps to smooth out the sound but it also reduces the sound level. Ben is completely uninterested with all of the technical talk and falls asleep in his chair.

About 20 minutes later when Ben is fully awake, Russ asks one of the teachers from the school to assist him with the hearing test. The results are very encouraging. Ben responds to regular speaking voices in the 50-60db range (which is normal) as well as to startle responses. At one point, Russ asks us if Ben listens to or watches Barney. "Occasionally," we tell him. With that, Russ begins singing into the microphone,

"I love you. You love me . . ."

Ben raises his eyes in the direction of his voice. I would have expected Russ to play a tape of Barney's music but he really gets into this part of his job. I can't imagine Jennifer, the audiologist we met on Day 1, ever doing something like this.

Russ is quite impressed with how well Ben performs at "turn taking" as he first hears a voice, waits until it stops, then makes his own noises. He then pauses and waits to hear the voice again. Russ remarks that this is quite an advanced skill and is a little surprising given that many profoundly deaf kids, even aided, do not show much response in the audiogram. Oh, yeah!

After replacing the outer casing on one of Ben's aids, Russ makes new ear mold impressions. Just like Pierre in Toronto, he is a pro, completing the task in less than 15 minutes. As the impressions are forming, Russ recommends that we try an FM system for a while. A new system costs close to $1,600 but we can borrow a refurbished one at no charge, and when Ben is enrolled in school, APSEA will cover most of the cost of a new one.

If I ignore my mother's untimely intrusion, today's appointments have been fantastic, way beyond my expectations. We now have two people in key roles that we can lean on for support. I'm sure they will teach us a great deal.

* * *

Don't we have enough to deal with?

I flop down on the bed beside Ben, sighing heavily. What a day! A great day for Ben but for me, the stress of the intrusion of my mother and Rosalee is beginning to sink in. As I stare at the ceiling, thinking about what tomorrow will bring, how early we'll have to get him up, I feel nauseous. The phone beside my head rings. At first, I'm a little confused, unable to figure who would be calling our room. I lift the receiver and hear my mother on the other end. She is now back home and is phoning to see how we made out today.

I have little interest in speaking with her right now but what choice do I have? I wish this phone had had "call display". She tells me that I seemed uptight at the seating appointment. Rather than agree with her and try to end the conversation quickly, my fatigue takes over and I tell her, in a somewhat intense voice, that I was upset that she and Rosalee intruded on our personal business, that I was very uncomfortable talking about Ben in front of her, and she should have figured that out.

Taken off guard, she responds with, "Oh." After a few moments of silence and a few other questions, my mother processes my statements more completely and shoots back at me that I should not have said that to her.

"Rosalee is good friend of mine and if it bothered you that we were there, you should keep that to yourself."

Now I'm really angry.

"Well, you asked me and I told you. I can't help it if you don't like my answer. You know, both of you should have had the common sense to give us some privacy once the appointment started. We were meeting these people for the first time and it was really awkward and inappropriate to have a complete stranger there! Ben is my personal business, not yours, and if I wanted to share that with Rosalee, that's my decision!"

I'm really digging a big hole for myself but I can't stop. I don't want to stop. Doesn't she understand that it's not about her? Doesn't she realize that maybe we're uptight because Ben is going to have surgery tomorrow?

My mother's response is that Rosalee was an appropriate person to be there since she was a nurse for many years and had a son with a disability.

Huh? What kind of logic is that? She's trying to justify her presence rather than listening to what's bothering me. As usual. this has turned into my fault. I'm the bad person here, I guess.

I cut her off and tell her I have to go. Something tells me I won't be getting a call tomorrow to see how Ben has fared.

* * *

His first dental surgery

It can't be time to get up yet. I've been asleep for less than an hour. The alarm continues to buzz despite my protests, telling me it really is 4:45 a.m. With burning eyes and heavy limbs, I gently tap Ben to awaken him. It doesn't take much and he springs to life, obviously realizing what's in store today.

A half hour later, he has his *Prepulsid* with ease and cooperates getting dressed, a nice change. By 6:15 a.m., we're in the car, heading for the IWK. Reporting to the day surgery clerk 15 minutes later, we discover yet another person employed in the health-care system who doesn't know what she's doing. She can't find Ben's file and doesn't see him listed on the daily report. As far as she can tell, Ben is not scheduled for any surgery today! I try to contain my frustration. After a few minutes of shuffling paper, she finds the file. Pulling out the top sheet, she says,

"OK. Yes, Benjamin is scheduled for 8 a.m. with Dr. Anthony."

What? Dr. Who? What's going on? Who is Dr. Anthony?

"No", I respond as politely as I can. "It's supposed to be Dr. Rundle."

"No, that's what it says here," she retorts as her eyes gaze upon the piece of paper she said didn't exist a few minutes ago.

"They sometimes switch if one doctor is called to an emergency."

We retreat to the waiting room, not quite sure what to do. While it's likely this new dental surgeon is just as experienced as Dr. Rundle, it's the surprise that bothers me the most. We have a relationship with Dr. Rundle and so does Ben, so we know what to expect. After several minutes of dismay, we are greeted by one of the day-surgery nurses. She is very professional and nicely handles the mix-up, telling us that Dr. Anthony is actually the head of the department and an excellent dental surgeon. She instructs us to get Ben changed into his greens and watch a video that will describe both the procedure itself and how the Recovery Room works.

The video is mildly interesting and I only half listen. I just want this to be over and everything to be magically fixed. We wait and wait some more.

The halls suddenly get busy and we notice a very tall woman, dressed in operating room garb, approach us. She introduces herself as Dr. Wyse and says that she will be the anaesthesiologist for the procedure. Her accent is very thick and difficult to understand. She takes us into a small examining room down the hall to explain what will happen.

Her words and tone are serious in nature as she tells us that she is very concerned about Ben's reflux. She goes into great detail about what she will do if he does "reflux" during the procedure (I didn't know you could use it as a verb). Up until now, I really hadn't thought about the dangers of reflux while under anaesthesia. What is with these doctors who like to scare the bejeezus out of you before anything has started?

Another doctor rescues us from this chilling conversation: it's Dr. Anthony. By contrast, he is very friendly and makes us feel at ease, assuring us that we have a top-notch team with Ben today. A few minutes later, a confident nurse enters the room to tell us she will be with Ben at all times. Ben catches her eye and smiles. He gets it—a good sign. This acknowledgment seals it for me.

At 8:15 a.m., Ben is wheeled into the O/R followed closely by Dr. Wyse. Jan shouts to her to take care of him. And she responds,

"Oh, *I* will!"

Her tone has shifted from serious to caring.

Two and half hours later, Dr. Anthony finds us in the waiting room and tells us that we can stop sweating. There were no problems and no extractions needed. He compliments us on the great work we have been doing taking care of his teeth and gums, since only a minimal amount of bleeding occurred. He also sings Dr. Wyse's praises, telling us that she is the best anaetshesiologist they have. If she is looking after Ben, then we will never have any worries.

We are allowed into the Recovery Room shortly after noon. Ben is lying on his back, his head elevated and his eyes a little groggy. He seems only slightly agitated, and sleeps off and on. Shortly after 2 p.m., Dr. Wyse drops by to check on him. She is pleased with how things went and tells us a bit about what she did. At this point, I realize that she really is good, that she treats her patients as if they are family, and her attention to detail is part of what makes her the best. She is another example of how her profession is really a vocation (another angel).

* * *

Where did this guy come from?

It's Friday. Our last day here. It begins with getting X-rays of Ben's hips. Despite being under an anesthetic yesterday, Ben is alert and cooperative, and with no line-up, the X-rays are ready within a half hour.

With time to spare, we make our way to the ortho clinic, an hour early for our 2:30 p.m. appointment. We discover that Ben's regular ortho surgeon, Dr. Ramsay, is not in today (this seems to be a common occurrence) which prompts the receptionist to page that day's on-call doctor, Dr. Breen. We are immediately shown to an examination room and within 15 minutes, a tall, burly man enters abruptly, a little like Kramer making an entrance on Seinfeld. His eyes squint as he flips through the pages on Ben's chart. He forgets to introduce himself—we assume it's Dr. Breen—and begins mumbling as he reads through Ben's historical record, looking up occasionally. He confirms to himself aloud that it was CMV that caused Ben's problems and, out of the blue, asks if we do any stretches. Then he asks,

"So why are you here?" He really has no idea.

Great. Another well-prepared, engaged health-care professional. Jan mentions the pain that Ben has been experiencing with his legs over the past month when we try to stretch and straighten them. Dr. Breen huffs a little and then directs Jan to place Ben on the examination table. With little care, Dr. Breen starts twisting Ben's limbs. Ben is caught off guard and not quite sure what's going on. Neither are we. He then hurriedly turns Ben onto his side towards him, with Ben's legs dangling over the edge of the table. Dr. Breen's continual pulling and twisting of Ben's legs is scary to watch. With Ben throwing his arms out in obvious discomfort and his face beet red, Jan has had enough and rushes to scoop Ben up into her arms.

Unfazed, Dr. Breen starts into a rant, telling us about cutting/ lengthening Ben's hamstrings will be needed as he grows but not for at least another year. He expresses his disgust and bitterness about the turmoil in the department, how he'll be retiring within a year, how these "young whipper-snappers" (his words, if you can believe it) of surgeons are taking over one day then leaving for places like Saudi Arabia the next. I'm trying to figure out what this has to do with Ben.

He makes it clear that we are wasting our time doing any stretches with Ben, that they have little effect, and physiotherapy won't help us at all. There is nothing anyone can do that will help him learn how to walk, he tells us. If Ben has the capability, he will walk with or without our help.

I'm not convinced that stretches are a waste of time but I know listening to this Neanderthal surely is. I'm sure that if we let Ben lie on his back all day in a beanbag chair, he will never learn to do anything.

Dr. Breen continues on his soap box remarking how if some "expert" said Ben wouldn't begin walking until 10 years of age but somehow he began at an earlier age, you might be tempted to say that it was the stretching or the surgery that made him walk earlier. Or if Ben didn't begin walking until a year or two later, then perhaps the "experts" would say that Ben should have had the surgery earlier, or we didn't stretch him enough. This is all nonsense, according to Dr. Breen. His point is that the magic number of 10 years of age is wrong from the outset and whenever Ben learns to walk, it will have had little to do with any intervention.

He emphasizes to us how continuity of service from one surgeon is very important and that he wouldn't consider surgery until he got to know us. Good thing, because I know I would never let him near Ben with a scalpel.

When we ask about the X-rays and Ben's hips, he tells us they are okay right now but his thigh bones are too straight, too in-line with his body, and they should really be pointing into his hips. As time goes on, he believes they will slip further away from his hips and dislocate, which would require surgery to correct. He closes his diatribe by suggesting that stretching may actually expedite this process.

It's quite amazing: in 15 minutes, he has trashed the department, discredited all physiotherapists, and said that stretching is both a waste of time and can be harmful.

Jan and I look at each other and then thank him for his time. He huffs again and exits as quickly as he came. I can't wait to get away from this crazy place.

* * *

18

9-1-1

As the week begins, Ben is bang on: alert, attentive, energetic and verbalizing constantly. He's found his "on" switch. I wish I knew where it is hiding. During the home visit made by one Ben's APSEA teachers, he shows off. At supper time, he is ravenous, almost insatiable.

The next day, at his playschool's Hallowe'en party, he enjoys every minute. He thrives in the attention shown by his teacher, who paints a pumpkin on his cheek, and his friend, Emily, who paints some design on his hand. Trick or treating that evening is exciting. Ben is dressed as a bumble bee, Conor becomes a Ninja Warrior and Tori looks great as Pocahontas. The air is cool, just below freezing, but there is no wind. Ben doesn't seem to care that winter is not far away. Tagging along with his brother and sister, outside, in the dark, is a new experience. His eyes say it all. They always do. When his treat bag fills to capacity, we make our way home.

An hour or so later, he is lying in my arms, having just finished his night bottle. His breathing is peaceful, slow and rhythmic, and his eyes are relaxed and heavy. It's not long before he falls asleep.

No sooner does the calendar change to November than cold and flu season descends on our house. After the revelry of Hallowe'en, Conor is stricken with a fever and nausea. My first conclusion is that he has consumed far too much candy—but that wouldn't cause his fever. He stays home from school and tries to get better. I had expected to have at least made it through this month before the viruses invade our part of the world.

After that streak of incredibly good days, I now wait nervously for the other shoe to drop, for Ben to catch this 24-hour flu bug. Though a little listless through the day, his demeanour is upbeat and his appetite is unaffected. Going to bed is effortless.

This can't last.

Reflux, again!

Fresh from our IWK adventure, Jan takes Ben for an afternoon OT appointment with Marsha who wants to observe how he eats and drinks. After a few spoonfuls of applesauce, Ben has a major reflux episode. His head turns and locks to one side, and his face turns very blotchy. In CPR fashion, Jan jumps to attention to administer back blows, convinced he is choking on some food. These don't work. She can't get her finger into his mouth because his teeth are clenched so, so tightly. Even the end of the spoon can't pry open his jaw.

Marsha is quite worried, even scared, and they head for the emergency department. As they get to the waiting room of the OT department, Ben begins turning grey, unable to catch a breath. Marsha's eyes widen, almost panicky. A few seconds later, Ben heaves a huge sigh and starts breathing more regularly. His complexion quickly returns to a healthy hue but he is exhausted. The appointment is over.

Marsha tells Jan that she is convinced it was a seizure. She can't believe how calm Jan has been through all of this. Jan tells her it is reflux and how the pain from it can make it look like a seizure.

"I was a nervous wreck!", she tells Jan. The healthcare professional—a nervous wreck. Nice. So now we have to add "coaching" to our list of responsibilities.

The next morning, as Jan gets Ben dressed for playschool, he has another episode. Lying on his back, his eyes widen, his eyebrows raise and his head gets locked to the left. His arms fly outstretched briefly but not like yesterday. It doesn't last long but long enough for Jan to keep him home from school. This is something new, having them after breakfast.

In the evening, Jan and I find some rare time to just talk. We ask each other why does Ben experience these episodes some days and not others. If we give him the same dose of medicine every day and feed him roughly the same types of food and drink in the same amounts, what is the trigger? We wonder if there is any connection to his sluggish bowel habits or the times he doesn't get enough sleep. Does fatigue make it more likely that an episode will occur?

What we do know is that they are not dependent on his position since most have happened while he was in an upright position. We start to recall how many times did we think he was having a seizure when it was really reflux. I start to wonder whether or not he really needed to be on *Phenobarbital* and how much time have we wasted. Should we have investigated more vigorously the reflux diagnosis as Dr. Smythe had recommended in early days?

We are realizing that there are not enough hours in the day—to compile our daily logs, to learn Lilli Nielsen's techniques, to learn more about the MOVE programme, to cope with reflux episodes, to deal with crazy surgeons and stunned receptionists, to coach health-care professionals, to build new relationships with specialists from afar, and, of course, to be caring and supportive parents to Conor, Tori and Ben.

* * *

Eight in a day!

The weekend arrives and Ben wakes bright eyed and quite content. After skipping his mid-morning juice, he is content to play in his Little Room. A short while later, I return to check on him and am surprised to see him not moving. Worse, his head is locked looking left and his eyes are bouncing. Like an automaton, I scoop him from the floor and place him on my shoulder. He can't seem to get control of his body and it takes a lengthy 5 minutes before he comes round. Not long after, he begins to cry relentlessly, for nearly a half hour. At about 12:45 p.m., I am able to get him to swallow his dose of *Prepulsid* and attempt to give him a bottle of Isomil, thinking that maybe that would cool his throat.

The first trials are unsuccessful since he is still in a lot of discomfort. As I try to make him more comfortable in my arms, the back door opens and in walk my mother and father. I have always tried to encourage them to simply drop in from time to time, to make them feel welcome and have told them that they don't need a special invitation to visit. Today's spontaneous stop-over, however, couldn't have come at a worse time. My mother seems unfazed that Ben is sobbing off and on, and is unsympathetic when I tell her he just had a lengthy reflux episode. Where's my caring mother who "got it" back in the summer when Ben was in hospital? My father completely ignores Ben and proudly displays the award he had received that day at a luncheon for the Kidney Foundation. He had brought the first dialysis unit to the Atlantic region a number of years ago, a treatment that is now commonplace. A remarkable achievement that deserves such honour but something I couldn't care less about today.

Despite my efforts to get Ben to drink some liquid, he refuses. Mid-conversation with my mother, I feel Ben's body stiffen, watch his arms outstretch in that all too familiar pose, and his neck contort into another reflux episode. My mother notices Ben's peculiar position and comments that she thinks it looks like a seizure. I tell her how it can be mistaken for a seizure but it's really reflux. Both of them seem to shrug it off and continue talking to Conor and Tori, as if Ben were just sneezing a few times.

His breathing becomes more shallow than the last episode and remains that way for several minutes, making me more worried. Since I am unable to provide my parents much attention, they don't stay for long.

Just as Ben is returning to a more coherent state, Jan walks through the door. I begin my replay of the day's events much to her dismay. A few minutes later, Ben goes into another episode. We reason that he is experiencing the same flu symptoms as those of his siblings who have been suffering from it for the past few days. We conclude that he is trying to throw up but his body isn't letting him. (We really have no idea.)

To try to break the cycle and calm things down, I give him a *Gravol* suppository. It seems to work, at least temporarily. In the meantime, we place a call to Dr. Campbell. He is not on call this weekend but Dr. Smythe is and so we ask that he call us back. Within a few minutes, Dr. Smythe is on the phone, listening to me describe what has been happening. He comments how it's best to treat common things commonly, to not over-react, how we have done all of the right things and to keep doing what we're doing. When I inquire about Ben's shallow breathing, he says that if doesn't improve or we begin to feel uncomfortable about his condition to bring him in. He is allowing us control of the situation but will step in to help carry our burden, if we want him to. He's a wonderful person.

After 40 minutes pass, we call Dr. Smythe to ask him to meet us at the hospital. We're somewhat anxious and uncertain, and want him to intervene. Mary Ann, our neighbour, comes over to watch Conor and Tori. On the ride to the hospital, Ben has another episode, his sixth today, but this time he coughs a lot and actually starts to make noises, some moans and some groans, something he had not been doing for the last three hours. As we pull up to the hospital, his breathing still isn't that great.

Once inside, we are subjected to a really clueless triage nurse who wants to take his temperature rectally. She tells us that the head of the ER has said that anyone under the age of 6 must have their temperature taken this way since it would be the most accurate. I quickly respond by mentioning that Ben was in PICU a few months ago and they constantly took it in his ear. She can't seem to process this information, like a *fembot* from Star Trek, saying she doesn't know anything about that.

We are shown to an examining room to wait. A few minutes later, the same triage nurse pokes her head into the room to tell us that I was right—that it is anyone under two years of age must have their temperature taken rectally and that children from ages two to 6 could be taken in the ear. Amazing.

We don't have to wait long before Dr. Smythe and a resident show up. We begin explaining Ben's day, and how his breathing was concerning to us. We tell them that we believe that he has caught the flu from his siblings and was having problems vomiting. Throughout the conversation, Jan is trying to hold Ben in her arms. Despite the fact that his eyes remain closed, he is quite squirmy and agitated, and repeatedly moans and groans. Dr. Smythe wants to examine Ben so we carefully lay him on the table. Within minutes, Ben begins vomiting. I am perplexed that both doctors just stand and watch. The resident retrieves a small metal pan but only after Ben is finished his retching.

Dr. Smythe listens to Ben's chest thoroughly and reports that is it clear. The vomiting seems to have cleaned things out and his breathing is no longer noisy and labored. We discuss Ben's reflux episode in late July and how Dr. Campbell thought he might have aspirated which caused his seizure. Dr. Smythe replied that he had looked at that X-ray and he didn't believe that he had aspirated.

He suggests that Ben be admitted for 24-hour observation to try to determine what is bothering him. I am reluctant. Staying overnight in this stressful place is not something I can handle today. Dr. Smythe leaves the room so that we can talk it over. We decide to stay in the ER for a few hours and if his condition improves, then we would leave; otherwise, Dr. Smythe can admit him. Dr. Smythe agrees with our approach and tells us that he would check back at 5:30 p.m.

The resident remains and talks to us a little longer. He appears to be a very practical person and actually listens quite carefully—a rarity in such a new physician. At one point, he comments on how difficult it must be to carry Ben for long periods of time. This guy might actually have a bright future in medicine ahead of him! During the conversation, Ben throws up again, though not nearly as much this time. A few minutes later, exhaustion takes over and he falls asleep.

As 5:30 p.m. draws near, we are feeling much better about him and want to leave. The resident calls Dr. Smythe to update him on Ben's progress but he wants to speak with me. In his gentle tone, he asks me how I feel and instructs me that if Ben worsens, we should not hesitate to bring him back to the hospital and he would admit him. Dr. Smythe goes on to say that if Ben's siblings had not had the flu, he would have definitely kept him for observation. But he did agree that it is reasonable to think that Ben has the same bug that his brother and sister contracted.

In a strange way, I am always left in a relaxed state arriving home after spending an unplanned hospital visit. Relaxed but physically and mentally exhausted. The events leading up to the visit build up in a stressful crescendo until I feel out of control and very agitated. Once it's all over, and Ben begins to feel a bit better, the huge weight that has been making it hard for me to breathe is lifted from my chest but not before I am drained of every last shred of energy and feel as if my lifespan had just been shortened by six months. Relief quickly settles in and for the next several hours I am comforted that Ben is too tired to do much of anything, too tired to be sick or have a seizure or anything worse. I don't have to *do anything* for a change.

Tonight is no different. Ben is wiped out from the day and sleeps in my arms while we all watch "The Santa Clause" movie. I carry him upstairs when the movie is over and he nestles into his covers easily, opening his eyes for only a few minutes.

We have made the right decision. Both this time and back in July. We are thankful that Dr. Smythe involved us in the decision process and really listened to what we had to say. I wish all physicians would take a page out of Dr. Smythe's book.

* * *

For the best, it is a vocation

Sunday afternoon, the phone rings. I hope it is my mother checking up on her grandson. It's Dr. Smythe. At first, I am a little stunned, not knowing quite how to respond, since neither Jan or I had called him for anything. He is concerned about Ben and very interested to know how he coped overnight. I tell him that we were all glad to be home and his sleep was rather peaceful. I thank him for the care and attention he gave us yesterday and for calling. The system needs more Dr. Smythes.

As evening settles upon us, so does a high fever for Ben. His body is hot stuff all through the night, though his sleep is relatively restful. The next day, we talk with Dr. Campbell about it. After being satisfied that Ben is battling only a fever and not having any breathing issues, he tells us to monitor it for the next 24 hours to see if things improve. There are many bugs floating around but some are viral so we need to see what other symptoms occur.

Ben becomes more and more restless throughout the evening with a constant fever. He wakes at 12:15 a.m., rather unhappy and agitated and stays that way for a good three hours. His fever does not lessen even a tenth of degree and he can't lie down without crying. Administering *Abenol* suppositories every four hours accomplishes little. By 3 a.m., Jan suggests changing him into lighter clothing and rubbing him down with cool cloths. After 20 minutes of his skin absorbing the moisture, he begins to show signs of cooling.

Tuesday morning, Ben is fatigued from his sleep-deprived night. Surprisingly, he chooses to drink some juice and some *Isomil* throughout the morning but by early afternoon, his fever returns, this time close to 40°C. I don't like what I'm hearing and come home early from work. We discuss things with Dr. Campbell again and he tells us that he will meet us tomorrow morning to check things out. His lack of urgency has a temporary calming effect on me. By 5 p.m., Ben seems much more content and is drinking quite easily. My fears of his dehydration are fading. Jan encourages me to attend a company meeting in Fredericton for the evening, saying she's sure he'll be fine.

As I return home late, she has been proven right. The evening was fine and his overnight sleep better than the night before.

On Wednesday morning, his throat seems to be bothering him. We are scheduled to meet Dr. Campbell at around 10:30 a.m. and so we leave a little early to battle the cold November wind and icy rain. As usual, Dr. Campbell arrives late. He is not in a good mood after he learns that there are no examining rooms he can use. He finds an empty room but the nurse tells us it was being used by Dr. Wentzel.

Dr. Campbell retorts, "Well he's not here now!"

Disgusted, he finds a large room at the end of the hall that looks more like a storage room than an examination room. Dr. Campbell looks around and finds a box of nutrition bars. He opens the box and offers me one while taking one himself.

"His chest is clear," he reports after listening to nearly every square inch of it. Dr. Campbell is always thorough and careful. Holding a tongue depressor in his right hand, he opens Ben's mouth rather roughly and immediately sees that his tonsils are very inflamed and oozing a good deal of puss. Ben looks up at Dr. Campbell and appears that he wants to cry but doesn't. Without missing a beat, Dr. Campbell touches Ben's back in a father-like manner and asks him to be calm.

"I guess he must think that I'm comforting and I know what I'm doing!", he exclaims. What a comedian!

We discuss antibiotics, how they really mess up his gut, and how the *Suprax* last time caused a lot of reflux

"OK, no more *Suprax*-ista!", he responds excitedly. We tell him what Dr. Sanderson had said and thought that *Amoxil* would be more gentle on his stomach.

We give Ben his first dose shortly after returning home. With little effort, he swallows all 10 ml. I hate every time he needs an antibiotic.

After a weekend of reflux, I am anxious to see what will unfold. We can be sure that nothing ever stays the same for very long.

* * *

Moving at 100 mph!!

Never has Remembrance Day been anything other than cold, damp, dark and depressing. The somber drizzle and gray-laden sky is an unmistakable sign that winter's nastiness is ever so close. On this November long weekend, Ben has an insatiable appetite. For three straight days, he readily gobbles all food that is placed in front of him. He is also much more gassy, burpy, and spitty than I've seen him. Perhaps it's the increased volume of food or the efficiency with which he consumes every morsel. Nevertheless, his alertness and bumped-up energy level alleviates any concern of reflux I might conjure up, concerns that are constantly brewing and are never far from the surface. My novice diagnostic skills have led me to the conclusion that several days on *Amoxil* is likely the cause for the increase in his gas and tummy activity and not what he has been eating.

Supper is later than usual tonight, not beginning until nearly 6:30 p.m., a result of a late afternoon nap. An hour after finishing every last bite, Ben becomes eerily quiet. My spider-sense is warning me that something isn't right. I can see his mood change from excitement to worry and the colour begin to drain from his face. The reflux tornado is touching down.

Only slightly flustered, I follow my normal routine to bring him around. Three minutes pass but my attempts to quell his reflux have no effect. I try to disturb things somewhat by sticking my finger to the back of his throat, trying to stimulate his gag reflex, anything to unlock his body. Nothing.

My anxiety is increasing and I begin to panic. I'm alone tonight since Jan is at the hospital visiting her father who has recently been having some problems. Our neighbour, Trish, a nurse, has been down and out with the flu for a few days so I can't call her to help. With Ben on my shoulder, I call another neighbour, Mary Ann. One of her sons answers my call to tell me that she's in Halifax. I hang up feeling even more unsettled. It has been eight minutes and he's still not responding to my consoling.

After pacing the floor several times, I decide to call Mary Ann's house again and ask for her husband. One of their other sons, Alec, tells me that he, also, is in Halifax. I think to myself, why didn't you tell me that when I called before. I ask who is looking after them and he tells me their regular sitter. Now I'm really alone. We pass the 10-minute mark and I'm feeling more and more panicky.

The doorbell rings: it's Alec, asking if there's anything he can do to help. I am touched that a 10-year-old wants to offer his assistance but there's nothing he can do. I'm going to be forced to call an ambulance. I don't know what Ben's doing. He's never been "out of it" for this long.

I have to sit down. My back is breaking. With Ben still on my shoulder, I frantically try to reach Jan. A few more minutes tick by and the phone rings. It's Jan. She instructs me to call Tom and Francine to stay with Conor and Tori, and to get Ben to the hospital right away. For some reason, I needed her to make that decision for me.

I immediately call 9-1-1 as Trish walks into the house via the back door. I am perplexed how she knew to come up but quickly realize that Jan must have gotten in touch with her.

The 9-1-1 dispatcher says, "St. Croix Court?", referring to our street name.

"No," I snap back. "St. Coeur Court!!" I don't believe this guy. Does he not have the info right there in front of him? I look over at Ben, held in Trish's arms, and witness him progress into a full-blown seizure. The dispatcher noticeably changes his tone and tells me the paramedics will be there very soon.

In less than two minutes, a fire truck is squealing in front of our house with sirens blaring and lights fully flashing. Three concerned firefighters enter our small family room dressed in full garb. It seems overkill to be wearing their heavy coats to tend to Ben. Nearly 25 minutes have gone by since Ben began his reflux episode. This is too much for him and his whole body starts convulsing. It's becoming too much for me. We need to make this stop.

The firefighters really do nothing more than hold Ben upright and wait for the ambulance to arrive.

It is not long before more flashing red and white lights invade our family room. The paramedics hurry inside and begin to examine Ben, who has just stopped seizing. I tell them about his reflux condition and about his recent seizure. The same firefighter continues to hold Ben as his vitals are checked. His heart rate and respiration seem fine but they decide to take him to the ER.

Strapping him onto the stretcher that is much too big for him, the paramedics quickly wheel him into the back of the ambulance. They instruct me to ride in front. I pause momentarily, thinking they've made a mistake. Seeing one paramedic and the firefighter stay with Ben, I hesitate no more and buckle up for the ride, craning my neck to get a glimpse of Ben as frequently as I can. No sooner do we pull away from our house does Ben begin convulsing again. They let him get through it but give him oxygen to help with his shallow breathing.

As we pull onto the freeway, the driver cranks up the speed, effortlessly surpassing 160 km per hour. For a moment, I forget about Ben's condition, amazed that this vehicle can travel so fast. Approaching the toll booth of the Harbour Bridge, a 1.5 mile span of steel and concrete that marks the dividing line between downtown and west Saint John, the bridge attendant waves us through—as if he has a choice.

Already at the hospital, Jan briefs the ER staff on Ben and the incident from July. Minutes later, Ben is whisked past the ER security guard and into the closest curtained examination space. We try explaining Ben's issue with reflux to the attending physician and how the pain and distress it causes can push Ben into a seizure. He has no idea what we're talking about and has never heard of reflux in children. I have to control myself to not scream, which is very tough to do. Sensing that I'm ready to lose it, Jan intervenes and provides an abbreviated summary. The ER doc stands there expressionless and waits for Jan to finish. With little confidence, he tells the nurses to remove all of Ben's clothes so that he can examine him. I'm not quite sure why Ben has to be stripped. Lying on his back, nearly naked, without a covering blanket and blinded by overhead florescent lighting seems more like abuse to me than treatment.

Before this physician can say any more stupid things, we are greeted by Dr. Ali, a new paediatrician. Without hesitation, she orders *Valium* both rectally and by IV. And to calm him down, she instructs the attending nurse to administer *Dilantin*. The nurse is unsure of how to fulfill this command and asks Dr. Ali how she wants the medication and to what dilution. I can't believe my ears. First a clued-out physician and now a nurse with no skills. Why does Ben always have to be subjected to the bottom 10% of the graduating class? Dr. Ali can't believe her ears either and snaps back at the nurse that she doesn't care about the dilution—she needs 150 mg right away.

Within 10 minutes, Ben's convulsing body relaxes. The meds are working. I knew they would. This time, I didn't fear that he would die. Perhaps I'm getting stronger.

Exhausted, he turns his head towards us and slowly blinks his blood red eyes. I am relieved that he has returned from that unreachable *SeizureWorld*, a place where he is all alone and on his own. All I can do is wait since I have no way to help him back to our world. This helplessness is so, so draining, and frustrating at the same time. A few hours earlier he was showing how smart he is, how happy he can be. Now, without cause or justification, he is none of those things and is forced to stay another horrendous night in PICU.

Dr. Ali is pleased that his oxygen sats are 96% but she wants to keep him at least overnight and run some tests. What choice do we have? He is in no condition to go home right now. His journey from *SeizureWorld* always passes through PICU. We have to stop these before they kill us all.

His cramping and discomfort later in the evening convinces me that reflux really is the sole cause. He doesn't have seizures for no reason. But no one can really tell us why it happens, when it will happen next, how severe the next one will be, or how to stop them. Seizures are always on my mind. I can't seem to let them go. There is a chronic knot in the pit of my stomach that I know is real. Solving his gut issues should be our goal but right now my focus is just to get him home.

*　　*　　*

19

HOW MUCH CAN WE TAKE?

This winter doesn't want to end. Spring officially arrived three days ago but the calendar seems to mean nothing. Mother Nature is just as furious as she was a few months back and nasty winter viruses continue to make our lives miserable.

Last evening, Ben's sleep was interrupted several times with a fever that just wouldn't go away. He vomited twice: not just gagging or coughing that got out of control but all-out heaving.

Today, Ben is feeling worse and worse. Just after lunch, he becomes very listless, not interested in eating or drinking. I take his temperature under the arm, add the degree to make the real core temperature and it's more than 40°C. Now, I'm scared. As Jan and I get ready to take him the ER, he starts convulsing. This one is different from his reflux episodes. It must be because of his really high fever.

Rushing through the ER doors, we tell the admitting person about his fever and his seizure. That's enough for Ben to jump to the front of the queue. The triage nurse asks us when it was that we last gave him Tylenol and then proceeds to give him another dose using a suppository. Within five minutes we are seen by a physician of about Dr. Campbell's age. He introduces himself as Dr. Kerrigan and takes us into the casting room since the other examining rooms are full. Things are hopping in the ER today.

"George, George", he mutters to himself. "Are you any relation to Dr. George?"

"He's my father", I reply.

I'm not sure if that's an asset or a liability the way he responds but he does give Ben the once-over. Again, a lot like Dr. Campbell. Ben is shivery under the bright lights as Dr. Kerrigan looks in his ears. He tells us both are very inflamed and likely the reason for his high fever. After listening to us describe the horrors of reflux, he responds that we likely know Ben best and that if we think Ben can fight the infection without antibiotics then that's perfectly reasonable.

Wow, someone with common sense and the first ER doc who really understands us. Can we reserve this guy every time?

Always on my mind

Waiting for the next major episode is a feeling that never goes away. My anxiety ebbs and flows but it is always there. It doesn't matter if I'm sleeping or awake, tired or energetic, it continues to swirl. And it seems more prevalent when I'm alone. Like this morning. Jan's shift ended at 3 a.m. and she needs her sleep, so it's my turn to feed Ben breakfast and get him ready for playschool. Conor and Tori are quite independent now and have little problem getting themselves ready.

As I get him washed and dressed, he grows a little quiet, likely from flipping him back and forth to get his clothes on properly. Nothing more comes of it but my anxiety level moves from green to yellow. His bus driver is a few minutes late—thankfully, since I'm not nearly as efficient as Jan. There is just enough time for Lonnie to reposition his jacket and mitts. His morning at school is stimulating and he is eager to learn today despite his messed up gastro parts.

In the afternoon, Lisa makes a rare home visit to see Ben in his stander. This is so much more convenient than having to drag Ben and the stander to the hospital. The quality of its construction makes it easy to get properly positioned. It is padded in all of the appropriate spots and very easy to adjust. I guess it *should* be for $2,200.

Lisa is pleasantly surprised at how Ben is able to keep his head upright and in midline. After tightening the rear belts and arm straps, I begin to quell my reflux worries and feel a hint of positive energy that maybe getting him upright will be a good thing, to let gravity help. This is a new experience for Ben, a new position, being on his feet instead of his bum. I think he likes it.

Ben's success is enough to give me the courage to reach out to the principal of a MOVE school in Baltimore, Maryland to ask her about the stander and how we could start using the curriculum. She congratulates us for getting the mobile stander for Ben and suggests that we, along with Ben's therapists, get some formal training from MOVE's creator, Linda Bidabe. She tells that it's one thing to read the curriculum guide but there would be incredible value from working with Linda.

I tell her that that's not likely to happen since we can't get anyone here to buy into the programme. I ask her if we videotaped Ben in various settings, including in his stander, could she and her team provide some direction and guidance on how we might work with the programme—kind of like a virtual consultation. She welcomed my suggestion and told me they would look forward to seeing what Ben is all about.

I'm sure bringing someone like Linda Bidabe to town or even visiting the school in Baltimore would be money well spent, but it's money we don't have. In the end, that's what it always comes down to. Ben's development shouldn't be dependent on how much money we have: It shouldn't but it is what it is.

* * *

One step forward, two steps back

December descends upon us. The darkness and frigid desolation of winter is creeping into our lives without our permission. The first Saturday of the month presents us with an opportunity to enjoy another neighbourhood potluck. The wind chill outside hovers near -20°C but the warmth of our conversations inside and a few glasses of wine overcome winter's power. Ben decides that his parents need a break and he falls asleep with little effort.

The next weekend, we're part of the audience to watch Conor assume the role of *The Colonel* in the short play, "The Cactus Wildcat". He has been part of a community-based theatre for a few months, culminating in today's performance. Donning layers of white makeup to transform his face into that of a 67-year-old, he rattles off his lines flawlessly, even *ad libbing* a bit. Again, Ben cooperates and gives us a break.

A few days later, Jan is back on the night shift and I'm home with everyone. Ben is tired tonight and goes to bed early. Not a sound is heard from his room for quite a while until a few soft noises trickle through the monitor. I enter his room to check on him. He is flat on his back in a reflux position, panicky, scared, and struggling to breathe. My eyes widen, not knowing how long he has been this way. Immediately, I scoop him from his bed being sure that this is a serious episode. He is unbelievably stiff, almost frozen, and not straightening out his body as he has the last few times—perhaps because he had been asleep? (or was he?); perhaps because I wasn't there soon enough to pick him up?

This is turning into an ER visit. I page Jan at work who makes quick calls to her sister, Rita, and to our neighbour, Mary Ann. A crowd of concerned people descend on our tiny home within minutes and we all try to get Ben to come round. Dr. Gamble, a paediatrician with whom we are somewhat familiar, is on call tonight and I describe to him Ben's condition. He tells me he will get in touch with Dr. Norris.

Ben continues to take very shallow breaths. Jan and I debate giving him *Valium*. He's not convulsing so we wait. After a few more minutes of no improvement, Rita's husband, a cop, suggests taking us to the ER in his police cruiser. We acquiesce.

Flying through intersections and traffic lights, I wonder if Ben is starting to convulse. It's so hard to tell.

Once past the admitting personnel, we are met with the physician on-call. Of course, he knows nothing about Ben. It's not his fault but it doesn't change the fact that we have to go back to square one yet again! He thinks the reflux episodes sound like seizures (everyone keeps saying that) and ponders whether to give Ben a dose of *Valium*. We push back, believing Ben is starting to come around since he is now very irritable and squirming, a typical reaction after a bad episode.

The nurses attempt to start an IV but struggle to find a vein, as is often the case. I shake my head. Is this improper training, inexperience, or a lousy staffing schedule? Shouldn't there be an "expert" on every shift? Why does Ben have to suffer from second-raters? A short time later, Dr. Gamble arrives and is furious that no one had kept him up to date on what was happening. After four unsuccessful pokes by the nurses to find a vein, Dr. Gamble tries and finds a site close to the bend of Ben's wrist.

The reflux continues off and on for a couple of hours. Just when we think it's all over and Ben seems to be coherent, he goes back into his locked state but only for about 30 seconds at a time. By 2:30 a.m., more than four hours after this nightmare began, Dr. Gamble orders *Valium*. Within a few minutes, Ben's body relaxes, the episodes fade away, and his fiery red bloodshot eyes begin to close. Is this because he is completely exhausted since we waited so long to recognize that he did, in fact, need *Valium*? If we had given it to him at home, could this visit have been avoided? I don't know anymore.

We arrive at PICU shortly after 3 a.m. and the nurse wheels Ben's gurney next to an empty crib. There is no way a three-and-a-half-year-old should be placed in a crib, and I'm sure if Ben had been "normal" that wouldn't have been considered. Jan and I exchange looks and then interrupt the nurse,

"The last time we were here, Dr. Campbell told us he prefers that Ben be in a bed, not a crib," Jan declares.

The nurse pauses. I'm sure she's too tired to argue with us and, without uttering a word, steers the gurney to the adjacent bed. Dr. Campbell really hadn't said that at all.

After being transferred to the bed, Ben opens his eyes slightly to see where he is. He puts up no resistance as his blood pressure is taken and his vitals are checked. A second nurse approaches us and says she needs to weigh him. I understand that there is a protocol to follow upon admission to the Unit but what purpose does it really serve at this moment, after all Ben has been through? Couldn't it wait until the morning to weigh him? Is everyone really that deficient of their common-sense quotient? I keep to myself but their actions only serve to reinforce my disdain for this wretched place.

Jan is on top of her game and says,

"Oh, he was just weighed last week and he was 30 lbs!"

This, of course, is a lie. (Not that he doesn't weigh somewhere close to 30 lbs—we know that to be true—but he really hadn't been weighed last week.) Taking Jan's word, they are content to record that weight. If that's all it takes, why disturb an exhausted child?

Several moments later, the resident comes to visit. She feels the need to turn the lights back on and tells us she's going to examine Ben. Hold on now—didn't the nurses just do that? She also feels it's important to test his reflexes. OK, whatever you think, I say to myself, but he's completely wiped and still has *Valium* circulating in his body. Fortunately, Ben is too tired to care.

I choose to stay with him for the night and find an upright, hard-back chair that I drag over beside his bed. I try to sleep, or at least close my eyes, until my head bobs and wakes me up. The nurses examine him every hour, listening to his chest, checking his pupils and taking his blood pressure. No wonder I can't sleep.

As the overhead clock ticks its way past 7 a.m., Ben opens his eyes and is a little confused. I jump to my feet and bend close to his hearing-aidless ears to console him. He goos a few times but I can tell he is still tired. He's probably tired of sleeping on the same side. I carefully turn his relaxed body and he easily falls back to sleep.

At a quarter to nine, Jan arrives looking a tiny bit more refreshed and certainly cleaner than I am. Not long after, Dr. Norris enters the Unit and makes his way to Ben's bedside. He does a cursory examination and then pulls up a chair to discuss what has happened.

After listening closely to our summary, he tells us that Ben could be so scared and so stiff from the pain of the reflux that it would be difficult for him to relax on his own to let the reflux subside. If we had given him *Valium*, it would likely have allowed his body to relax enough to stop the reflux cycle. The drug is very safe and has "a half life" of only 50 minutes. He says that Ben probably has dystonia, or sustained muscle contractions, which would keep the episode going. The turning of his head may be an indication of what's called the *Sandifer Response*, and not a seizure at all, at least not in the beginning of the episode.

Dr. Norris is a good listener, I'll give him that. He gives us a prescription for small ampoules of *Valium* and decides that there is no need to consider any long-term seizure meds at this point. As we finish up the conversation, Dr. Campbell comes into the Unit. Dr. Norris looks at his watch and jokes,

"It's a little early for you?" he says to Dr. Campbell. Turning to us, Dr. Norris quips, "He probably hasn't gone to bed yet!"

Dr. Campbell chuckles and mumbles something back. They have a good relationship.

After listening to Ben's chest and looking in his throat and ears, Dr. Campbell asks if we feel comfortable going home. He's catching on. We, of course, respond emphatically, "Yes!" Before leaving, he tells us he agrees with Dr. Norris's assessment and informs us that many people have reflux in one form or another.

Staying in this place gives me more than reflux. But somehow this time, we've managed to keep the hell to only 12 hours.

Shortly before noon, we pull into our driveway. Ben is exhausted. So am I, although my body hasn't been put through the wringer like his has. He falls asleep easily, thankful to be home. A few hours later, he opens his eyes, still devoid of energy but not unhappy. We give him a drink but don't even try any solid food, not with all of his reflux. At about 7:30 p.m., he manages to consume about 120 ml of *Isomil* but it doesn't settle well. Within in a few hours, he's asleep in his own bed. We're all grateful for that.

*   *   *

When he's good, he's really good

The next morning Ben awakes happy and somewhat refreshed. His appetite slowly returns as the day wears on. In the evening, he is lying on Tori's bed while I help her clean her room. Ben gets a burst of energy and begins kicking wildly. This is quite amazing given the events of the past 24 hours. He manages to inch his way to the edge of the bed leaving his legs dangling before he stops. It's clearly a game as he tries to figure out why his feet aren't touching anything. Tori scolds him for getting so close to falling.

On Saturday, he shows signs of hunger and is eager to eat a half bowl full of cereal. A good sign. Some friends get together with us in the evening for a relaxing meal. Ben is quite lively and enjoys the company. He is such a social person.

The weekend draws to a close too quickly but Jan still has time to prepare a meal for my parents and deliver it to them. My mother is laid up with recently operated toes and a cellulitis in her leg. She is in a pleasant mood today, thanking Jan for her thoughtfulness and commenting how resilient we are—in the emergency room one night, entertaining last night, and then having the energy to bring supper to them today. From time to time, like tonight, my mother shows flashes that she kind of understands our life.

Monday, Ben is great—active, bright, happy, and hungry. Tuesday, the same though he awakes a little later. The school buses are running an hour late due to the overnight accumulation of snow so Jan takes Conor and Tori to school by car. I start feeding Ben at 8:25 a.m. which doesn't leave a lot of time to get ready for his playschool. By 9 a.m., he is in his snowsuit, waiting in our driveway to be picked up. Snow is blowing across his face, the light flakes tickling as they dance across his cheeks. He smiles, enjoying the cool breeze. After being buckled inside the school van, Ben looks out his window and smiles again as he is driven away.

Wednesday arrives and he is up early, ready to go to school. It's our participation day today so I take him. I ride with him in the van, instead of Lonnie, and notice just how active he becomes on the five-minute ride to school. All day long, at school and at home, Ben is full of energy, kicking his legs, moving his body, and verbalizing constantly. He doesn't want to nap today—he wants to keep going—as if he is going to miss something. It's days like today when I feel he is able to do all kinds of things—he is certainly strong enough to do whatever he wants. Somehow, we must ensure he is always occupied with doing something, to maximize every second he is feeling well. I really can't remember when he has ever had back-to-back days as good as these.

That evening, he is sitting in his usual spot after supper, looking around as Tori and Conor dash into the room. When Tori approaches him, he immediately turns to look at her and gets quite vocal, his eyes wide with excitement. She walks by him and then turns quickly, running back in front of him. I'm not quite sure what she's doing but it doesn't matter to Ben. His head movements are instant and quick, following her every move. I get the sense that he wants to get up and follow her.

This is something new, showing a keener interest in his siblings. For the past few nights, after going to bed, Ben has been looking over at Conor, talking with his eyes, and Conor wastes no time jumping over to him to give his baby brother a good night kiss. Ben doesn't let his PICU stays get him down. He is enjoying life whenever he can.

* * *

A heavy sigh

The new week begins with a physio appointment with Lisa. I attend the appointment with Lonnie since Jan is with her father for some blood work and other tests. Lisa stretches Ben out on a mat on the floor and comments how he continues to have very good flexibility and range of motion. She attempts to get him to look at her stale and tired, uninteresting toys and, of course, he does not give them a glance. Something about insanity and doing the same thing repeatedly and expecting a different result is playing over and over in my head. Ben is, however, quite interested to look up over his head and kick.

Being prepared for an unproductive appointment, I have packed Ben's little mirror on wheels and the old standby—a blue/white coloured empty milk carton. After Lisa is unsuccessful in getting his interest, I pull out the mirror and he is drawn to it immediately. I follow this up with the milk carton and Ben, as he has done on many occasions, does his best to reach for it to touch it. Lisa is impressed that he is reaching for things and decides to put him on his belly. With the milk carton being moved back and forth in front of him, Ben pushes up on his forearms almost effortlessly and follows the carton. His movements are very quick.

Then she sits Ben on her lap and leans him from one side to the other to follow the carton. When leaning to the left he rights his head perfectly but when leaning to the right, to look back to his left to find the carton, it is more difficult for him. Next, Lisa stands him on the floor and he bears weight very well. She is equally impressed with this feat and suggests we get a set of AFOs (ankle-foot orthos) for his ankles to keep his feet in a better position. I raise my eyebrows and think to myself,

"You mean we're actually moving onto another stage in his development?"

I mention how much he is reaching and moving about as a result of the Little Room. Her only response is to talk about the "homemade" one they had in the department. I'm not sure where it came from but it is nothing more than a wooden box that I can't imagine would be interesting for anyone. Lilli Nielsen's design is made from light metal tubing and the walls are clear Plexiglas to allow an abundance of light and ventilation. And the walls resemble a pegboard that are interchangeable and provide auditory feedback. While I am certainly no expert, I think I've grasped the purpose behind the Little Room. It's clear that Lisa has not. I sigh in frustration, realizing that she still doesn't get it.

Does Ben have too many issues for her? Is that the reason? Or does she not believe that he will really ever achieve much so why bother? I want to be polite but it's getting tougher and tougher. Ben doesn't have forever to start learning.

*   *   *

A cross-town getaway

One of the things we are not, or at least *I* am not, is spontaneous. Not that I was really that way before Ben was born but now I'm definitely not. I'm too much on the edge of my seat, not knowing how Ben will react to things, when his next reflux episode will be, or his next seizure. I wish for consistency in my life, some small level of predictability, where I can go somewhere and do something fun without worrying what Ben might do.

However, something comes over us (something spontaneous) as we approach the last weekend in January, a month that has had its share of highs and lows, that never seems to end, that is simply long, arduous and depressing.

Jan decides we just need to get away for a night, with the kids, for a change of scenery. We have no money to go far—we never do—but we ponder spending a night in a local hotel. We could use the pool, rent some Nintendo games and escape the all-too familiar surroundings of home.

The Hilton on the waterfront is about as nice as it gets in our town. Built a little more than 10 years ago, it is still relatively new. Its rustic red-brick exterior and brass complements along with the covered entrance and cozy circular driveway bring a touch of class and elegance to this blue-collar town. Its *Turn-of-the-Tide* dining room is pricey but has a quiet and relaxing setting that allows an unfiltered view of the water. I think it's a great idea.

The hotel has plenty of room—it's January in Saint John. No one comes here on vacation at this time of year. And anyone on business wouldn't stay a weekend.

Conor and Tori are excited to stay overnight in a strange place although they don't quite understand why we would stay in a hotel this close to home. Ben is content to tag along but, I think, couldn't really care less that we've planned this cross-town getaway.

We arrive over the supper hour and choose to splurge on room service. It's a little pampering that we can't afford but definitely deserve. It's not really a vacation by any stretch but I find it relaxing, peaceful, and comforting. I can catch my breath for a brief time and not worry about the tiresome details of cleaning up, making meals, or doing laundry.

It's just different, staying overnight with Ben, not because of an IWK visit, or a PICU visit. But because we choose to do this. We have control over our lives tonight.

*   *   *

Someone sent to help

Shift work is a killer. Jan has been living it for far too long: 3 to 11; 5 to 1; 11 to 7—a.m. that is. The overnight ones are the hardest. Jan jumps at the offer of a 5 p.m.-1 a.m. shift for an extended period, with an occasional overnight. This forces us to find a permanent babysitter which is a big step for us, even though we had Tara look after everyone during our stay in Toronto. It will mean that Jan and I will be like two ships passing in the night but we need to get into a regular routine. Our pace is unsustainable.

We interview many people, some whom I would not want looking after our dog (if we had a dog). One candidate is a woman in her early 50s, soft spoken but confident. She isn't interested in full-time work (which is good because we can't afford full-time). She was the only one who asked to see Ben and to hold him. She wasn't afraid of him and her short conversation with him was genuine. There's something about this person, Gloria, that convinces us to take a chance.

Gloria's first week on the job is the first week of February. Conor and Tori are enjoying the new face and Ben is quite content. Arriving home mid-week, I find Gloria skimming through a book on "Early Learning" for kids with CP. She is very keen and seems quite natural in her approach. I have a really good feeling about her.

Each day when she arrives, she is ready to put him to work—getting him to stand, having him sit in front of his plastic *Gymfinity* toy, holding a variety of objects in his hands. On one occasion, I find Gloria getting Ben to stand and watch TV. Tori is standing behind him, moving one of his feet forward and then another, like he is walking. For the first time, I notice that his feet are almost flat on the floor.

On Saturday afternoon, Ben and I are in the living room and I position him standing, looking out of the window. I am amazed that he is able to bear weight for several minutes and remain fairly straight through it all. All the work that Gloria is putting him through is paying off, making him stronger and more coordinated, able to bear weight for several minutes at a time, allowing him to accomplish routine things like stand up and look out the living room windows.

Gloria has embraced the role much more quickly than we could have expected. She is driven to give Ben as much opportunity to develop as possible and to give us a break whenever we think we need it.

After a few hectic weeks of Jan's new schedule, she and I finally get to compare notes. I tell her that Gloria has been getting Ben to stand several times each day and he has actually become better at standing. He is displaying a new level of confidence.

We recall how Gloria had said she knew a good friend of my Aunt Vicki, and how Gloria still visits this friend to help her with day-to-day tasks. Jan believes that Vicki somehow "got through" to her friend to bring Gloria to us. It's a little spooky to really believe this but it also seems a little more than pure chance. Maybe Jan is right. Gloria does seem like someone chosen to help us. She has adapted so quickly and Ben has responded very well. At certain times in your life, there really are those who will help you along the way—champions, I like to call them. Perhaps she's one of them.

* * *

Waiting outside the doors

The weekend arrives rather calmly and we're glad. Adjusting to a new schedule has been tiring. We need the rest. Jan is exhausted today having spent a lot of time with her father over the past few weeks. His health is noticeably deteriorating. Since his car accident and ruptured aneurysm, life for Clem hasn't been the same. I can't help wondering what effect this traumatic event has had on his body. I'm sure it has upset his equilibrium and the mechanisms that have been keeping things in check for many years, weakening his body's compensatory systems. The suddenness and rapidity of his failing health is something no one expected.

After I return home with Conor and Tori from the neighbourhood rink, Jan decides to take a nap. Within minutes, Ben wakes from his nap, clutching in pain. Now, what's starting? It doesn't last, and for the rest of the afternoon and evening he is fine.

Less than an hour after Ben is snuggled into bed, we hear him breathing and snorting fast. I rush to his bedside and pick him up as he throws out his arms in pain: another reflux episode but one that lasts only a few minutes. He is quite tired and settles back to sleep. Twenty minutes later, he awakens, clutching in the same manner, and this time it lasts a little longer. I carry him downstairs to rock him while we watch TV. After nestling on Jan's shoulder, he falls asleep.

Like clockwork, another 20 minutes pass and his eyes fly open in panic, engulfed in another episode. I hate this. Jan passes Ben to me to see if he would be more comfortable on my shoulder. He lasts an hour this time before waking again.

Ben's body is now very rigid and his eyes are full of fear. This episode lasts more than 20 minutes as we dither about whether or not to give him *Valium*. In the heat of the moment, it's not an easy decision to make, one that we have never had to make before. His breathing isn't as shallow as other times but he does not want to come round on his own.

I bring him upstairs to the family room and lay him on the couch. Jan injects half of the dose, only 2.5 mg, still uncertain whether this is the right thing to do. His eyes are bloodshot and he remains rigid. After 10 minutes, Jan calls Dr. Campbell. Dr. Smythe is on call and almost instantly, he calls back. Jan explains the situation. Very calmly, Dr. Smythe instructs us to watch Ben's breathing carefully, and after 20 minutes or so (there's seems to be something special about 20-minute intervals), if he settles down and we feel comfortable, then it's okay to stay home.

Since the first half dose hasn't been effective, we decide to give him the rest of the dose of *Valium*. His body completely relaxes. Jan holds him on her shoulder as he becomes very squirmy and irritable. Even with his eyes closed, he is moaning a lot. In the meantime, Rita arrives, ready to stay with Conor and Tori if we plan to take Ben to the hospital. We can't decide.

Wanting to make sure the *Valium* isn't bothering him, we jump in the car and dash to the hospital. I hold him while Jan drives. He continues to squirm but is not refluxing at all. We arrive at the front doors of the ER and pause, hesitant about going in and content to wait it out. We can't really get any closer to the ER without actually being *in* it. If we go in, they'll ask the thousand questions that we have answered a thousand times before, and they will want to take his temperature and listen to his chest and start an IV and take some blood and on and on, and we will be there all night.

About 15 minutes pass and Ben begins to heave. It is successful this time though not much comes up. He seems more settled. We wait another half hour, idling outside the doors, before heading for home. Half way home Ben throws up again and we pull off the road to make it a little more comfortable for him. By 1 a.m., we are pulling into our driveway. Inside, everyone is asleep including Rita. Ben has to vomit again but there's nothing left to bring up.

There's no sense putting him in his own bed so Jan and I decide to pull out the bed in our family room couch. I lie down, holding Ben upright, while Jan sleeps a little. His poor body wretches again but it seems that this episode is nearing the end. We are able to lie him beside us, propped up on a couple of pillows.

At 2:30 a.m., I awake with a start, my mind playing tricks on me, capitalizing on my over-tiredness. Feeling his forehead, I realize Ben is burning up. Jan gives him an *Abenol* suppository. He remains asleep for another four hours until the phone rings. It's Dr. Smythe wanting to know how Ben is doing.

He is amazing. I tell him what we did, that we had sat in the parking lot, undecided, for almost an hour. He chuckles a bit but understands.

Ben opens his eyes shortly after 7 a.m. and is exhausted. I clue in that it's actually Monday morning, and quickly get showered and ready for work. I'm not sure how productive I'll be today. Before leaving, I check on him and Jan. They're both asleep and quite calm. I wish I were right there with them.

* * *

"He's gone!"

I don't know how Jan is surviving on so little sleep. Working the 5-to-1 shift, battling through Ben's reflux, rushing to the ER, and spending all other free time (whatever that is) at her father's bedside. Even the day after our stressful rush to the ER with Ben, she is back at the hospital in the palliative care unit with her father. It's not a subject we talk about in great detail but we both know we're going to be getting a call, soon.

She is extremely close to her father. From the time she was just a kid helping him with his deliveries, Clem has always been a special person in her life. He put his family first, no matter what the occasion or crisis, and had little time for bureaucracy and wastefulness. Jan relies on him for his wisdom and advice, and turns to him for love and compassion when things get tough, especially with Ben. Clem has helped in so many ways, from babysitting to keeping Conor and Tori occupied when we couldn't. Thoroughly enjoying his grandchildren is an under-statement and they are better people thanks to him.

Over the last several months, in particular since his awful car accident, Jan has returned his love and dedication to help him get through one hospital visit after another. It seems to be a place we see much too often. Her journey to the hospital this morning is with a heavy heart. The nurses have told her that he is slipping and they don't expect him to last more than a few days. The malignancies seem to be winning.

Two evenings later, all is quiet at home. Ben is finally starting to feel better, thank God! As I finish wiping clean the kitchen counter, the phone rings. The display shows "Unknown Name / Unknown Number". I guess that it's someone calling from a cell phone. I'm right.

"Hello", I answer. There are a few seconds of silence, and then, in a slow whisper, comes a trembling voice.

"He's gone!"

It's Jan. That's all she can say. I stare out the tiny kitchen window at the thin blanket of dirty, crusty snow. It's as desolate as this moment. I'm speechless again, like the day Ben was born. She's a mess, sobbing. No blessed wonder.

"Ah, Jan", I answer softly. "That's awful. I'm so sorry". I can't find the words. Even those I do find don't fit. I can't do anything. I feel helpless, again.

"Okay. I'll talk to you later," Jan replies, ending the conversation.

It doesn't seem fair. No, it isn't fair. How can someone so special be taken so early, after only 67 years? Why do Conor, Tori and Ben have to miss out on his teasing and loving ways?

What started out as a very stressful week has crescendoed into unbelievable sadness and grief, reminiscent of that first awful week nearly four years ago. The wake is on Friday. It doesn't seem real. Trish generously offers to look after the kids, at times nine of them at our house, so that both Jan and I can be at the wake.

Saturday morning arrives and we're all beyond tired. Fortunately, Ben has returned to normal and last Sunday's ER encounter feels like it was weeks ago. Without being asked, both Lonnie and Gloria arrive to help look after the kids while we attend the funeral. Conor and Tori feel our sorrow and tell us they'll be good. Of course, they will. They always are.

The day is cold and windy, and that in no way helps us get through it. Returning home, we find a house full of content children. Ben made out just fine and behaved himself as Gloria fed him for the first time. While I'm relieved that things went smoothly, I'm not sure I could have done anything had they not.

Our lives have suddenly become lonely again.

*   *   *

Too much to balance

It all doesn't seem real. Sitting in the quiet of our living room, I try to make sense of why life keeps getting more and more difficult. It seems the harder we try, the more things we do right, the bigger our burden grows. We are fortunate to now have a good support structure but we don't seem to be making any progress.

I try to reconcile the dread of the past four years, try to understand the purpose of it all. It's impossible today. My heart aches for Jan but at the same time it has been left empty. I search for a silver lining and find none.

Clem's eulogy provided no comfort. It was delivered by a wacko priest who insisted he had to be the one presiding over the ceremony even though he didn't know Clem at all. He made up some bizarre, unrelated story about tea and sandwiches that had nothing to do with Clem's life and left people very unsettled.

Looking back to March 1992, it began with the death of my Aunt Vicki. Three months later, Ben's arrival highlighted our unpreparedness and signaled a beginning of endless anxiety and uncertainty. Three months after that, Ummi died. And even though he told me to never give up, I don't know where I'm going to find the strength to live up to those final words.

Battling seizures, reflux, ER visits, ambulance rides, useless therapists, idiotic physicians, ever-conflicting information, financial stresses, unsupportive family members, and now death. How can we balance it all? Why do bad things keep happening to us? What is God's plan? Does He really have one? Have we somehow been forgotten?

There doesn't seem to be any stability at all in our lives. Any glimmer of hope gets snuffed out by a force ten times larger than required. Today, it is too much to handle.

*   *   *

20

MORE REFLUX

Several months ago, we acknowledged the fact that living with Ben in a home with stairs was not going to work. At three years of age, his lack of walking skills has made his care too complex. And, though he is small and light for his age, somewhere near the fifth percentile on the growth chart, he is only going to get bigger, heavier, and, some day, impossible for us to carry.

Through an acquaintance of Rita's husband, we found a skilled draftsman who offered to draw up engineering-quality house plans on the cheap. We chose a one-story, ranch-style home, that is essentially our current three-level-split home stretched out onto one level. It has extra-wide hallways and doorways for easy access, plus hardwood floors throughout to permit free movement of a wheelchair.

It is going to be a very expensive and risky venture. We have never attempted anything like this before and have no idea how it will all come together. Sooner or later, stairs will become too big a barrier to ignore so we really have little choice. After getting estimates from a number of local contractors, whose inflated prices grossly exceeded the appraisal cost of our future home, our only option is to build it ourselves (hiring the sub-contractors, that is). I try to ignore how we will balance this responsibility with all of the other craziness of our lives.

The parcel of land we want doesn't look like much: an uneven terrain overgrown with tangled dead grass. But it is a corner lot and a great location on the city's west side. Many of the lots in this 50-year-old subdivision are actually double lots. It hasn't been advertised but we find out that the owner wants to sell it. It's pricey but it's perfect. There are no competing offers so we close the deal fast.

We got lucky for a change. That doesn't happen very often.

Multi-tasking is the norm

Ben has been great all day and enjoys the 10-minute jaunt from our house to where our new home will be. In the open expanse, Conor is eager to run around while Tori is content to mosey back and forth, kicking her boots at some loose gravel. The overcast sky doesn't provide a lot of warmth but Ben doesn't complain, sitting quietly in his stroller. I try to picture where the garage will be and start pacing off its perimeter. Glancing over at Ben, I notice that his head is turned to one side and it appears to be locked. My eyes widen in a bit of panic. Not again!

I run to him, pick him up and start walking very quickly for home, compressing his back to help him breathe more deeply. It's impossible to run with him on my shoulder. Conor and Tori grab the stroller and push it back home. Within a few minutes, as I scurry across a neighbour's lawn, Mary Ann spots us and calls out, "Is Ben all right?" She knows it seems strange for me to be carrying Ben.

"NO!", I yell back.

She closes her car door and runs towards me to help. When we get inside our family room, Mary Ann finds a towel for me and proceeds to remove Ben's shoes and socks so that she can stroke the soles of his bare feet. Within seconds, he comes around and returns to a normal breathing pattern. His colour instantly improves but he is completely drained.

As the next few days pass, it becomes clear that he is having tummy issues, awaking early in the mornings, unable to fall back to sleep, very laughy with lots of gas. At the end of the week, we are off to the hospital to meet Dr. Campbell so he can check his ears and throat which seem to have been bothering him again.

Pulling onto University Avenue, just minutes away, Ben has a reflux episode. I find a open area next to the physical plant of the hospital to stop. Jan rubs his tummy, coaching him to relax, and he comes around on his own. It is brief but long enough to make him quiet.

We appreciate Dr. Campbell meeting us on short notice but he is never on time. Today, he's forty minutes late. The delay gives Ben some time to come back to normal. Ben's right ear is a little red and his throat is definitely irritated. However, Dr. Campbell believes that since this irritation has come and gone over the last few weeks, we should give Ben another week and see if it finally disappears. If not, then he will likely prescribe something. He tells us that the body can get a little weaker each time it comes back and won't be as effective fighting it.

Knowing that antibiotics bother Ben's tummy so much, he suggests trying the drug in its capsule form and mixing the powder with food or drink. He says that there are often a slew of additives and colouring in the liquid form, and those things may bother Ben. He mentions that a certain asthma medicine he used to prescribe contained a coloring that actually *aggravated* asthma in some people!

The next week is hectic. We finalize the details of the land purchase for the new house, Conor and Tori compete in the provincial music festival (it must be spring!), and we get ourselves ready for another IWK trip. Life is flying by.

* * *

A long, long day

Monday arrives a little too early. Travelling always hits us the next day. Ben was bright, happy and talkative when we arrived in Halifax yesterday but he is feeling none of that today. We have an incredibly long list of appointments to complete and we need to be very organized. Minutes before leaving our hotel room, Ben gets very quiet, lets out a little squeal and outstretches his arms. This reflux monster continues to torture all of us. It doesn't last long and on the short drive to the IWK Ben's mood bounces back. I don't want to deal with reflux today. I'm too tired. The continuing episodes are becoming increasingly burdensome.

The first appointment is with our audiologist friend, Russ. He is unusually late for our 9 a.m. appointment, which gives us a chance to eat our cinnamon buns from GrabbaJabba, our favourite coffee shop. The difference with Russ being late versus another specialist is that he is always respectful of our time, especially Ben's schedule. If Russ is late, it's not because he's disorganized, or inefficient, or had no idea that you were coming, or that he booked three people at the same time.

Ben's hearing test results are nearly identically to those of last November, which is surprising given his morning reflux. Russ notices the tubing of both hearing aids have formed small cracks and he replaces them with ease. Proudly, he tells of his upcoming trip to Colorado where he'll learn about cochlear implants. Jan and I are pleased that Russ is comfortable enough with us to share this. Clearly, our relationship with him is growing.

Before leaving, he reminds us of the benefit an FM system could provide to Ben, especially in school. Jan explains that we've been dealing with a lot of things recently, including the death of her father, but we are eager to try it soon.

Our 10:15 a.m. appointment with Dentistry turns into a 10:35 a.m. start. Dr. Anthony apologizes for his tardiness, welcomes Ben, and gets down to business. Since the dental chair is too big for Ben, we place his head on Dr. Anthony's lap and his legs on me. As each tooth is examined, he recommends brushing near the gum-line a little more to prevent small cavities from forming. But he does give us a 9 out of 10. Dr. Anthony points out where Ben's teeth have poked through even more since his dental surgery and is pleased to learn that we have begun the process of weaning Ben from a bottle.

I take Ben into an adjacent room for some quick X-rays of his jaw and teeth and then rush to our next appointment. Jan tells the dental receptionist that we will check back later with Dr. Anthony regarding the X-rays. We're already 15 minutes late for Remedial Seating. Jan takes everyone to the clinic while I retrieve Ben's custom seat and car seat from our rental van. We really need to purchase a new van. Sooner or later, with all of Ben's gear, we will be forced to reconcile this issue. A new house, a new van? I need to win the lottery!

Both Ben's stroller and car seat check out well. His custom seat is passable with two exceptions: the seat belt is not holding his growing pelvis properly and the lateral supports aren't doing their job at all. We leave it with Dan to make the adjustments and rely on the stroller to transport Ben for the next few hours. It's now lunch time and everyone is ravenous.

The cafeteria is busy today. Conor and Tori know exactly what they want for lunch and what lineup to be in. I am amazed by their confidence and comfort. To them it's familiar territory, perhaps a bit too familiar. What kind of childhood memories will they have about this place, I wonder? Despite the chaos of a few hundred people milling about, moving around us, in front of us, stopping to chat beside us, Ben eats a good lunch.

With reasonably full bellies, we make our way to the Ophthalmology department. They are running behind schedule and so we use the extra time to pick out a new pair of glasses frames for Ben in the adjacent optical storefront.

Forty minutes later, a voice summons Ben. It's now 2:25 p.m. We are taken into a narrow and dimly lit examining room and asked the usual questions. Another set of visual acuity tests are conducted but Ben's scores are higher this time: he is able to see lines that are quite difficult to distinguish. The technician exams the lenses in his glasses, writes down a few figures, and proceeds to deposit drops in Ben's eyes. As each drop lands on his eye, Ben inhales sharply and can't seem to catch his breath. He moans a little, and then blinks a thousand times. She instructs us to return in about 40 minutes.

We take a quick elevator ride down six floors to the basement and head for the seating clinic to get Ben's seat back. A lot of adjustments are made (stronger lateral supports; a wider, more durable seat belt; lengthened shoulder straps; and lowered foot plates) while Ben sleeps in the seat itself. As we leave, Judy stops to welcome us back and is happy that they were able to make Ben's seat more comfortable. We exchange email addresses to make booking our next appointment a little easier.

This extra conversation makes us five minutes late for Ben's orthopaedic appointment. I ask to see Dr. Harrison, the new ortho surgeon, and inform the admitting person that we have only half an hour since Ben has drops in his eyes. She stares back at me and tells me to take a seat. She doesn't even try to help.

While we wait, Conor and Tori find a new toy called a Space Piano. It is a tall wooden structure, about four feet wide and six feet high, but only about six inches thick. In the middle, there is an opening nearly the width of the structure where, if you place your hand inside, a note or group of notes will be heard. It is quite fascinating since your fingers do not touch anything. The faster you move your hands back and forth in mid air, the more notes are heard.

Ben's name is called just as the symphony is revving up. We are forced to first see an intern who collects a bit of history. One of these times I'm going to make it all up and tell complete lies, just to see if they are really listening. Ben has remained asleep since the seating clinic appointment and only after being deposited onto the examining table does he slowly open his enormous pupils. The young doctor in training informs us that Ben's hamstrings and heel cords are tight but that his hips are fine and his back is straight. Two out of four, I guess? Despite his fatigue, Ben is able to demonstrate that he can bear weight for a short period of time. The intern leaves and tells us that Dr. Harrison will be in shortly.

While we wait, I dash to Dentistry to find out the results of the X-rays. Dr. Anthony is standing at the front desk and informs me that ". . . they're perfect!" The only words I hear! Ben . . . perfect . . . hmm.

Hurrying back to the ortho clinic I find that Dr. Harrison has still not seen Ben. I catch the intern's attention, telling him that we were due back in the eye clinic 15 minutes ago and aren't sure how long the eye drops will last. He acknowledges my concern but simply carries on to another patient.

Within a few minutes, Dr. Harrison enters with the intern. He examines Ben's legs, commenting on his tight hamstrings and his straight back, repeating a similar description from the intern's analysis. He glances at the X-rays but doesn't say too much. It takes forever to actually get the X-rays taken, he could at least hem and haw a little longer to make the effort seem meaningful. Why bother having them taken at all if they're so uninteresting?

Without hesitation, Dr. Harrison expounds on his role in Ben's life which is to ensure he is able to sit comfortably since that is "all" Ben can do at the moment. I wouldn't have phrased it that way—Ben can do a lot more than just sit! As Ben grows, and starts standing or walking or whatever he is able to do, he tells us that he will help Ben to do those things properly too. Because we are not currently having issues, there isn't much he can do today. The tightness isn't good but it isn't interfering with Ben's sitting ability so he'll just leave things alone.

Dr. Harrison is pleased to learn that Ben is bearing more and more weight but predicts the tightness will only get worse and interfere in his progression to standing longer and taking steps. He tells us to see him in six months. He prefers this shorter time period in order to gather a series of snapshots to see how things are evolving.

Ben has had his eye-drops in for over an hour when we finally get back to see Dr. Lavoie. He begins by looking into Ben's eyes with a lens marked with tiny cross-hairs to determine if Ben can look straight at him or slightly off to the side. It's likely that looking slightly off-centre may permit Ben to see better what's in front of him because of the slight scarring on his left eye. Dr. Lavoie reports that things look fine. At some point, the visual acuity cards will begin to lose their effectiveness and it will become more of a challenge to figure out how well Ben actually sees. The cards only tell him how well the eye works. It may become necessary in a year or two to test how well Ben processes what he is seeing.

He declares that Ben's far-sightedness has actually worsened, which is usually the case when kids are young. He writes a new prescription and says that Ben's right eye is more like his left now. For the next six months, until we see him again, he wants us to monitor any turning in his eyes. If one eye turns more than the other, it may mean that the muscles are not working hard enough which can lead to loss of vision in that eye. Patching the eye may be needed again to correct this.

Every time I come here, I think back to Dr. Goderich saying that he wasn't convinced Ben had much vision. Can you imagine if we had taken what he said as the truth? It burns me up every time: how no one holds him accountable for his words; how he can just make such provocative statements without any evidence to back his claims; how wrong he was.

The day is finally over. More than eight hours of it. We're all wiped. Conor and Tori didn't complain at all as we wore a path through the maze of corridors. They're amazing. Despite my weariness, I am smiling inside, thankful that Ben has endured a grueling day, reflux and all.

It's interesting how a 30-second reflux episode can zap more energy from me than eight hours of hospital appointments.

*   *   *

No rest

May is just about upon us. The weather is getting warmer and the evenings, longer. There are signs of new life everywhere. Marg is opening the Camp this weekend, cleaning out the winter dirt and the dozens of lazy old houseflies. New life, new beginnings. Conor and Tori are eager to take part and want to help their Nana.

"Ben and I will be fine," I tell them. "It's just one night."

It's past midnight and I convince myself that I should get to bed. As I turn down the bedcovers, I hear Ben making unusual noises on the monitor. My fatigue vanishes with a rush of adrenaline and concern. Standing next to him, I watch him outstretch his arms in pain and listen to his rapid and noisy breathing. At least he's breathing well, not like during a reflux episode where his head is locked to one side. It appears to be abdominal cramps of some sort. Within a few minutes, his discomfort subsides but he remains awake. I change his position, and gently rub his hair and back with the hope of relaxing his agitated body. After his breathing settles into a peaceful rhythm, his eyes grow tired until he gradually drifts back to sleep.

Anxious and exhausted, I crawl into bed, hoping he'll sleep the night. My hopes are not met and I should know better by now. He makes it half an hour before waking to another wave of cramps. My response is the same but it is not as effective the second time. Realizing he is not going to go back to sleep, I bring him in with me. It doesn't stop the pain but it allows me to watch him without the effort of standing over him.

During the third wave, I pick him up and hold him close on my shoulder. It does little good. It's just wave after wave of cramps for two grueling hours. As the clock rolls past 4:15 a.m., he finally closes his eyes and so do I. We're given a 45-minute reprieve before enduring another round of cramps. Once 8 o'clock hits, we get up, both beaten and feeling lousy.

Jan returns late morning to discover two exhausted souls. Spring is supposed to bring new life. It seems to have passed us by.

* * *

Paged

Arriving at work on Monday morning, my pager rumbles. It's the home number. I rush down the ramp from the Parkade to call back and the pager rumbles again. "911" are the first three numbers of the new callback number. I find a desk phone near a security guard's desk and stumble over the buttons to make the call. My fingers are ten times bigger than normal right now and all fine motor control is hampered.

Bursting out of the heavy glass entrance doors of my office building, I hail a cab and ask him to hurry. It only takes 15 minutes to get home but that's still too long. I find Ben in Jan's arms, incoherent and becoming stiff. This is more than the abdominal cramps from the weekend. We give him 5 mg of *Valium* and wait. It's not obvious whether it's working so we jump into the car and head for the hospital.

As we make the turn from our street, we see a police car behind us. We signal to him and he pulls over. Jan gets out to explain why we need his help and realize it is a friend of ours. He recalls being at our house the last time we rushed to the hospital in January and asks if Ben is having a seizure again. He gives us a hurried escort and we follow him as close as we can. Even with sirens and horns blaring, some drivers ignore everything and do not pull over.

At the hospital, Ben is still not great. I jump out of the car just as a man meets me with a wheelchair. For a second, I don't quite understand what he's trying to do and then realize he thinks I'm the patient who needs help. We hurry inside. They are particularly efficient today and immediately hook him up to an O_2 monitor. Everything is fine on that front—it always is. Within a few minutes, he starts squirming and moaning, and his eyes are now closed. Several minutes ago, they were wide open, glazed and bouncing. He becomes irritable for about five minutes and then falls asleep.

From a distance, a slow-moving doctor approaches us, someone we have never met. He asks us to describe what has happened and questions whether or not it was a seizure. When we mention the *Sandifer Response* that Dr. Norris has suggested, his tone and body language immediately change. Apparently, we have somehow distinguished ourselves as "parents with a reasonable level of intelligence." Since it is only noon, we ask if Dr. Campbell is in the hospital. A loud voice pages him and within 45 minutes, Dr. Campbell arrives.

As he makes his way over to our curtained-off stretcher, Ben wakes up to vomit a little. I think this is what he was trying to do all morning. He cries out briefly and falls back to sleep. Dr. Campbell examines Ben while he stays asleep but can't detect any outward sign of anything: no fever, no infection, no nothing. We talk about maybe increasing his *Prepulsid* dose as well as the possibility of surgery to correct his reflux. Dr. Campbell surmises that giving Ben some *Gaviscon* just before every meal might help. We agree to give it a try. He asks if we are comfortable going home. The question is a rhetorical one.

I long for the day when we don't feel the need to rush to the ER every time Ben has a severe reflux episode or a seizure. But knowing that *Valium* can suppress his breathing, we can't risk *not* going.

Our car is back in the driveway shortly after 2 p.m. My whole work day is shot but I really don't care. I am exhausted emotionally and physically but I have no time to sleep. There is no relief. Even if I could sleep, I couldn't disconnect my mind from what has just happened or the continuing uncertainty, anxiety and stress that doesn't seem to diminish. Fortunately, Ben is also too tired to care right now and lies peacefully in a deep sleep on the downstairs couch. Expecting that the worst is over, at least for today, Jan gets ready for her 5-1 shift.

We can't stand still. There are too many pressures, too many responsibilities, too many things to do.

* * *

A Mother's Day to forget

As the week wears on, Ben's mood and energy improves. Each day, he drinks a little more, eats a little more, and smiles a little more. Time after time, he shows us his ability to bounce back, no matter how far or how often he is kicked. He attends playschool on Tuesday and is full of life, even using his walker at gym time. Thursday's school day is even better, his class taking advantage of the spring weather by holding gym time outside. Ben loves the change of venue, laughing and yelling at his friends as they run around.

This second week of May is a busy one for me. We will be breaking ground for our new home next Wednesday and there are so many (too many) things to organize. Getting this close to the official day, I'm not sure if I'm up to the challenge of this crazy balancing act but it's too late to turn back.

We roll into another weekend and I'm feeling very unprepared. It's Mother's Day and I haven't organized anything. I suppose I could blame it on our wild days of reflux and spending every waking hour on house construction activities. Regardless, I don't feel good about it.

The day is quiet, too quiet. I have this feeling bubbling inside me that I'm witnessing a lull before a reflux storm. Ben must be sending me some strong vibes as his tranquil state turns into his trademark terrified look. Another dreadful reflux episode consumes his body.

I rush to him and pick him up. The pain passes quickly and I position him back into his seat. Less than 10 minutes pass and he has another episode, though it's more like an attack of some sort, ending with him throwing up. A third episode surfaces. Anticipating it will play out like the rest, I don't pay much attention for the first few minutes. Jan checks on him only to find that he has begun a seizure. Reflux episodes present such a fine line. I can't believe that I was so nonchalant.

We lie him on the couch and see his eyes, now with huge pupils, bouncing, his eyebrows twitching rhythmically, and his lips moving in circles. We inject a dose of *Valium* and head for the hospital, but not before hastily dropping Tori off at Trish's. Conor is with Marg and Rita this afternoon as they visit Nana Brook for Mother's Day.

By the time we get to the hospital, Ben is still convulsing, which ensures we are seen right away. Another new doctor assesses the situation fairly quickly. She wants to start an IV right away but agrees to wait and see how he responds after another 5 mg of *Valium*. It works. He is now calm and falls asleep. She starts an IV to be ready for any new issues, since Ben has been convulsing in varying degrees for more than half an hour.

We wait and watch him for a few hours before returning home.

Two days later we get in touch with Dr. Campbell. He has read the report from the Mother's Day episode and recommends that we increase Ben's *Prepulsid* dose. He also shares his belief that surgery is looking more and more like the only viable option to stop these episodes. I can't imagine putting Ben through another operation but we can't continue giving *Valium* and rushing to ER every week, either.

With heavy hearts, we consult Dr. Sanderson, a gastroenterologist we have recently been seeing at the IWK. She puts a different spin on things. She believes that it is very possible that Ben has sensed all of the events over the last few months, in particular his grandfather's death, on top of the chaos of building a house. She advises staying the course and says she wouldn't be surprised if everything calms down once our lives calm down.

Anxiety and sadness: sure, why shouldn't Ben experience those emotions? Just because his life is complicated doesn't mean he's less of a person. He's not some case study or clinical artifact: he's Ben, a living, breathing, playful and loving child, our child. Have we once again let his differences cloud our attitudes and behaviours? How did we get this way? It's got to stop!

*   *   *

Reaching my limit!

Another brutal week is over and I'm feeling uptight. Instead of being able to unwind, I find myself worrying about the next reflux episode. It is paralyzing me. Person or not, Ben is a big worry. The weather today is dull and chilly. We're less than a month away from the summer solstice but it seems as if we're going in reverse. It also seems as if Ben is going in reverse. I can't bring myself to say that he's regressing but two hospital visits in two weeks . . . Are they reflux? Are they seizures? Maybe I'm in denial. Emotionally drained is what I really am.

It is becoming clear that all of the turmoil of the last few months is taking its toll on everyone. I feel helpless that Conor and Tori are victims, too. Last night Tori didn't want us to go to a neighbourhood potluck. This is not like her.

Sunday is another terrible day. There is no day of rest in our house. At breakfast, Ben is content one minute and the next his head is locked, his arms are outstretched, his lips are pursed, and his eyes show fear.

Monday evening, he has another severe reflux episode. After being lively and in tune all day, he progresses into his contorted position during supper. He moves off and on throughout the episode but he can't come out it. He gets more and more grey in the face and then starts to convulse. I place him on the couch and rush to get the *Valium*. My heart is racing, panic is rising. I have never given *Valium* to him before; Jan always did but she's at work.

Marg comes through the back door as I fumble with the vial. Tori is with her and doesn't like what she sees. I pull out a 5 ml syringe but it's too big for the tiny glass vial. Rifling through the *Ziploc* bag of supplies,

I find a smaller one. I draw 1 ml of liquid from the vial and deposit it into his bum. I stand there, squeezing his bum so the *Valium* doesn't drip out. It takes only 30 seconds and Ben comes around, squirming a lot and crying, his breathing returning to normal. It takes him about two hours to completely recover. No hospital visit this time: I guess I can look at this as an improvement.

By Tuesday, he is almost back to normal, talking a lot, eating fairly well, and having a lot more energy. Wednesday, even better, along with experimenting with making different sounds.

That evening, Dr. Campbell calls us at home and talks to Jan about Ben's first day on his new drug, *Omeprazole*, which is a stomach acid blocker. It was prescribed by Dr. Sanderson. He tells Jan that even though it significantly cuts down on the amount of acid in the stomach, it does have side effects and, ironically, can cause diarrhea, constipation and cramps. That about covers the spectrum of bowel issues.

The next day, I talk with Dr. Norris to bring him up to date. Though he doesn't often have encouraging words for us, he is always a steady hand. I mention our discussion with Dr. Sanderson about performing a fundoplication procedure, in which the upper part of the stomach is "wrapped" around the oesophagus to help keep stomach acid in the stomach. And about inserting a gastric button. In his usual thoughtful manner, he agrees with me that inserting a gastric button would be a step backwards for Ben and really believes that the *Omeprazole* will make a difference.

I hope he's right.

*   *   *

21

A TUMULTUOUS YEAR

We're less than a week away from moving to our temporary home, a rental townhouse that is close to Marg, where we'll stay until our new house is ready. Our current house, which closes very soon, is a disaster zone with things half-packed and boxes scattered in every room. Ben's end-of-year school picnic is today and we debate whether or not to attend, given the craziness of our lives. The weather conditions are tempting us. What have we got to lose? It will at least be a distraction.

Arriving at the park just before the lunch hour, we have trouble finding a suitable parking spot. The lot is filled with vehicles. As we climb out of our car, one of Ben's teachers spots us and yells a friendly hello. Conor and Tori are eager to enjoy unrestricted access to the adjoining beach and playgrounds. Jan and I are hoping for a relaxing few hours.

After giving Ben his lunch time dose of Prepulsid, I notice his head wants to turn to one side. His posturing is subtle except for the way he is holding his mouth and curving his tongue. I spot that his eyes are a tiny bit bouncy as I get closer to him. Though his head isn't locked into one position, he doesn't seem to be very coherent.

My restless mind brings me back to Conor's birthday party a few years ago, at the smoky, smelly bowling alley. That day was supposed to be fun, like today. I'm starting to sense the world closing in and, at the same time, feel exposed.

Everyone could be watching Ben have a seizure and there's nothing I can do to stop it. As horrible as these episodes are, they are private, they are personal. No one needs to know anything about them.

We attempt to carry on normally, conversing with others without letting on that Ben isn't quite right. The father of one of Ben's classmates approaches us and greets Ben. He informs us how he used to work at the old Dr. Roberts Hospital. This was a place, most would call an institution, established in the 1960s where they would send all of the "retarded" kids. He remarks how special he believes Ben to be. I agree with him, of course, but tell him that Ben isn't feeling himself right now. His brow furrows, seemingly unaware that there is anything wrong with Ben. Perhaps my fear of being on display is an over-reaction. Maybe no one really knows, except for us.

A different kind of party

Ben's episode has now lasted more than 20 minutes. He hasn't turned grey or displayed that terrified look but both Jan and I are getting concerned and a little antsy. We begin to pack up our things and head for the car. Opening the rear door, I lie him on the back seat, getting prepared to give him a dose of *Valium*, while trying to be as discreet as possible and not embarrass Ben in front of his classmates. Within a few minutes of lying down, he out-stretches his legs, giving a little kick, and begins to breathe more normally. It is over. We get out of the car and stay for the remainder of the picnic.

It has been 12 days since his last episode, not a long time but it's the longest span in the last six weeks. And all of the recent episodes that have lasted more than 20 minutes, like this one, have not progressed into a seizure. Is this some small victory?

We are back home by mid-afternoon but Ben is looking quite tired and pale. These episodes always suck the life out of him. I lie him down on the family room couch, thinking he wants to sleep, but he really wants to throw up: and does he ever, unabashedly and without restraint. It's instant relief for him and he falls asleep in minutes.

Two hours pass before Ben wakes, this time with a start and a puzzled look on his face. He appears disoriented. I sit down next to him and talk softly to him. Making eye contact with me, he begins to smile and tell me a story. His day has been anything but enjoyable. Somehow he is able to pick himself up and get on with life. He continues to show us the way.

* * *

A kindred spirit

The local newspaper is carrying a special section today on *spina bifida* and is flooded with articles and letters to the Editor on the subject. Scanning the volume of prose from the contributors, I spot one that hits home. Jan or I could have written it:

> *"I've always looked at life as a large roller coaster ride. It has its ups, downs, and wild twists and turns. But, whether you enjoy the ride or not depends on your attitude. If you're pessimistic, you won't enjoy the ride. But if you look forward to the ups, and grin and bear the downs, overall you'll enjoy it. All this seems so much more true when I consider the past 28 months.*
>
> *A little over two years ago, I was blessed with my son Corey, who was born with spina bifida. That's when my family started the largest and wildest roller coaster ride we could have ever imagined.*
>
> *Throughout the ride, we've learned to appreciate the small achievements that most people don't. We also learned not to take things for granted and to take time for the very special moments we have together as a family. With each surgery and medical procedure, Corey shows me such incredible strength. Even when he's recovering from surgery, he's full of smiles, hugs, and kisses for everyone.*

A wise person once told me that "You're never given more than you have the strength to handle." This is so true. So when I'm in the middle of the wild twists and turns, I'm scared and don't think I can go on any farther, I have to remember what that wise person once told me. I must draw upon my inner strength not only for me but for Corey and his three big sisters.

Most times we ride the waves of our roller coaster. Little ups and downs that don't shake us up too much. Like our frequent appointments to the doctor, physio, and OT. But we always try to prepare ourselves for the "big dip" that's somewhere around the next turn.

Whether it's another surgery (we've had 10 so far) or an out-of-province trip to hospital, we can never take for granted that our "ups" will last forever.

I'd be lying if I said I wasn't scared on this lifelong ride with Corey and his disability. But like I wrote earlier, it's all in the attitude.

So next time you meet a family that has a child with spina bifida or another disability, don't feel sorry for our turbulent ride but support us in our times of need and celebrate with us the small achievements our children make each day. Because like every roller coaster, there's always a point where the ride is calm and smooth, until it reaches a point where you can get off.

This is "wow" moment for me. Here is someone who feels what we feel, is stressed the way we are stressed, and knows all about the crazy ride we're on. We have found a kindred spirit. A spirit that reminds us that we are not alone in our tumultuous journey. I am energized again.

* * *

Breaking new ground

The hulking excavator that roamed the terrain for the last few days has gone, leaving a huge hole in the middle of our new piece of property. Also gone are the two very large, majestic spruce trees that sheltered the rear of the lot thanks to the City's power-tripping Planning Advisory Committee. I had applied for a "variance" to place my house a mere four feet closer to the roadway so that I could spare nature's towering wonders. I had numerous letters of support from my neighbours and assumed the granting of the variance would be a formality. I was wrong. Perhaps the naivety and inexperience of my 32 years had me fooled.

Standing near the edge of the 10-foot deep hole, I feel the early morning sunshine warm my face and the ground around me as I wait for the foundation contractor to arrive. I still can't believe we're doing this. Acting as my own general contractor, I have little choice but to visit the job site three times a day—in the morning before everyone arrives (no later than 7:30 a.m.), once during the lunch hour, and then at the end of the workday to keep track of the day's progress.

Each morning, I order the supplies needed for the next working day and ensure that everything gets delivered from the previous day's order. That I am trying to keep ahead of everything *and* hold down a busy, full-time job is something I try not to dwell on.

By the first week of June, we begin the process of settling into our temporary home. Only a small roadway and a postage-stamp lawn separates each townhouse. Our layout is a good fit for Marg but not for Ben. The bedrooms sit a floor above the main level and can only be reached by climbing a narrow set of stairs with a cramped landing in the middle. Manoeuvering a wheelchair is virtually impossible on any level. But it's nearby, it's convenient and can be had for a short-term rental period.

We unpack most of our things but can't find the energy to fully set up at this transient location. It's frustrating to search for something and not find it, never sure whether or not we lost it or if it's in storage. Especially if it's something Ben needs.

But it's only for four months. And it's close to Marg. And it's the summer. It shouldn't be a problem, right?

* * *

Constant nervousness

I'm sure my continual state of nervousness is heightened by the daunting task of building a new house—a project whose budget might easily spiral out of control. On the sunny Sunday afternoon, going for a walk seems like the thing to do. There is a park about 15 minutes away, and Conor and Tori are more than eager to go there. Marg comes with us to play and to help. I don't want to inhibit their fun, and Ben is certainly enjoying himself. I am still nervous, though. I'm not sure when this feeling will go away. It seems that I've been conditioned to expect something no matter where I take him.

He is great the whole day, even into the evening. I'm always nervous about that too—it seems that whenever he has a bang-on day something bad always follows. I am really becoming paranoid.

Two days later, I arrive home from work to find Gloria holding Ben who is wrapped in a blanket. She tells me his arms and legs were cold having been outside for quite a while as he watched Conor and her throw a baseball back and forth. She tells me he has been happy and lively all day.

A few minutes after Gloria leaves, I take him upstairs while I get changed. Glancing across the room, I notice that he is glazed-looking. His pupils are noticeably large and his response and movements are slow. I pick him up as I do every time. His breathing is very soft and he is forcefully swallowing, repeatedly. He isn't in distress or clutching, just very quiet and motionless. This must be reflux but this time it's silent. At least 20 minutes pass before he lets out a couple of good burps, confirming my suspicions. His pupils return to normal size and he becomes more responsive, though still somewhat tired. I am amazed that he fought through this episode on his own.

Not long after, Ben and I sit in our small kitchen, both sideways against the window. This has turned into his spot to eat. He likes the natural light and occasionally glances out at the front walkway. He begins his supper a little slowly but not unusually so. Every day, I hear a relentless voice in the back of head telling me to feed him as much as possible at every meal, always pushing to give him as much nourishment, energy and strength as possible. It's a fear of him losing weight and suffering dehydration—it's a slippery slope to both of these problems if I'm not focused on his intake. Today, my obsession is misplaced.

After a few mouthfuls, he turns his head and appears to be in discomfort. I pick him up but his eyes tell the story as he outstretches his arms. He is fighting it, moving his head from time to time, and finally lets go a series of burps. Thinking it's over, I let my guard down. Within seconds, he transforms into a locked state while his eyes immediately start bouncing in rhythm with this arms. I can't believe he has gone into an all-out seizure.

With my heart racing, I carry him to the living room, lay him on his side and inject the same half-dose of *Valium* that had brought him around the last time. Within 10 minutes, his condition doesn't improve much with the exception of a calming of his arms. He remains very limp and his eyes are still bouncing.

I call Jan to see where she is. I give him another half-dose but don't do a very good job—most of it dribbles out of his bum. I pick him up but he is still in that far-away state. I decide to give him a little more since he really can have as much as 10mg.

When Jan arrives, we drive to the hospital. As we arrive in the emergency parking lot, he comes around and starts to squirm like he always does. I put a call into Dr. Campbell who is actually on call. We sit in the parking lot, awaiting his call. Ten minutes pass. Dr. Campbell apologizes for not calling back sooner as he tells us that he was in his car *en route* to the hospital. He instructs us to meet him inside the emergency department. We tell him that we're actually sitting outside the front doors.

Jan waits near the reception area with Ben as I walk towards the main lobby to try to meet Dr. Campbell. I get all of the way around to the elevators and spot Dr. Smythe waiting for an elevator. I just make eye contact with him, not uttering a word, and he responds with, "He went into emergency," meaning Dr. Campbell, of course. These guys are good.

We find a spare stretcher and I leave to register while Dr. Campbell examines Ben. Unconcerned, he says that Ben is now quite stable so there's no need for us to stay here. I describe to him the sequence of events and how I likely should not have tried to keep feeding Ben. Dr. Campbell disagrees and tells me that the only way to see what is his capacity is to try to feed him. His words help to lessen some of my guilt.

Nervousness, paranoia, guilt. What a life!

*   *   *

He keeps on trying

I feel good about Ben as a new week begins. I can't explain why. Perhaps it's his alertness and insatiable appetite. Clearly, he must be growing with all that he eats. This week, I don't feel that something terrible is lurking just around the corner. My mind is telling me that there is hope, that he will conquer this reflux bogeyman.

He gets in his Little Room today, completely stretched out, his head all the way inside, and he is loving it. This is the first time in over six months that we've had the courage to lay him on his back with little support—the fear of reflux has paralyzed us so much. Ben shows us why we can't live in fear. His reaching, kicking, vocalizing and total body movement tell us that he remembers how enjoyable it is to play in his Little Room. He doesn't worry about the next episode and neither should we.

The weekend comes and so does his fourth birthday. We're smart this year and keep the celebrations low key. There has been far too much instability over these last few months to feel like planning any party. Between reflux and house building and living at what seems like no-fixed-address, I'm in no condition to celebrate.

The month of July flies by. Our new residence is really taking shape, with images of crisp new floors, sun-drenched decks and manicured grounds becoming more and more clear. Most importantly, Ben has avoided any reflux, mild or otherwise. This run of good days gives Jan the boost she needs to invite about a dozen of her co-workers to a barbeque. Ben seems up for it and welcomes the new faces. It is encouraging to witness his social side developing. For a few hours, we feel some sense of normalcy brought to our lives again. No reflux means no stress, or at least less stress. Our new friend *Omeprazole* is clearly making a difference.

Ben survives the turmoil and chaos of moving into our new house at the end of August. Thankfully, we all do. Having a little more stability allows him to easily make the transition into a three-day playschool programme and he is loving it. Each morning brings a smiley and lively Ben into our lives—a stark contrast to the days when reflux and seizures stole his good nature and banished him to some far, far place. Each morning, Ben gets to see something other than the inside of our four walls, and to interact with children his own age.

Whether it's the stimulation from school or the launching of a new routine, Ben has sustained a level of energy and enthusiasm that is certainly new to us. It must be pleasing to him. Even when placed on his belly, a position that often tires him quickly, brings forth a stronger, more deliberate Ben. His eye tracking abilities have become smooth and rapid, too, compared to the delayed and uncontrolled ones of only a few months ago.

Each day that passes without reflux is a day that Ben gets brighter and livelier. I rationalize with myself that even if next week turns awful, I can say that I have thoroughly enjoyed this week. Nothing can take that feeling away. My new found confidence is encouraging me to do things that interest me and not feel guilty. Ben's never-give-up spirit is beginning to help me find the energy to want more.

*   *   *

It eventually catches up with you

Before leaving for work, I approach Ben's bedside to give him a kiss and wish him a fun Monday at school. As he turns his head towards me, I notice that he is having a difficult time opening his eyes. There is a hard crust gluing his eye lashes together. He seems afraid of opening them very far as each lash must feel like it is being pulled from his eye lids. With a warm, damp cloth, I gently moisten the lashes to soften the brownish coloured crust. He is not enjoying this but after a few applications, he blinks repeatedly to loosen any remaining stickiness. Ah, relief.

I check in with Jan over the lunch hour and she tells me that Ben has some green pus oozing from the corner of his eyes and is somewhat moany. I don't have a good feeling and decide to work from home in the afternoon. As I walk through the back door, Ben is looking bothered. With a heavy heart, I ask Jan what's the trouble. She says that just as she began feeding him his lunch, he had a reflux episode. It lasted only a few minutes but he is clearly in some sort of discomfort. I feel so helpless. Reflux, eye infections, what's next?

Before I can really get myself down, Ben is overcome by another episode. This time, a bad one. Within a few seconds, he starts convulsing, brought to life by mild twitching of his eyes, lips, and tongue. Frantically, we grab a vial of *Valium* from the small kitchen cupboard that doubles for a medicine cabinet and rectally inject 5 mg. His rectum is full of stool and the drug does not have much effect. We have no choice but to get to the hospital as fast as we can.

The nurses quickly set up an IV and administer another 5mg of *Valium* over a 20-minute period. It's now 3 p.m. Ben's twitching slows down so that only his eyes are bouncing, just a little, crustiness and all. Sensing that Ben must be somewhat stabilized, the nurses leave us alone—for 45 minutes.

Ben remains incoherent and I am very agitated. I make my way to the central desk where all the nurses, doctors and other staff congregate, trying to get someone's attention. They do a wonderful job of ignoring me and ensuring I feel like I am imposing. I catch the eye of one physician. I remember him from a previous visit. After seeing Ben, he gets that Ben is still convulsing to some degree and gives him another 2.5 mg of Valium. This does the trick for Ben. His twitching ceases and he falls into a sound sleep.

The doctor tells us that he has spoken with Dr. Campbell and that he is going to give Ben some *Dilantin* to ensure that he didn't start a seizure again when he wakes. We express our reluctance to give him additional drugs, describing for him that once Ben stops convulsing, he never starts again. He tells us that Dr. Campbell is currently in the hospital and he would get him to come see us first so that we could discuss this with him. I am somewhat in disbelief that Dr. Campbell is still here—his office hours start at 2 p.m. every day and it's almost now 4 o'clock.

Less than 30 seconds later, two nurses enter our draped-off area with a small IV bag. I ask them what they are doing and they tell us that they are going to give Ben some *Dilantin*. Defensively, I retort that we don't want to do that until we speak with Dr. Campbell. I recognize one of the nurses from an earlier visit—her gaudy purple eyeglasses and long blonde ponytail are hard to forget—when she took Ben's temperature rectally, even though he was four years old, even though we insisted that no one under two years of age has it taken that way. Hearing our defiance of not wanting the drug, she storms away shouting,

"The family refuses the *Dilantin*! The family refuses the *Dilantin*!"

Nice. How professional is that? But, of course, anything goes in this out-of-control health-care system, where it doesn't matter how the patient is treated.

Within a few minutes, a medical student who is working with Dr. Campbell comes to talk with us. He apologizes for the confusion and behaviour of some of the staff. After speaking with us, he calls Dr. Campbell to give him the complete story. He signals to us that Dr. Campbell would like to speak with us. I'm just about out of my mind so I mutter to Jan to talk with him. The conversation doesn't last long. He wants to know if we would feel comfortable taking Ben home. The answer is—you guessed it—an emphatic, "Yes". The med student says that someone will be by shortly to remove Ben's IV and then we can go home.

A half hour passes and no one comes near. It's as if we're being punished for refusing the *Dilantin*. Once again, I make my way to the centre circle of medical professionals to request Ben's IV be removed. We are told that Ben has to be "transferred" to the ER Paeds doctor who can then authorize the removal of the IV. When I ask how long it will be, a clerk tells me he'll be over in a few minutes.

I continue my pacing until a young man, likely mid-thirties, with a bushy moustache and thick, wavy brown hair stands up from behind the nurses' station and walks sternly towards us. He introduces himself as Dr. Cormier, the ER Paeds doctor. Clearly, he is not in a good mood. Neither am I. He tries to tell us that it would not be wise for us to take Ben home, how he is very concerned that the seizure activity that lasted for more than an hour, and that our refusal of *Dilantin* was a mistake. Neither of us are impressed by this doctor's tone. Jan and I both respond quickly with how we know Ben better than anyone, how Dr. Campbell knows what Ben is like, and we know the pattern that Ben follows after a seizure. I feel like asking him to step outside. I want to tell him what a loser staff he has, how we were left for over three quarters of an hour while Ben continued to convulse, how disorganized this place is, and how we don't appreciate being addressed as if we're subordinates. I want to tell him all of this and more, but I want to get away from this wretched place even more. Clearly, I'm not making any friends but I don't care. Within minutes, Ben is unhooked and we kiss this horrible place good-bye.

As the rest of week unfolds, Ben shows us how resilient he is . . . again. By Thursday, he is back to feeling himself, albeit a little less energetic, eating his usual amounts, talking and moving while watching TV, sleeping through the night, and not waking up laughing. On Friday, he makes it back to school, the first time in 10 days. He loves it and shows his pleasure through non-stop talking.

By Sunday, I am feeling lousy, zapped of energy, with a booming headache and repeated nausea that keeps me down and out for the entire day. When evening approaches, Jan complains of abdominal pains and is burning up with a high fever. We rely on Conor and Tori to help us with kitchen cleanup and bath time for Ben. On Monday morning, Jan can't get out of bed. This life is killing us. I want off this carousel of pain.

* * *

A full slate

The entire main level of our new house is blanketed in hardwood except for the entrances and the bathrooms. This was done to allow easy access for Ben's wheelchair and other equipment. Anything with wheels. The local floor-finishing contractor I hired and the *just-got-out-of-jail* reject he sent left every square inch of hardwood a disaster—dull and uneven, with large areas rough to the touch. There were even pools of dried varnish in corners of some of the rooms. I wanted to throw up when I discovered in late July what a mess had been made. I couldn't believe someone could perform such a horrendous job. They had to go out of their way to be that bad. At that point in the project, we had no choice but to continue with the rest of the house-building activities and leave the ruined floors to be dealt with at a later date.

With the calendar moving into October and the busy season behind most contractors, we were able to secure the top refinisher in town, the person we had wanted to hire originally. To fix our mess means we must move every stick of furniture, every toy, every shoe, everything that touches to floor to either our basement or our garage. At the same time, we have to pack for four long days of appointments at the IWK. We planned the floor refinishing exercise deliberately when we would be away from home anyway. We thought that would be efficient. But going to the IWK is never easy and this chaos is troubling to everyone. Needless to say, we're all out-of-sorts and not sleeping well. Fatigue and insecurity only worsen my stress level. Our lives continue to get more and more complicated. I find I am saying that a lot these days.

Most of the furniture has found its way off of the main floor by Saturday, just one day prior to our departure. Most everything, except for our beds. Ben doesn't like the fact that his room is so barren. My tiredness is directly proportional to the restlessness of his sleep. When Sunday morning arrives, we tackle the rest of furniture, filling the garage as much as possible but leaving the moving of our piano to professionals. They deposit it in the front foyer but not completely off of the hardwood. I don't notice their error until they are long gone. Jan and I struggle to push it closer to the front door but the tiny, fetched up, warped metal wheels on this century-old goliath of an instrument leave a small, permanent path on the floor. I can't win.

Ben is eager to leave this turmoil and travels well to Truro, almost thankful to be getting away. We arrive quite late, about 6:30 p.m., but he still manages to eat well. A few hours later, he falls asleep with little effort. We all do.

Our first appointment on Monday morning is with Dr. Harrison. Today, Ben weighs in at the 31.8 lb mark. We're happy with that. About 15 minutes later, Dr. Harrison greets us and attempts to manipulate Ben's legs and ankles, telling us that both are quite tight. As a matter of routine, he instructs us to get an X-ray of his hips so he can see how things are progressing. By the time we leave the clinic and return with the films, the clinic is now overflowing with kids of all ages, some with casts and others in wheelchairs.

Looking at the latest X-rays, Dr. Harrison points out a slight increase towards Ben's hips dislocating but not a huge difference. He expects an increase over time, which happens as kids get older. It is now more likely that Ben will require his heel cords lengthened as well as his hamstrings, and possibly in the groin area, too. However, this would not be for at least six months and he will make a decision when we come down next spring. Trying to be reassuring, he informs us that it is a very simple operation that will help Ben stand and sit more easily and comfortably. Dr. Harrison says that we can still try the AFOs but the fact that his ankles are so tight may mean that they will not work very well. The bones of children with CP grow at a faster rate than do the muscles and tendons; hence, the tightness.

He asks us what is the biggest problem we are facing. "Reflux!" is our response. We are surprised that an ortho surgeon would be well aware of kids and reflux. He tells us that he can very much appreciate what Ben goes through, what we go through, when he struggles with these episodes. It is quite refreshing to talk to someone who knows what we're talking about.

Following this 2½ hour appointment, we make our way to the seating clinic to check in with Judy. Ben has grown again since we last saw her which means that she must increase the seat depth and lower the foot rests. His car seat checks out okay but it won't be for long. I shake my head when Judy tells us that the price of new one is more than $800. She shows us how enormous these Gorilla seats are (aptly named, it would seem). I can't see how this will ever fit in our car. We're going to be forced into purchasing a larger vehicle—whether or not we can afford to is not going to stop Ben's growth.

We take advantage of an ophthalmology appointment cancellation and see Dr. Lavoie after leaving Judy. He performs the standard visual acuity test, shifting his rolling stool in quick, short movements, and mumbling to himself. The last set of cards displays lines that are extremely thin and close together. I can't imagine that Ben can distinguish those. In his usual emotionless manner, Dr. Lavoie informs us that Ben responded well and is quite normal for a four-year old.

Peering into Ben's eyes using a variety of lenses, Dr. Lavoie determines that the prescription that we have still works for Ben, and reports that the scar remains unchanged. As a result, we don't have return for a year instead of the usual six-month interval. A great way to end the first marathon day.

Tuesday morning brings us to APSEA for a hearing test with Russ. His demeanour is always calm and welcoming, a real treat among a surplus of drones. This is our fourth visit and yet I'm still fascinated by his silver hair. It is very striking and leaves me wondering his true age.

After assuring us that the hearing aids are in proper working order, he chooses to test Ben's hearing with the FM system. Before clipping the mic to his shirt, Russ positions the receiver on Ben's tray. Ben is somewhat combative this morning and repeatedly attempts to knock the receiver off of his tray. Russ tells us this is good way to teach Ben how to localize a sound, by talking to him from in front, behind and on either side. Before leaving, we initiate a short discussion concerning kindergarten. Russ knows a teacher at a local Saint John school who is very experienced with students with multiple disabilities and will put us in contact with her.

Our one o'clock dentistry appointment is with Dr. Anthony. His casual, welcoming approach is refreshing and relaxing. It almost makes me want to have him as *my* dentist. Today, Ben is quite accommodating. Dr. Anthony is pleased that we are doing a great job with Ben's oral hygiene as evidenced by the lack of any gum bleeding during the cleaning. Through the examination, a tiny hole is discovered in one of Ben's new teeth. Dr. Anthony tells us that this is nothing of concern but that it may need to be filled (or silver capped) within the next six months. Since Ben is such a model patient and always lies still, the filling could probably be done in the clinic. He instructs us to keep him informed if any surgical procedures are planned in the near term since he may be able to coordinate that with any fillings. Easy for me to say, since no one was probing and pulling and scraping inside my mouth, but this appointment was effortless: no delays, no stress, no anxiety.

Even though we're half an hour early for our next appointment, we make our way to the GI wing of the hospital and wait for Dr. Sanderson. This part of the hospital is strangely set up. A short distance from the elevator is a door that seals off the GI wing from the rest of the floor.

Entering through this door gives way immediately to a hallway and you have no choice but to turn left or right. Dr. Sanderson's clinic rooms and offices are on the left and a small waiting room, equipped with a TV and lots of children's books, appears out of nowhere.

Helen, Dr. Sanderson's nurse, greets us a few minutes ahead of schedule. Helen has only one speed (high) and she flits about like a hummingbird. She weighs Ben and tries to get an accurate length measurement but he's not interested in cooperating. As she further examines Ben and takes his blood pressure, we give her an update about his meds and his episodes, especially that he hasn't had one in 15 days.

A short time later, Dr. Sanderson greets us before Helen gives her a brief summary of our conversation. We inform her that we did not have the upper GI barium swallow procedure done that she had requested because both Jan and I had been ill and we ran out of time to reschedule before today's visit. We also bare our emotions as we tell of our stressful ER visit a few weeks ago. Dr. Sanderson is a very no-nonsense person as well as a very caring one. Hearing this ER adventure, she sighs and shakes her head, sympathizing with what we had to go through, almost apologizing for their behavior.

We mention that Ben has not had any reflux episodes since we have stopped giving him *Gaviscon*, even though Dr. Campbell thought that it would help. She nods saying that some kids can tolerate a drug well in the beginning but later build up an intolerance to it, and that it could certainly interfere with Ben's ability to vomit when he was sick a couple of weeks ago. She compared *Gaviscon* to giving someone a rubber glove to swallow. She isn't a big fan of it, needless to say.

She tells us that we should still have the upper GI procedure done and to follow it up with a gastroscopy just to verify that there are no ulcers or physical damage occurring to his esophagus.

During her examination of Ben, which includes multiple pokes and pushes of his belly and around his abdomen, she describes a patient of hers, a 20-year-old, who is on a "horse dose" of *Omeprazole*—some 120 mg daily—and that within only a few hours the acid level in his gut still rises dramatically. She is convinced that some kids produce stomach acid in "overload mode" and you just have to deal with these anomalies as they occur. She also reiterates her concerns about putting Ben through a fundoplication procedure, how it isn't always successful, how he would not be able to "belch" or throw up afterward. But mostly that he would permanently have a gastric button in his abdomen and would need to be fed using it for the rest of his life. This kind of discussion scares me to death. Life with reflux is awful but it's going to have to get a whole lot "more awful" to even consider something like this.

As always, our appointments with Dr. Sanderson are not only informative but also comforting. She is never afraid to speak her mind and does so with confidence. Her devotion to her patients is like Dr. Campbell's and, like him, she always has time to listen.

Worn out from this three-day marathon, we all need some fun time. About 30 minutes from downtown is the community of Spryfield, and we learn from Helen that they have a large indoor wave pool, all at ground level, completely wheelchair accessible. Sounds like a prescription for relaxation.

Having never been to that part of the metro area, we miss the exit from the highway but still manage to find the road for the Spryfield Community Centre. The clock tower on top of the main building can be seen from quite a distance, and we eventually find the long, circular driveway that leads us to the front entrance.

It's mid-afternoon and the place is nearly deserted. With the rustling of the fall leaves beneath their feet, Conor and Tori can't wait to get inside and do something fun. The many pitches of the building's stark red roof contrast warmly with the hazy, overcast autumn sky. There is a gentle, humid breeze that tousles Ben's wispy hair, a reminder of the summer we missed and of a fall season that will quickly lose its battle to winter.

Jan, Ben and I follow Conor and Tori across the newly finished sidewalk and through the automatic sliding glass doors that open quickly to a large, brightly lit lobby. To the left is another set of glass doors that take us to the pool. Ben's siblings have led the way and are now eagerly waiting for us to catch up.

Once inside, we are overwhelmed by the hugeness of the pool area. Large windows surround us on three sides and the ceiling is constructed completely of panes of glass. Being drenched in so much natural light brings a certain sense of comfort and calmness, something that is quite foreign to us these days.

The floor of the giant pool disappears gradually from the walkway that surrounds it, much like the slope of a real beachfront, gradually becoming deeper and deeper. It's a perfect setup to get Ben's feet wet. The stillness of the warm, chlorinated water allows Ben to enjoy himself for a change. He is fascinated by the room's openness and the brightness of the never ending sky overhead. Within minutes of soaking his toes, he sits up erect after hearing a very loud buzzer echo across the water. Soon thereafter, waves appear in the water, getting larger and more forceful with each undulation, splashing the sides of the pool area and licking at Ben's calves and knees. This is great.

For a full half hour, we have the entire pool to ourselves. A full half hour of normal time, of family time; away from hospitals; with no thoughts of reflux; with no stress or worries in Ben's mind either. The half hour is just a teaser but we'll take it!

* * *

Multiple clusters

The month of November passes without incident. But winter has snuck in and the days are much too short now and un-invigorating. Nevertheless, our daily pace does not slow down with the reduced level of daylight. My project work is moving at breakneck speed and Jan is in her third of five days of training. As I pack up for the day and begin tying my boots for the bus ride home, my pager jolts my hip with the prefix "911". It doesn't matter what the display reads; the vibration of this torture device always makes my heart skip a beat and then revs it to an agitated level, making me forget how to breathe, while my hands tremble.

Gloria answers my call home and calmly tells me that Ben is having "the reflux." I struggle with using the word "the" in front of reflux. You can have "a heart attack" or "a seizure" but to me it seems you should simply call it "reflux," like saying he's having distress. You wouldn't say, "the distress." These thoughts race through my mind in the first half second after hearing her words, perhaps my mind's way of buffering the news. As she tells me that he had had an episode earlier in the day when they were out for a walk, her voice pauses.

"He's now out of it. Seems okay," she now says, relieved.

She goes on to say that the incident during their walk included his face turning blotchy, his head turned and eyes bouncing a bit, while both arms were outstretched. These are certainly the classic signs of Ben having reflux.

In the evening, Ben devours his night bottle in rapid fashion. He was not interested in his supper, perhaps due to his multiple episodes. Sitting up easily, he lets go his usual string of three burps but after his last one, he suddenly becomes very laughy. I put him on his my shoulder to help him stretch his torso. This does not give him any relief. I stand him in front of me, holding him under the arm pits. Seconds later, he stretches out his arms. At first, I think he is afraid of falling and then notice the dreaded head-turning., This is his third episode today. It lasts less than a minute and his mood quickly returns to one of excitement. Somehow he has managed to work through the pain and has decided it's not going to slow him down.

The week draws to a close with the reflux count standing at five. A few days ago, my pager throttled me with news of another episode, shortly after I left for work early that morning. My hatred for these episodes has not diminished but Ben does seem to be gaining control of them on his own. And he does not seem to be nearly as terrified as he used to be. In between these dreaded incidents, it is obvious that he wants to be happy. In fact, he tries hard to be happy and demonstrates a strength of character that I need to learn how to emulate.

Five days before Christmas, I am once again in the office very early. Trying to feel good about taking the next week off, I desperately try to tidy up a last set of deliverables and straggling emails. At noon, I check in with Jan and Ben at home and learn that he has had four reflux episodes that morning. Jan tells me that there was no need for me to rush home since he came around on his own, so she chose to not call. Part of me is thankful that I didn't know but a larger part of me doesn't want to be kept in the dark. She describes how his first episode began shortly after he started his breakfast, with head turning and rigid limbs. She began getting concerned as the episode passed the seven-minute mark. The other three episodes were much milder and briefer, and didn't seem to have any lasting effects.

We can't seem to go a week without them. In fact, the four episodes today brings the total for the year to 70. There is no pattern. They are unpredictable and unnerving. I feel like I'm starting to unravel.

* * *

A rush of feelings

It is probably safe to say that we have lived through more than two dozen so-called "severe reflux episodes." (I can't bring myself to call them seizures.) More importantly, of course, so has Ben. Each time these episodes appear, a rush of feelings courses through me.

With any episode a sick feeling begins deep inside me, as if someone is twisting my stomach round and round. For the severe ones, a hint of panic creeps in, too, usually stemming from the ever-present uncertainty about whether or not it has been "long" enough, of whether or not he has *really* started to convulse or it is just distress. Most of the time we guess right, and it is really only a guess since symptoms progress along a subtle continuum and express themselves slightly differently each time.

If the episode continues beyond the 10-minute mark and my back is twisting and collapsing from carrying him on my shoulder, making sure he gets good breaths, my adrenaline releases and my heart pumps even faster. Each time, without fail, a painful memory is immediately brought to life—that we might have to take him to the hospital. These dreadful thoughts play over and over in my mind for what seems like hours, all the while trying to decide whether to give him *Valium* to prevent an untimely, stressful, and drawn-out emergency room visit.

When I lay him on his side on the couch to first check to see if he is convulsing, he almost always has that distant, frightened look in his eyes, which are then somewhat bloodshot. His face, too, will be blotchy and worrisome to look at. If any part of him is twitching, and sometimes it is his arms that are involved, this scares me even more, and I try to shoo Conor and Tori off to their rooms. (Seeing Ben like this can be quite unpleasant and disturbing for them.) At that moment, a helpless feeling comes over me because no matter what I say to Ben to console him, I can't get him to snap out of it. This only aggravates the sick feeling I had at the beginning, and the dreadful thoughts replay faster and faster, leading me to believe that they will come true. At this point, my mind is pleading for the seizure to stop. There is no way to predict the duration of the episodes, at least I have never been able to do so.

I begin to feel sorry for Conor and Tori for, suddenly, without mercy, their daily routine is halted and they must wait for the outcome of this seemingly uncontrollable chain of events. I feel frustrated that they are burdened with this hardship that steals their brother from them at the most inopportune times, and drains, if only temporarily, the enthusiasm and happiness from their parents.

After the first dose of *Valium* is given, I can only wait, with my heart still pumping wildly, hoping that the medication will take effect soon.

Two minutes pass, nothing.

Three minutes, nothing.

Four minutes.

"What's he doing?", I question myself. "No, nothing. No, it's hard to tell."

This indecision has replaced the pain and sadness for a few minutes. The second dose of *Valium* finds its way into his body and it's over as quickly as it started. The twitching ceases, his breathing is regular, the blotchiness fades, his terrified look has disappeared, and his whole body is now so, so relaxed. At this point, maybe 25 minutes have passed since I entered this altered state, and I heave a sigh knowing that we had dodged a bullet for another day, that we can stay home.

When I try to resume the activities of a half-hour ago, they seem like a half-day ago. Ben just rests. I watch him from time-to-time knowing that I don't have to worry about another reflux episode today since he is too relaxed from the drugs. I can let go a bit knowing that I don't have to play with him or feed him or make sure he's occupied because he hasn't the energy to do any of those things. I can actually do something uninterrupted, or play or read with Conor and Tori. I am thankful that I do not have to go to the hospital, appreciative that it could have been worse, and wonder if the day will ever come when we can predict these things or eliminate them altogether.

*   *   *

A wild winter

Winters are never kind to us. The frigidness of the outdoors keeps us locked inside for days and days. We can't help but get a little stir-crazy as the threat of influenza is waiting just outside the door, taunting us, daring us to venture outside.

We almost got through the month of January without any reflux episodes. Influenza? Hah! You're nothing compared to reflux! The episode at the end of the month that took over his body was a bad one and the first one that he had experienced after going to bed. This was really troublesome since we always thought that once he fell asleep we would have nothing to worry about. I picked him up from his bed but he was quite tight and very scared. It continued for 15 minutes and needed *Valium* to stop it.

The arrival of February brought a tag-team of both reflux and the flu. Not one or the other, or one *then* the other, but a complete ambush, culminating in six episodes one day, each one lasting longer than the one before, each showing how Ben really wanted to throw up. Given his fever earlier in the day, we concluded that he must have the flu on top of a bad gut. Even administering *Gravol*, then *Abenol*, and finally *Valium* in the late evening didn't stop him from going into a seizure. On the dash to the hospital, the seizure stopped but we weren't sure what effect the drug combo would have on him or his breathing.

By the time we got to see Dr. Campbell, Ben was sleeping with no signs of reflux or convulsions. He listened to his chest for a long while and said that he wasn't taking very deep breaths. A nurse came and gave him an aerosol treatment to open up the airways—sometimes these can be in spasms because of the reflux. It helped but Dr. Campbell wanted an X-ray just to be sure. It was negative and we went home. We were lucky that time, having someone who knew Ben and who could get right down to business.

That was two and half months of reflux and winter haze. Fortunately, the spring equinox today helps to break the cycle but only to help us to remember that Dr. Harrison will likely need to perform heel cord and hamstring releases very soon. Why can't we ever forget about and then suddenly remember *exciting* events that are coming up? Probably because there aren't any.

Heading to Ben's appointment with Dr. Norris today, the first regularly scheduled visit in quite a while, I feel a little unsettled. He's not the most exciting person to be around and his expectations of Ben are always muted.

His examination is fairly routine as he comments on the remarkable range of motion Ben has in spite of being so neurologically compromised. I want to feel good about that but he says it almost suspiciously, as if

Ben is somehow playing a trick on him, or we shouldn't get our hopes up too much since this ability will likely not last. He doesn't say any of those things—it's just my turbulent mind.

He goes on to tell us not to worry about nutrition since Ben is obviously growing and will always be thinner than most. It's Nature's way of helping with his care, he believes, by keeping him from being too big and heavy. When asked about the constant coldness of Ben's feet and hands, he says it's a result of the neurological signals not working properly, that the blood tends to pool in these areas and not circulate efficiently. It's not a result of poor circulation like someone with arteriosclerosis, and his feet are likely not "asleep" even though they are cold. I wonder how he knows that.

After pressing him for an opinion (I really have to beat the words out of him), he suggests that we do not proceed with the releases of the hamstrings and heel cords since Ben has a good range of motion, in his view. He tells us that he tends to be conservative concerning these measures and if it's not causing other serious problems (like hip dislocation), he would "press the pause button" for now.

I want to "press the rewind button" to restart Ben's life.

*   *   *

The debate

Facing the likelihood of Ben having surgery leaves the summer somewhat unsettled. Not only are we bothered by the fact that the procedure is so invasive (releasing his hamstrings and heel cords means actually cutting them) but we are also struggling with whether or not it is the right thing to do for Ben.

On many occasions, we have witnessed surgeons and physiotherapists, as well as occupational therapists, take stands on opposite sides of an issue. While both points-of-view are reasonable and convincing, they are often contradictory. Given this dilemma, we seek out the advice of a physiatrist, a medical doctor who focuses on physical medicine and rehabilitation, especially for persons with physical impairments or disabilities. Kind of a Dr. Harrison/Lisa hybrid—an interesting mix, for sure.

His name is Dr. Kelly and he is one of the coordinators at a nearby rehab centre, a place we never knew existed. Half an hour past our appointment's start time (*"Keep your patients waiting."* must be part of the Hippocratic Oath), Dr. Kelly greets us and apologizes for the delay. He is very young—we guess, our age. We neatly describe Ben's life of the last five years (we're getting quite good at this) and our uncertainty around the impending surgery.

After examining Ben, focusing on the extension of his legs and feet and taking angle measurements, he recommends a series of stretches that we could try on Ben over the next six weeks. He would examine Ben at the end of that period to see if any improvements have been made but cautions us not to be too hopeful. I'm latching on to anything at this point and dismiss his lack of hope.

We spend the rest of summer faithfully performing the stretches. Ben has a pretty good summer, too, with just three reflux episodes, only one of which was severe enough to require *Valium*. It's amazing how this can become so routine.

Getting both ourselves and Ben organized for any sort of appointment is never a simple task, and today we are delayed leaving our house for the hour-long trip to the rehab centre for our six-week follow-up appointment with Dr. Kelly. Checking in with the receptionist about 20 minutes late, we learn that Dr. Kelly couldn't wait for us and has had to attend an off-site meeting. We're far from impressed. Clearly, a double standard.

As we turn to leave, we catch a glimpse of Dr. Kelly leaving his office and scurry down the hall to catch him before he leaves. It is obvious he doesn't want to deal with us today, especially in our unorthodox fashion. Raising Ben for the last five years has forced us to be aggressive, much to the chagrin of some. His terse demeanour, very different from the first time we met, and his rushed manner demonstrate his disapproval for our tardiness. But I don't care. We have to live with Ben for the rest of our lives—Dr. Kelly doesn't.

In a very uncaring tone, he tells us that while Ben's legs and feet can be more easily stretched, there is no significant improvement in his range of motion. Surgery is the only option, in his view.

A few days later, I decide to call the principal of the MOVE school in Baltimore and get her thoughts. She agrees that it is not an easy decision to make. In her experience, she has heard of some horror stories with this procedure as well as some successes, but she can't say one way or the other which approach she would recommend. She mentions that some children with tight hamstrings and heel cords have actually improved through extensive use of a gait trainer, and suggests that we try that before having surgery. That would have been a great idea six months ago but the surgery date is less than two weeks away. And, actually, Dr. Harrison suggests the opposite—that Ben can not effectively use a gait trainer until he has the releases done.

I don't know! I don't know!! I don't know!!!

*   *   *

22

THE RELEASES

With less than a week to go before Ben's surgery, we call Dr. Harrison. Our heads are trying to say "yes" but we just can't commit to it.

"It's unfortunate that others have put doubt in your minds. The physical evidence speaks for itself," declares Dr. Harrison. "The procedure is very routine, and it will be a very good opportunity to coordinate with Dr. Anthony for Ben's dental work and Dr. Sanderson for the gastroscopy, which will be done before the releases. I honestly view surgery as a last resort but a necessary step, nonetheless, to enable Ben to achieve future goals," he tells us with genuine compassion.

"I don't make this recommendation lightly and any thoughts of ' . . . of course a surgeon would recommend surgery, that's how he makes a living . . .' should not come into play at all. The worst possible scenario, in my opinion, is that no improvement will be seen but there is virtually no chance of things getting worse, and most likely that significant improvement will be achieved."

Hanging up from the call has settled us quite a bit but it's still a tough decision to make. For four months, we have battled with so many questions. Have we done enough? Have we exhausted every possibility? How would we know when we've done enough? How would we know how he will turn out five years from now if we do nothing? The physical evidence may speak for itself but it's not a life-threatening decision.

Most of the opinions are pointing to surgery. Even the physiotherapist we visited in Halifax as part of Ben's pre-school assessment a few months ago thought that the releases would probably be worthwhile. She could see the tightness in his legs and commented that he would find it difficult to walk in his current state.

It's a real dilemma. I hate it . . . but we have to do it!

The Trek

It is a dull September morning—overcast, cool, windy—as we pack up the van. Conor and Tori are milling around and helping us but Conor is a little show-offy. I think they are both showing their distress that we will be away for a week and their routine is upset. And I'm sure that they really don't know what is going to happen to Ben.

Wiskers, our cat, is busily devouring one of his cans of food and really has no idea that we are going to be gone for a week, maybe more. Tori gives him a quick pat on the head and races Conor to Nana's car. We say our good-byes as Tori remarks that she will say an extra prayer for Ben so that he will make out all right. Is that to help her brother or ease the worry of her parents?

We get away without a problem. As we make the turn from our street, I turn on the wipers. The weather matches our mood this morning. It's now 10:15 a.m., about an hour later than we had hoped to leave but what else is new?

Ben is very much at ease travelling this time. Making his way to school three times a week on a bus has created a positive pattern for him on what leaving the house is all about—that going out doesn't always mean a trip to the hospital. There is still some nervousness with each journey he makes, no matter how long or how short, but it's not like it used to be.

We make our way to Steeves Mountain Truck Stop, about an hour and 15 minutes into the journey, and give Ben his juice. He isn't really interested in drinking very much so we press on to Sackville. Since it opened a year ago, the Wendy's/Tim Horton's restaurant there has hauled us off the highway for lunch every time. But this time it's different since Conor and Tori are not with us. Ben feels the difference, the absence of his brother and sister clamouring about, running off to the washroom, and emptying the trays.

Within 15 kilometers of Truro, brightening skies help our mood. After unloading Jan and Ben, I run off to meet Terry and a few others at the golf course to try to unwind before the big week. This round of golf is different, too, nowhere nearly as enjoyable as the ones I played in the summer. I'm sure it's because it's September 20th and not the middle of July; but also because I know it will be the last time I golf on this course, since Terry and Val are moving to Ottawa in a few weeks; and because nothing can stop, even suspend for a brief time, my continuous mental churning and anxiety about the coming week's events.

That evening, back at Terry and Val's, there is no relaxing "midnight" dip in their pool as we did in the summer; no time for shopping; no time for just doing nothing. We have a quiet dinner to celebrate their transfer but it will be the last dinner we share for a long time.

*   *   *

The day before

We are late leaving for the hospital, arriving nearly two hours past our planned 2 p.m. check-in. Jan takes Ben up to his room on 5-North while I check into the Fairview Lodge a few blocks away. It is a basic apartment-hotel complex, one step up from a university dorm. Our rented room is tiny, with stark wall colours and cold, white vinyl flooring. The one small light fixture in the middle of the ceiling dulls the room's interior even more. The room is cheap—that's the only good thing I can say about it.

As Jan gets to the floor, Dr. Wyse, our favourite anaesthesiologist, is waiting for them despite our tardiness. She tells Jan she is actually on vacation, the last day of it, in fact, but understands the importance of meeting with us the day before. Did we ever make the right decision, requesting her for this procedure!

After getting somewhat settled in the room, she and Dr. Wyse discuss what will happen:

"Tonight, he will have his finger poked to do a blood test for electrolytes and CBC and white cell count," Dr. Wyse explains.

"Intubation will be done with a clamp to prevent aspiration as much as possible . . . . He will be given narcotics for pain . . . . He should have his morning *Cisapride* dose by 6:30 a.m . . . ." and on and on. She has everything planned to the minute.

A short time later, the orthopaedics resident, Dr. Trent, arrives with consent forms for us to sign. He explains the upcoming procedures and advises that complications are possible with any surgery, and may include bleeding, nerve damage, and the requirement for additional surgery. We know those words have to be said, for legal reasons if nothing else, but they would have seemed more humane if he had also spoken words of support. Nope, not today.

In the evening, one of Ben's nurses gives us a short tour of the floor, showing us the kitchen, the supply room, the washrooms, and most importantly, tells us that we can reserve videos for Ben since the TV in his room cannot get *The Weather Network* channel, his favourite. (Nothing about complications and bleeding this time.)

An hour later, the three of us venture to the basement of the hospital to the Remedial Seating Clinic to see what final adjustments are needed for Ben's new chair. It's a little eerie making our way to the Clinic at night on a Sunday without Conor and Tori. Judy greets us, eight months pregnant and having made a special trip to accommodate our schedule. The new chair looks great with its metallic purple frame and rugged wheels. He's going to be the coolest kindergarten student, by far! She makes a few quick measurements and tells us to see her again on Wednesday for a final fitting.

After having Ben's blood taken and vitals done, we are left with an awkward time in which there is nothing to do except to get him ready for bed and get ourselves mentally prepared. It takes a while for him to fall asleep, being in a strange bed, sharing a room with a stranger, but Ben is so calm that he is actually helping *us* to relax. I don't feel that feeling of helplessness that "*he has no idea of what is going to happen to him*," unlike the surgery to remove his adenoids—when he was wheeled briskly through the corridors to the doors of the operating room, how we had almost no time to comfort him (or maybe he was comforting us).

I cover him up a little more and stand at the foot of his bed just watching him sleep. For a moment, I am overcome with sadness and fright at the same time.

"Our life, his life, is by no means perfect," I say to myself, "but we are, dare I say, somewhat comfortable and I keep asking myself if we are upsetting that comfortable state for the better or the worse by doing this surgery?

Or maybe we have no choice: if we want him to progress, we have to do this. Maybe, if we want Ben to achieve more, we have to make decisions that will not allow us to return to the way things are now, that we have to get out of our comfort zone, to a new and better comfort zone."

I say my usual nightly prayers for him and ask that he come through with flying colors, that he recover in record time so that we can go home in only a few days. The thought of staying at the IWK isn't giving me that horrible feeling that I get whenever we visit our hospital, but I still want to get home as fast as possible; I want it to be over now.

An hour later, as I open the door to the room at the Fairview Lodge, I feel very empty and lonely: Ben is in the hospital, and although Jan is with him, I am somewhere else. Lying in the dark, I can't get to sleep. I turn on the TV but it doesn't help. I glance at my watch—it's 1:30 a.m.

*   *   *

The day

My eyes are crusted shut as I wake up to the chirping sound of my watch, telling me I'm already late. I'm sure I never really got to sleep. Despite being sick with fatigue, I manage to hustle myself enough to get to the IWK by shortly after 6 a.m. As I rush through the doorway, I can see that Ben is awake, talking, in Jan's arms, craning his neck and eyes to see me. She says that he had a good night and woke up at around 5:45 a.m. He knows. He's a smart kid.

The nurse comes in at 6:30 a.m. exactly, just as the order reads, carrying with her Ben's *Prepulsid* dose (Dr. Wyse called it by its generic name) and some numbing cream for his hand where the IV will be inserted. Once he's completely prepped, he falls back to sleep. What else is there to do?

A few minutes before 8 o'clock, a team of people arrives to take us to the O/R. Ben is very relaxed as I carry him in my arms. He's telling me everything is going to be fine. After the five-minute walk, we are greeted by the O/R nurses as well as the gastro resident. She very calmly explains the procedure of how they would put a small amount of air into his belly to insert the gastroscope and then take the air out before finished. There is a slight risk of damage as the gastroscope is inserted but it's very unlikely.

A few moments later, we speak with Dr. Wyse in her O/R garb. As Dr. Harrison enters the room, she catches his eye to tell him (in her broken English) that she has ". . . *reserved ICU bed . . .*" but he shakes his head and says that the bed is not likely to be needed. Dr. Wyse informs him that she believes it is better to be prepared and mentions something about his office agreeing with her approach. Dr. Harrison responds that he is unaware that his office has said that. She then describes how she was involved in a three-hour dental procedure "last time" (with Ben, that is) and how she had done the same, as if to say, "I know what I'm doing; I know how to care for Ben," a certain pride shining through.

She ends her conversation by telling Dr. Harrison that we had specifically requested her for this procedure.

At 8:10 a.m., they take Ben inside. He is very peaceful, lying on the gurney. I can't help but relax somewhat. Everyone is so gentle, compassionate and calm. Jan and I head straight to Dentistry and find Dr. Anthony to sign the dental consent form.

In reading the procedure I notice the phrase "plus or minus extractions". I am unclear what a "+" extraction would be. After telling Dr. Anthony about the conversation between Dr. Wyse and Dr. Harrison, he chuckles a bit and tells us that Dr. Wyse is certainly the best and that Dr. Harrison doesn't always get along with everyone.

With a few hours to kill, Jan stops at our rented room to get cleaned up. The bathroom is equipped with only one towel (you get what you pay for) so I head to a nearby Wal-Mart to buy a couple more.

As I leave the mall, my cell phone rings . . . and my heart stops. I can't answer it. I freeze. What if something has gone wrong? Doesn't matter. I have to see who is calling.

"Mr. George?", the voice asks.

"Yes?", I respond nervously. The voice is Dr. Sanford, the gastro resident. "You can stop worrying. Ben is just fine. All went well with the gastroscopy."

She goes on to say that there was some redness above Ben's gastric "something-or-other" but otherwise everything is normal, and that we should continue his meds as usual. She tells me that Dentistry is just going in to do their work. So far, so good.

All pumped up and eager to share the good news, I head straight for the Lodge, driving a little fast for city streets. Jan is delighted. With too much time on our hands, we stop at the Dalhousie University (our alma mater) bookstore to find some cool clothing for Conor and Tori. Selection is poor today, it being so early in the year. Our shopping excursion a bust, we attempt to reach a friend of ours who works in Halifax but learn that he is away on vacation. With all of our options used up, we retreat to the IWK.

By 11:45 a.m., we seat ourselves in the day-surgery waiting room. Before Jan can call Ben's floor nurse to inquire about things, Dr. Anthony enters, fully dressed in street clothes.

"Things went well", he declares happily. "I was able to fix two small cavities, one on each side on the top, along with a little more fixing on the two teeth on top that have come down more. I gave Ben a flouride treatment and took X-rays that show new teeth ready to replace Ben's two top middle teeth."

"He's a great patient and you two are doing a good job at keeping his teeth clean."

Two down. One big one to go.

We rush our lunch and proceed quickly to the surgical floor, waiting to be called to the Recovery Room. It doesn't take long: Jan goes first and I follow 20 minutes later.

We were told that only one parent would be allowed in Recovery at any one time but we quietly ignore that rule. Dr. Wyse is nearby. She approaches us to say how pleased she is with everything and that there is no need for ICU.

Ben is very groggy but not unhappy, with rather large casts on his legs, from just below his knees to his toes. Dr. Wyse goes on to say that there was no sign of aspiration in the O/R and that Ben was given morphine for pain during the procedures. She also mentions that Dr. Harrison gave him a broad spectrum of antibiotics at the beginning of the procedure so there was no need for Dr. Anthony to worry about that. We learn that whenever you invade the mouth during surgery, there is a good chance that bacteria can complicate things, especially by infecting areas already operated on. Today, everything went as planned.

Ben is back in his room by 2 p.m., awake and talking a little. The remainder of the afternoon he spends resting, getting some drugs for pain, even mustering the effort to drink a few ounces of watery apple prune juice. We are amazed that he is able to drink so much today.

Ben's roommate, a seven-year-old boy, has been away from the room for the last several hours, which is a big relief for us. There have been so many people visiting this child it is difficult to tell who are the parents, if in fact there are two in this child's life. The young woman Jan and I think is the mother left him earlier in the day, left him crying uncontrollably for a long time. When she finally returned, she repeatedly told his nurse, "*I didn't hear no page!*", apparently in response to the nurse's attempt to contact her to tend to her son. I fought hard to keep my mouth shut then and not say something like, "This isn't a babysitting service. You can't leave on a smoke break for over an hour!"

Throughout the evening, Ben continues to comfort me by being so content and peaceful. Dr. Wyse makes another visit (I think she likes Ben) to sign his casts, inscribing the initials "BMW". He is thirsty for more watery juice and ingests more *Abenol, Codeine* and *Prepulsid* at 8 p.m. An hour and a half later, he falls effortlessly to sleep. This is too easy.

*   *   *

Day 1 post-op

Sleeping all night is wishful thinking on my part. With my watch barely displaying 3 a.m., Ben stirs and moans. Jan and I change his position but he remains laughy and agitated. His pull-up needs changing and his shirt is soaked from drooling. Getting this off requires feeding the clothing along the length of his IV line and over the bag itself. Quite a feat so early in the morning. A full two hours pass before he settles back to sleep. Twice more, his nurse makes a visit to check his IV, and twice more I'm awakened by her footsteps.

By 7:30 a.m., sleep is over as Dr. Trent and a group of interns storm into Ben's room to check him out. They're all dressed in their white lab coats with shiny new stethoscopes dangling around their necks. Jan and I come to attention, rub the crust from our eyes, and attempt to unknot our tousled hair and straighten our wrinkled clothes. Ben checks out okay and the resident signs his cast.

A few moments later, Dr. Sanderson stops by also to sign his cast. Ben is becoming quite the celebrity. She comments that Ben is doing wonderfully (her words are very comforting right now) and mentions that his blood work was fine, showing no sign of vitamin B_{12} deficiency (a side-effect from one of his anti-reflux meds). Since people can have B_{12} reserves for up to two years, she says that she will continue to monitor these levels and deal with problems if they arise in the future.

It isn't long before Ben's nurse disconnects him from the monitor *and* removes his IV! What a great feeling—for both him and us. It's an acknowledgement that he is on the uptick and one step closer to going home. We can sense that he is starting to feel better as he sits on Jan's lap with his casted legs propped onto the side of the bed and enjoys some of his usual breakfast mixture.

Shortly before noon, Judy and Dan from the Seating Clinic arrive with Ben's new wheelchair—it *is* really cool. Judy suggests that we try him in it when he is ready and any fine-tuning adjustments can be made before we leave.

Ben tries some lunch—a bowl of runny peas and another of sloppy pears—in the same feeding position as before. He even manages a few ounces to drink. He can't seem to get enough. A few loud burps, though, quickly turn into repeated heaving. Obviously, we're pushing him too much. Maybe the peas were too heavy or perhaps the feeding position kept his belly crunched.

After getting him cleaned up, we put him back in bed so that he can watch a movie. He is delighted and watches it with good concentration, moving his arms a lot. An hour passes and he suddenly turns pale and throws up again. That settles him enough to allow a good long nap.

By early evening, both Dr. Harrison and Dr. Trent stop by to examine Ben. Everything is as it should be, even Ben's discoloured toes. Jan hits them with a number of questions:

> *"Is any particular care needed when changing his pullup?."*

> *"Who will give us instructions for exercising and positioning at home?"*

> *"Driving home in a car seat with his legs dangling with two big casts on? Is this okay?"*

> *"Who should remove his casts?"*

> *"We have other appointments that we would like to coordinate with our return in November. Can we book our follow-up appointment while we are here?"*

> *"What is the earliest date in November that we can come back since we are nervous about traveling that late in the year . . ."*

Dr. Harrison answers all of our questions but seems to be in a hurry, inching his way closer to the door as each question is asked. He suggests that we not give Ben any more *Codeine* since that is likely the cause of his nausea. However, being nauseated 24 hours after having five procedures is certainly normal according to Dr. Harrison, and is something that you would expect. He tells us not to fret about it. That's not easy to do when I haven't slept in three nights, when my mind exaggerates every detail, when anxiety floods every thought, and I can't stop expecting the worst.

Not long before bedtime, Ben's nurse makes one last visit to check his vitals and is surprised to see he has a fever. It's not that high at 38.2°C but high enough to make my gut churn, believing that, if it continues to climb, he may start having seizures. I know it's my mental and physical exhaustion killing my ability to absorb anything other than good news but I can't help it.

We have a discussion with his nurse about the recommended dosage of *Tylenol* versus what he really requires. I am brought back to the time of his adenoid surgery, still annoyed by the miniscule dose that was given at that time, how he was in such pain and how the nurses ignored our requests. Some things I just can't let go. Until Ben was born, I was never like this.

Within an hour, his temperature returns to normal and so do my emotions. I'm shaking, I'm so tired. Before he falls asleep, Jan and I help to give his legs a good stretch, casts and all. It is instant relief for him and his face transforms to a very relaxed state, as if all pain and tension has instantly left his body. I so wish he could talk to tell us what he needs.

A new baby moves into bed #1 whose parents seem a lot more functional and capable. Another stressor has been removed. I decide to spend the night with Jan and Ben, and squeeze myself into the corner of the room. I can't be away from him no matter how exhausted I am.

* * *

Day 2 post-op

It is still dark outside when Dr. Trent and crew come in to check Ben. They are very discreet, very quiet, using only a pen flashlight and a gentle lifting of his covers to check his bandages. "All dry and everything looks good," they report. And Ben is good, too, remaining asleep through the whole routine.

Ben's body is clearly telling itself it has to rest, has to heal, since his eyes are still closed as the clock comes up to 10 a.m. Dr. Wyse pokes her head into the doorway to see how her patient is recovering. She tells us that this is her day off but just needed to make sure things were still progressing smoothly. She had wanted to stop in last night but decided against it at 1 a.m.

Jan mentions to her how surprised we were to see Ben so alert shortly after his surgery and asks why that would be.

"I can't tell you all of my secrets!" she responds with a grin.

During the conversation, she tells us that while *Codeine* can certainly help with managing pain, it can also make you sick and constipated. Jan compares Ben coming out of surgery to her own surgery five years ago when she was very gaggy and nauseated afterward. "Things are improving all the time," Dr. Wyse tells us, "including having to use less and less of the anti-inflammatory drugs that can cause the nausea."

Once all of his visitors have gone, we give Ben a sponge bath in bed and wash his hair, to help him feel more human. He displays his approval with repeated smiles and pleasurable moans. As we finish combing is hair, two ortho residents enter the room, looking to remove Ben's leg bandages. It's an effortless exercise. We are told to watch for swelling, which can occur up to three days post-op, as well as for infection, which can take as long as a week to show itself. Somehow, their tone and descriptions of these complications isn't helping us feel good about how great Ben really is. I know they're trying.

They tell us that assuming no swelling and that Ben is able to eat his regular menu again, we would be discharged. Ah, now you're talking. Now you're making me feel good.

The rest of the day and night go remarkably smoothly with no codeine and some semi-solid food. By 9 p.m., he is snuggled into bed and asleep within half an hour.

* * *

Getting sprung

Wednesday's Hospital Rounds begin at 7:15 a.m. and the ortho residents, along with the Head Nurse, pay us a visit. Ben is getting used to ignoring their intrusions and sleeps through the entire examination. All are pleased with the results.

"What time will Dr. Harrison be stopping in today?" asks Jan.

"He's out of town for the rest of the week," one of the residents replies.

They must have it wrong. He told us he would discuss the details about removing Ben's cast. Who would do this now? Not these junior apprentices.

"All it will it take is a simple phone call to his office to talk about this," another rookie claims.

"But it was Dr. Harrison who had said he would discuss this with us later in the week, not wait until next week!"

Pushed into a corner, the first resident admits that maybe Dr. Harrison had forgotten about this but repeats nervously that this topic can be easily discussed by phone. The Head Nurse rolls her eyes and shakes her head slightly.

"We'd really like to be released today," I tell the crowd. "Ben had a very peaceful night, he ate well yesterday, and we are kind of getting the heebie-jeebies."

None of them is keen to let us leave before tomorrow. Jan tells them we would only go as far as Truro today and stay with Jan's sister.

"I guess that's a reasonable approach," the Head Nurse replies. "I'll get things ready for Ben's discharge."

Woo hoo! Our day is set. We feed Ben breakfast a little later than normal and take him to his 10:30 a.m. dentistry appointment. Everything looks great with his teeth and the X-rays show quite noticeably where all his new teeth will be coming in.

Before visiting the seating clinic to have his wheelchair adjusted, Jan delivers a note to Dr. Harrison's office, asking him to call us next week. We find a kindred spirit in Judy as we discuss the antics of Dr. Harrison and vent our frustration about people making things so difficult.

In the next two hours, we give Ben his lunch, run some errands, drop off a small gift for Dr. Wyse (even though no one is really sure where to find her office), pick up Ben's newly adjusted car seat along with a plywood insert to support his cast while travelling, and finish the last of the packing.

Shortly before 3:30 p.m., we say our goodbyes and carefully load Ben into the van. He is now sporting a fiberglass coating on his casts with an opening cut for his toes. Finally, all done! We eagerly pull away, tired but glad to be leaving.

We make it Truro in the usual hour's drive but it is a crazy stay at Val and Terry's. We really shouldn't be staying here since they are in the middle of packing and getting ready to move. They have just had their front stairs varnished, their bathroom painted, and boxes are everywhere. Ben doesn't mind—he is happy to be out of the hospital and on his way home to get a good night's sleep in his own bed.

23

A SYSTEM UNPREPARED

Ben's foray into the public school system had begun a few weeks before his release surgery. On the day after Labour Day at about 8:15 a.m., the doorbell rang, an unusual sound for a weekday morning. I thought that it was Conor or Tori, returning frantically from the bus stop after discovering they had forgotten something important like a favourite ball cap or Barbie doll. After all, it was their first day back to school following the summer vacation.

As I opened the door, a middle-aged lady with a fairly slight build stood before me, her body half wanting to come in and half wanting to rush away.

"Hi. Here for Benjamin George.", she stated in a raspy voice.

I paused for a few seconds as I peered into the driveway to see an abbreviated yellow school bus parked precariously there. Now, you have to see our driveway with its unbelievable slope to get the full effect of this vision, but the first thought that crossed my mind was why a bus designed for students in wheelchairs would be parked in such an inaccessible manner. Rather than blurt out something stupid since it was early in the morning, I politely told the lady that Ben didn't go to school on Tuesdays, only Mondays, Wednesdays, and Fridays.

"And not only that", I went on to say, "you're too early. He isn't to be picked up until 9 o'clock."

"Oh! We'll be out to Simonds by then!" she retorted. I'm not sure what that meant.

After I told her what I thought the arrangements were, she said that she would contact "Sue" to try to straighten things out, whoever Sue was.

As I walked back into the kitchen, Ben was sitting patiently in his seat, waiting for breakfast, oblivious of the false start that had just occurred.

A unfriendly welcome

A different bus arrives for Ben the next day—not a cramped yellow bus but a newer, cleaner, and roomier privately-operated "handi-bus." The driver, Paul, welcomes Ben and takes extra care securing his wheelchair. Riding the bus with Ben is someone new to us. Her name is Gerry and she has recently replaced Carly as Ben's human-services counselor. Having a new face with Ben in a new environment is a bit unsettling but, then again, Carly had never adjusted well to the job: she was nervous all the time and quite disorganized. Jan and I couldn't see how she would have managed taking Ben to school.

We had asked a number of people about the best school for Ben to attend, given that there are several elementary schools in close proximity. The answers kept pointing to the one equipped with a specialized resource room for students with disabilities. We thought that made sense and signed him up for Mrs. Murray's kindergarten class.

Arriving at school shortly after 9 a.m. that first morning, Ben disembarks with Gerry and Jan and I meet them in the front lobby. We find our way to Mrs. Murray's classroom, and, though we have never met her, think it appropriate to knock on the classroom door to announce our arrival. Classes are already under way at school, starting a bit too early for Ben's schedule. A second knock is needed before a tall woman, likely mid-thirties, opens the door.

"Yes?", asked the woman, seeming a bit annoyed.

"Mrs. Murray?", asked Jan. The lady nods hesitantly.

"I'm Jan George, and this is Ben." Mrs. Murray looks a bit surprised, as if she has no idea that Ben is in her class, or, perhaps more accurately, that she really doesn't want a student in a wheelchair in her class.

After Gerry is introduced, they both enter the classroom and join the circle of other students. Jan explains to Mrs. Murray that Ben will start out attending only three mornings a week until he adjusts to the routine. This has been agreed to by the school's administration but Mrs. Murray clearly has no idea what Jan is talking about. Jan also tells her that either she or I will remain in the school building while Ben is in class, in case he has any issues like a seizure. She appears to know nothing about Ben or his challenges. We tell her that we have never left Ben away from home before and want to be close by. It was as if Jan were speaking a foreign language. No response comes from Mrs. Murray, only a blank stare. Perhaps the seizure remark has frightened her.

Two weeks pass and never once does Mrs. Murray venture out of her classroom to talk to either one of us, not even to say that Ben was enjoying "this" or participating in "that," or that she is happy to see that he is becoming more accustomed to the classroom. Her only conversations with us concern her obsession with a particular medical form and the possibility of reflux and seizures.

One morning during those weeks, I notice that terrified look in his eyes and his blotchy skin as he gets off the bus. I call to Gerry that Ben is having a reflux episode. I whip off both the tray of his wheelchair and the straps holding him, pick him up, and rest his head on my shoulder. I hurry up the concrete ramp that leads to the school entrance and get inside as fast as I can. Massaging his back, I walk back and forth in the hallway, waiting for him to get through it. Within a few minutes he lets out a big sigh and it is over. Gerry is right there with me when he comes round, having brought his wheelchair inside out of the pouring rain.

We get Ben back into his wheelchair and slowly walk down the hall to his classroom. As we get closer, I whisper to Gerry not to mention this episode to Mrs. Murray, since I think it will only aggravate our already-tense relationship. Gerry agrees and we go inside, interrupting circle-time as we always do. At that moment, I begin to wonder whether or not Ben is becoming uneasy with school. I also wonder why Mrs. Murray can't wait an extra 15 minutes to begin the circle-time.

After a few minutes of listening to Mrs. Murray read the latest book to the class, Gerry notices that she is not wearing the FM system that connects to Ben's hearing aids to allow him to hear more clearly. She reminds Mrs. Murray of her oversight and receives a lengthy glare for her comments. As she was untangling the wires of the system's microphone, one of Ben's classmates asks, "Mrs. Murray, what's that?" pointing to the FM system.

She whirls her head to stare down at the child and nervously replies, "You know what it is!".

When Ben returns to school two weeks after his surgery, Mrs. Murray completely ignores the new additions to his legs, despite the curiosity of 24 other five-year olds, and makes no attempt to ask how he has fared. She also neglects to inform us that class pictures will be taken the next day. We find out only after arriving at school and learn that they were being taken on the upper floor. Since the building has no elevator, Ben has no way to participate. Jan asks the photographer if he can take Ben's picture downstairs but he doesn't like that idea and instead offers to carry Ben up the stairs. Really? You're going to carry Ben in his wheelchair up two dozen stairs? By yourself? You think that's safe? Is everyone in this school completely messed up?

When it comes time for the class Halloween party, Ben wears his costume to school. I have spent several days "modifying" his wheelchair to look like a Formula 1 racer. When his classmates see him roll into the classroom, they all run to welcome him and compliment him on how cool his costume is. Mrs. Murray doesn't give Ben even a glance, let alone acknowledge the excitement of the other students. This was, of course, because she has scheduled the party for the afternoon without bothering to tell us, excluding Ben since he attends school only in the mornings. This teacher appears to be going out of her way to reject Ben and us.

It takes us a while to put all the pieces together and to learn that we are the talk of the school district and that Ben is the centre of it all. Ben is doing nothing wrong, not causing any disturbances, not annoying or bullying anyone, just showing up to learn like all of the other students. Yet, somehow, his attendance has become something of a spectacle.

A few days after the Halloween party snub, we discover that the city's Public Health Nurse has distributed an article on CMV to every teacher at the school, including Mrs. Murray. This isn't a random newsletter highlighting upcoming events; it is directed specifically at Ben. I'm sure she has violated a dozen privacy laws. The fact that Ben was born with CMV more than 5 years ago is old news and no one should care. How did she get this information? How is she even allowed to do this? If we had had enough emotional and financial resources, we would have sued.

"Ben is not the child you should be wary of since you know for certain that he has actually had CMV", I want to tell this nurse and Mrs. Murray.

"No, ladies. It's little Johnny over there who appears 'normal' that could just as easily, and is actually more likely, to be carrying the virus right now, and you wouldn't know it!"

That might have sent her over the edge. Filled with vengefulness and anger, I really wanted to go down that route to inflict as much pain as possible!

Instead, we choose to remove Ben from this school and look for a better one.

*   *   *

Kindergarten—take 2

Jan and I are escorted to a brightly decorated classroom and invited to take a seat. The room is overflowing with tiny, multi-coloured chairs, the walls are covered with a multitude of water-colour drawings of outdoor scenes, and the whole room exudes a sense of warmth and comfort. A few moments later, Mrs. Mallory, Ben's new kindergarten teacher, and Mr. Green, the principal of his new school, greet us and thank us for coming to visit.

They both apologize for the grief that we have been put through at the neighbouring school, even though they weren't responsible for any of it. Mrs. Mallory admits she has never had a student with Ben's challenges but makes it clear that she is not afraid of him and can't wait for him to start in her class. Instantly, the weight of the world is lifted from our shoulders. It suddenly becomes a very normal conversation in which Jan and I don't feel the need to defend ourselves. I realize only now that Mrs. Murray is dealing with something greater than the strain of having a student like Ben in her class, that she is having difficulty dealing with a class of five-year-olds in general. If she had been only a little odd or gruff, we likely would not have been led to Mrs. Mallory, a perfect match for Ben.

On Ben's first day at the new school, Mrs. Mallory appoints him "leader for the day," meaning that he must help pass out the morning snack. His classmates instantly accept him and treat him as one of the crowd, even though we are already a few months into the school year. She also alters her class routine, knowing that Ben is not attending full days, and includes a big welcome to Ben in the school's November newsletter. She isn't afraid to try things with Ben, to expose him to new experiences every day. And the trips to the gym are especially enjoyable, where he thrives on being wheeled about, the faster the better.

Three weeks pass and Mrs. Mallory wants to chat with us about how things are going.

"Am I doing enough?" she asks sincerely, as if she might be falling short of our expectations. Kindergarten is mostly play-based, of course, so how could she be falling short? Making him an integral part of the class is huge.

"You know, whenever Ben's school bus arrives, *all* his classmates rush to the windows and press their faces against the glass to get a glimpse of him coming up the ramp," she reports to us with glee.

"Ben is a real joy to have in my class. Every student is excited when he is around, talking to him constantly, wanting to push him in his wheelchair. When he was absent for his IWK visit last week, they wanted to know when he was coming back. And they ask me why he can't come with them, outside, during recess".

Her words are amazing. Her desire to learn more and more about Ben, to discover how she can create different ways to help him get the most benefit out of his time at school, is over the top.

The education system still doesn't know what to do with someone like Ben—maybe *that's* what Dr. Norris meant. But all of that does not matter when you have someone like Mrs. Mallory in your life.

*   *   *

24

HE AIN'T HEAVY

He is still sleeping at 7:45 a.m. when I open his bedroom window blinds. Looking across the front lawn, I can see that it is a typical December morning, partly sunny, not too cold. It wouldn't matter if there were a foot of snow on the ground, we can't be late for school today. I help him push through his tiredness, though his tight arms and legs don't cooperate. After finishing getting ready for work, I take over feeding Ben his breakfast. With so much anticipation, I am a little nervous. I know I am putting pressure on myself, likely setting myself up for disappointment. But today is Ben's first Christmas show at school and I want this day to be special, and for Ben to perform well.

Conor and Tori ride on the Handi-Bus with Ben, and the driver lets Conor work the lift. Jan videotapes them getting off the bus at school, displaying Ben's happiness and excitement. She calls me a short time later to tell me that she expects Ben's class will be on stage at about 10:15 a.m. I'm not sure why I went to the office this morning, since I really don't get much accomplished. I am too wound up, worried that something will happen to make me late.

After picking up a handful of Christmas cards—for Mrs. Mallory who is the biggest reason for all this excitement, for Gerry for all her work with Ben, for Mr. Green for his support and welcoming us to the school, and Mrs. Lawrence who helps Mrs. Mallory run the class—I burst through the front doors of the school. Conor and Jan greet me to say that things are running behind. We have at least a half hour wait. I ask how Ben is.

"Great. Really happy!", is the response.

As I enter the classroom, I spot him in the lineup sitting comfortably and content in his purple wheelchair, without his tray, and wearing his purple Smartie costume. He has drooled a little on his costume, and the purple paint has stained his chin. I am so proud, so happy. He fits in so well. Even though I know he can't really perform on stage, I am still so happy. Jan tells me I'm beaming. What a feeling.

We joke with one of the teachers about him having a big reflux episode in front of everyone while on stage. Right now, I'm not worried about that. Getting him to school this morning and having him in such a great mood was the biggest hurdle overcome. Nothing can dampen my mood now.

Front and centre

We move out into the hall; his classmates are overflowing with excitement. Talking, laughing, moving from side to side. Ben is at the end of the line, craning his neck to get a glimpse of me standing behind him. Older kids stream past us in both directions. The place is buzzing. Mrs. Mallory realizes that we have lined up too early and makes us return to the classroom. Ben doesn't mind.

About 10 minutes later, we line up in the hall again, this time with Ben as the leader. When the next stream of kids file past us, we start down the hall—the excitement is really building. We arrive at the narrow stairs of the stage and Gerry helps me carry him up. There are only three small steps, so carrying him is easy. The curtains are drawn, only every second overhead light is on, but two blinding white floodlights shine up from the floor at centre stage. Mrs. Mallory asks the kids to move aside to let Ben take centre stage. After I position him in front, Mrs. Mallory reminds me to make sure the brake is on. I love this lady! I snatch the towel away that is in place to catch drool and dash to grab a seat in the audience.

I crouch down in front with Jan, Conor and Tori. We all see Santa off to the left, sitting up high, and booming in a loud voice, "*I wonder what's on channel 6 again*".

And with that, the large green velvet curtains open. There he is, head hung a little to the right as it always does. The lights shine perfectly on him and the kids start singing "*When you eat your* Smarties *do you eat the red ones last . . .*".

Ben doesn't do much, his head hanging even further as the song progresses, but I keep snapping pictures, hoping to get a good pose. I find it a bit hard to believe that it really is Ben up on stage with his kindergarten class. I couldn't have imagined this day five-and-a-half years ago after being told that he might never walk, talk, or go to school. It doesn't matter in the least that he just sits there—that isn't the point. As the song approaches the end, his classmates twirl around, lifting their costumes a little. One of them accidentally hits him with her costume. Ben raises his head, looks over at the offender, and smiles.

As their voices get louder his smile gets bigger, and he raises his body to a perfectly upright position just as the performance ends. He is star of the show.

The curtains close and I run backstage. Mrs. Mallory is happy that everything worked out. Gerry is happy; Jan is happy; I am ecstatic. He did it and I got to see it!

* * *

A lump of coal

It's two days before Christmas. He isn't right after lunch—quiet, even a little pale, with that all too familiar reflux aura present. I can feel it in the air. As my mind is predicting reflux, his eyes get stuck to one side and then it starts. I pick him up to comfort his rigid frame but no massaging helps this time. After 15 minutes, we decide to give him a shot of *Valium*. The first dose has no effect, so we gave him another. Within seconds, his stiffness disappears and he lies very still on the couch. I am swept with an uneasiness that something still is not right—his usual appearance after an episode, after *Valium*, where his eyes are usually in tune with his surroundings, as he drifts off to sleep, is not there. His eyes stare right through me, very incoherently. Ten minutes pass and he suddenly starts convulsing, with eyes bouncing, tongue thrusting, and arms pulsing slightly, all in the typical rhythmic fashion. Instead of calling an ambulance, we choose to pile into our van and rush ourselves to the hospital.

The ER doc remembers us from a recent visit and acts very quickly, setting up an IV to get more *Valium* into his system. Ben's fragile nervous system is back under control within 30 minutes of arriving—what a relief—though he just lies there, exhausted.

We mention to the ER doc that Ben has been restless the past few nights, waking up early, laughing, even yelling at times, and quite active. He responds that some of his epileptic patients have told him that up to 24 hours in advance they can tell that they were going to have a seizure. Maybe by waking up at 4 a.m. the last two nights, Ben was telling us that something was wrong.

Not long after that, Dr. Norris joins us in the ER. He examines Ben and observes that his ear canals look somewhat inflamed. Maybe that's the cause. "Does anyone really know?" I ask myself.

We discuss the events of the day and Ben's EEG that was done at the IWK last month. During that test, Ben was having brief seizures, quite frequently, in fact. The neurologist compared them to a bolt of lightning coursing through Ben's brain and told us if they occurred too often, they would definitely affect his concentration and could cause more damage. In light of this, Dr. Norris recommends a new anti-convulsant medication called *Frisium*, something that is supposed to have very few side effects and should not make Ben too sleepy, as many of these drugs often do. He hands Jan a prescription for about two months' worth and tells us to give it a try.

We leave the ER a short time later, with Ben quiet and peaceful, but exhausted. The early winter evening is cool and dark and so is our house when we enter. It is just as we had left it earlier in the day, with things half picked up and chores undone: another day wasted; another incident to recover from; another hospital visit over. It just doesn't read like a Christmas script but we decide to carry on with our holiday plans.

On Christmas morning, after discovering how generous Santa was to everyone, I bring Ben from his bedroom to the family room couch. He is like a rag doll with no tone in his arms, no strength in his neck, and sheer exhaustion in his eyes. Conor and Tori actively bring his presents over to him, do most of the opening for him while performing a little "Vanna White" to show what he got.

"Not interested," is his response.

On Boxing Day, we go through the same routine—Ben wakes late, I carry his floppy frame to the couch, and persist in getting some fluids into him: not interested. Jan convinces me that we need to take him to the hospital. (At Christmas. Why not? We've been there on just about every other holiday.)

Despite a full waiting room, the ER is particularly efficient that day, making us wait only 15 minutes. After a resident exams Ben, the paediatrician on-call assesses the data and informs us that he likely has something viral and that he is somewhat dehydrated. Not surprising given the absence of any drooling. She recommends that Ben be admitted, at least overnight, so that he can get some fluids back into his system. Despite my detest for this place, I agree with her recommendation since it would do no good to return home. There would be no PICU this time, either, but rather a "normal" hospital stay. I decide to stay the night with Ben.

Once we're settled in our double room, with no roommate, my father makes a visit. He is concerned for us and his grandson. We had spent Christmas Day with them but it was far from enjoyable. I had felt a little guilty that none of us could enjoy the day. Sensing our exasperation, my mother wanted to provide some comfort food to lighten the load and my father opens a small cookie tin of goodies that she has made.

Ben lies very content in the oversized bed while we talk. This is far more relaxing than Christmas Day. I never thought I could ever feel relaxed in this place. Lights are out by 10 p.m. and I cuddle in the cot beside his bed. Not long afterward, a nurse makes her way to Ben's bedside, carrying a small flashlight. She checks his IV and temperature, and listens to his chest.

After she leaves the room, I peer out into the hallway and spy Dr. Campbell even though he is not on-call tonight. He catches my eye and comes in to talk to me. Amazing. He recommends waiting until Ben can drink on his own before we go home—maybe even tomorrow.

In the morning, Ben is like a new person. Jan brings me a change of clothes and I get cleaned up in one of the parent showers. Both Conor and Tori are participating in a basketball tournament that begins today and we can't disappoint them. Since Ben had such a good night, I take Conor to his morning game while Jan stays with Ben. Watching Conor play is strangely comforting. It doesn't matter that Ben is in hospital during this season. Taking him there was the right thing to do. Being with Conor now is also the right thing to do.

By late afternoon, Ben is quite happy, consuming healthy amounts of food and liquids. This is his signal that he's ready to go home. When we disembark in our garage, Conor and Tori come running to greet us and see that their little brother is feeling better. Everyone is happy to finally be home.

The year closes with an unplanned outing to a local restaurant with Jan's sisters and their husbands. New Year's Eve for our family is usually quite bland. Ordering take-out and watching "Dick Clark's Rockin' New Year's Eve" is about as exciting as it gets in our house so getting out for a few hours is a real treat. We savour every moment.

With a few minutes to spare before midnight, we find a spot on the docks, shivering in sub-zero temperatures, and watch the carefully timed explosions of fireworks that signal the new year. We must continue to do things like this from time to time if for no other reason than to give us the strength to face the next crisis.

* * *

Keep breathing

"What choice do you have?", asked Paul, a co-worker of mine, in a somewhat rhetorical manner.

"You're his parents. You have to do whatever it takes."

Our conversation about all that Jan and I have gone through, what the future holds, and how we will ever find the strength to continue at this pace when we're 40 years old let alone 50, ended with this very matter-of-fact statement. He was telling me something that I intrinsically knew, that really it doesn't matter whether I want to keep dealing with seizures and reflux, useless specialists or a dysfunctional education system. It doesn't matter what I want.

"That's life, Mike. You can't run away from it. Figure it out. Deal with it! Find a way to make it better!"

These words start reverberating in my head as I watch the ending of the movie, "Castaway."

"I had to keep breathing even though there was no reason to hope . . .", exclaimed Tom Hanks, aka Chuck Noland, a modern day Robinson Crusoe who found a way to survive alone for more than seven years on a remote island in the South Pacific. Even though he felt he had control over nothing, he knew he had to stay alive, that he couldn't give up. Something good, something, eventually, would come his way, even though that went against all logic, all rational thought, and he knew he would never get off that island.

Then, one day, that logic was proven all wrong when the tide came in and gave him a sail. And he found his way from that tiny, uncharted island all the way back to Memphis, his home. Though his former fiancé had moved on during those seven years and had eventually married, which made him lose her all over again, he knew what he had to do.

"I have to keep breathing, 'cause tomorrow, the sun will rise. Who knows what the tide could bring?"

He's right. He's absolutely right. Tomorrow, there will be new signs, new choices, new life. We can never give up, as Ummi told me, because we're all Ben's got. Any day he could come alive. Maybe one morning he'll wake up and speak to us, or climb out of bed.

We have to believe that we will eventually get what we want, even simple things, as we did a few weeks ago when we finally got to the Sheraton for our Christmas party, despite enduring a reflux episode on the hour's drive to the hotel.

If I truly believe that life is a journey, where the timeline is not nearly as important as having a proper compass to keep us heading in the right direction, then the future is not so scary. We have made it five years and we're still here. Still breathing.

Not long after the movie ends, I tuck Ben into bed and glance up at the picture hanging above him, the same picture that hung in my bedroom growing up on Wentworth Street. In it a teen carries a younger boy on his back, trudging through the snow with a large school-like brick building and adjacent church in the distant background. This scene is really the symbol of a community for homeless boys, called Boys Town, that was set up by a Catholic priest named Father Flanagan. That's not the reason it hangs on the wall—it's just an appropriate scene for a boy's bedroom. Tonight, it looks different.

The caption on the picture reads, "He ain't heavy, Father. He's m' brother." I instantly recall the song by the same name, which talks

356 □   THIRD TIME LUCKY

about a long, long road "... *with many a winding turn that leads us to who knows where* ..."

The song goes on to say how "... *I'm strong enough to carry him* ...", "... *his welfare is my concern* ...", and how "... *the load doesn't weigh me down at all* ...".

It all makes perfect sense. Life's true purpose is embodied in this simple picture. To serve and care for others, especially the poor, the marginalized, and the forgotten.

Even though most days we're barely surviving, tonight I am overcome with a peace that is washing over me like warm rain: calming, soothing. There's no way Jan and I have been led this far with Ben to have it all end horribly.

Everything will be all right.

AFTERWORD

Thinking outside the box!

It is a hot and humid 4th of July when the bell sounds from the back door. Peering through the kitchen window, Jan can see the top of a ball cap on the little visitor. As she opens the door, she almost begins with, "Sorry, but Conor is away in Ottawa . . ."

But the little voice interrupts that thought pattern and asks, "Can Ben come out to play?"

Taken off guard, Jan responds hesitantly, "Uh, . . . okay. Who are you?"

"I'm Colin, a friend of Ben's," he says confidently.

"Well, wait just a minute. I'll get him in his wheelchair.", Jan replies.

With Colin waiting patiently, Ben emerges from the mud room and enters the bright sunshine that warms the deck.

"Hi, Ben," he says cheerfully. "Can I take him across the street to the tennis court?" he asks. Jan pauses for a moment and says that she doesn't think that would be a good idea (Colin is only six years old, after all); they can play on the deck, though.

Without missing a beat, Colin begins into what most would view as a very one-sided conversation with Ben. However, it is obvious that Colin doesn't view it that way. At one point, seeing a big gob of drool on Ben's chin, Colin stops mid-sentence and says, "Oh, here, let me get that for you, Ben," as he wipes his chin.

The next words are something like, "Hey, Ben. I got a new tooth! See!?" and he holds his mouth open wide to let Ben see. Colin plays with Ben for about 20 minutes, asking him questions and telling him stories, until he waves goodbye and pedals down the ramp for home.

I can't begin to describe the feelings of happiness that run through me when Jan tells me this story. Here is a six-year-old who truly sees Ben as his friend, as someone he can call on, as someone he can play with. Talk about "thinking outside the box" and seeing beyond the barriers that most people put up when they encounter someone like Ben, even those who have known Ben all his life. In fact, *we* still do that sometimes, letting Ben's challenges cloud our attitudes and behaviours.

We must always remember that how Ben approaches life is more dramatic, not different. He desires to love and be loved, to move, to play, to learn, to interact with his friends, and to feel safe and included.

We should all try to be like Colin. We would definitely be better off.

Ben today at 19—happy, energetic, fun to be with